The Franklin Trail: A Dark Memoir

The author's first book, *The Franklin Trail,* is a story of overcoming adversity and eventually meeting Mary Jo; they faced life together—clean and sober—for forty-two years.

This is our story:
I was a young boy hated by thugs, feared by foes, respected by peers. I walked the wild side, searching for answers without knowing the questions. Along the way I met a fellow traveler by the name of Mary Jo. We were two drifters—both loners. Mary Jo lost her parents at a young age. We both learned life's lessons the hard way.

Comments/reviews about *The Franklin Trail: A Dark Memoir*:

"I found *The Franklin Trail* to be a remarkable recount of what was the author's troubled past. His journey is both intriguing and fascinating and deserves the sub-title of *A Dark Memoir*. His perseverance to get through his trials of life is admirable and can be an example for others."

~ Mark Even, Book Author

"Memoirs are not in my usual line of reading—and I also receive a lot of review requests that I seldom accept—so, frankly, I dreaded reading it. I was pleasantly surprised. The narrative is engaging, a little wry, a bit matter-of-fact, not at all apologetic, and candid—kudos there. The writing dwells in passive voice more than I'd advise, but not so much that it lost my interest. The author's multiple voices—his, Andy's, and Andrew's—come through clearly…"

~ Avid Reader

THE BLUE HIGHWAY:

Memoir of an IBM Guy

THE BLUE HIGHWAY:

Memoir of an IBM Guy

D. R. Cruikshank

Published by Palidan Books, LLC
Sedona, AZ 86636
email: drcruikshank@me.com

I have tried to recreate events, locales, and conversations from my memories of them. To maintain their anonymity, in some instances I have changed the names of individuals and places. I may have changed some identifying characteristics and details such as physical properties, occupations, and places of residence.

ISBN: 978-1-7351484-6-5

Printed in the United States of America
First Printing 2020

DEDICATION

To my children and grandchildren, who have
been given, and taken, opportunities to see a
world outside of their own comfort zones.

In fond memory of my mother,
Lois Irene (Wisti) Cruikshank (1926-2014),
who never gave up on me.

In memory of Ronald J. Peterson
(April 12, 1945-August 25, 2012) and
Joseph Kozlowski
(February 19, 1946-June 9, 2006)
Partners in life; soul mates forever

In memory of Rick Turner
(February 7, 1936-January 30, 2021)
My AS/400 System Performance Mentor

To the IBM i database engineers worldwide—
all two of them.

To the memory of my wife,
Mary Jo (Peterson) Cruikshank.
(August 22, 1952-June 24, 2020)

*"I feel that last night was a giant step backwards. Now that we've
learned to sleep with our backs turned,
next time we will be sleeping apart. I am scared."*
~ Mary Jo Peterson, Couples Counseling, June 18, 1978

*Together, we learned how to live life—apart.
Our forty years of married life together were extraordinary.*
~ Dan Cruikshank

Epigraph

"Ain't no amount of book learnin' gonna teach you common sense."
~ Unknown

"There is no tool that will do your thinking for you."
~ Unknown

"It is easier for me to teach someone my bad habits, than it is to break them of someone else's."
~D. R. Cruikshank

"I have few friends, and I don't need anymore."
~ D.R.Cruikshank to his IBM 2nd Line manager

Contents

Acknowledgments

Chris Atkins—she was my first copy editor, and I was her first client. Since she lives in the UK, I thought I could get by teaching her my bad habits, but she flipped the table on me—turning my bad habits into best practices.

A special thank you to Deb (Cruikshank) O'Connor and my nephew, Jamison O'Connor, for their excellent illustration of **The Blue Highway**, and to Deb for her rendition of the Direct Deposit Workflow. You have captured the essence of my life during my IT career.

Special thanks to my early readers: Laura McGuire, Mark Even, Tom Edgerton. Your comments and thoughts were greatly appreciated.

I greatly appreciate the feedback from: Jon H., Brian R. Smith, Lou Antionelli, Kyle Nowell, David Lewis, Jim Denton, and especially Mark Anderson.

And, as always, special thanks to my editor, and friend, Marion Johnson.(www.memoryworkspublishing.com)I can always count on your expertise in bringing my story to fruition.

Introduction

I was a shy, quiet boy, with a speech impediment. I would become a humble, soft-spoken man, with a voice that would be heard around the world.

"Are you shitting me?"

That's what I would've said back in 1970 if someone had told me I'd travel to six continents, wearing a black suit, tie, and carrying a brief-case that held a laptop computer, my passport—and maybe a change of underwear.

"No way, you're shitting me, right?"

In 1970, I was nineteen, still living at home with my parents, living life like there was no tomorrow. The previous year I'd been expelled from high school. I had no decent job prospects. I spent my days listening to music and recording 8-track tapes, mostly for myself, and occasionally for friends and strangers who were willing to part with a six-pack of Colt 45 in exchange for some musical sweet dreams.

Around the world? I still can't believe it. What's that? Clean and sober?

"You have got to be shitting me?"

It's true. It would never have happened if it weren't for Mom and that aptitude test she had me take.

Summer 1970

Mom was working as a secretary at the University of Minnesota when she heard about a test for a new area of study—computer programming. Mom made a copy of the test and brought it home. That night she found me in my usual spot, wearing my new set of Stanton stereo headphones.

She shook me and said, "Danny, I want you to take this test."

I took the test and gave it back to her. The next thing I knew I was attending the fall session which began in August. I had to quit my job as a sand-trap edge trimmer. I hoped I wasn't making another mistake.

August 1970

After the first two weeks of the course, I was ready to quit. It had been an introduction to computers—the 80-column punch card, keypunching, hard wiring card readers, blah, blah, blah. To top it off, they introduced us to *third generation programming languages* (3GL), like COBOL and Report Program Generator (RPG). My ECPI counselor persuaded me to stay.

"Daniel, the first two weeks are just a warm-up…get you introduced to some computer fundamentals. You're going to like the instructor—Mr. G."

The following Monday I was introduced to Mr. G. The guy looked like a pear in a suit. I couldn't imagine Mr. G. coming up with anything that would hold my interest.

"Good morning, and welcome," Mr. G. said. "Starting today you'll be taught how to design a computer program. Last week you heard about writing 3GL programs. You will not, I repeat, you will not write one line of program code without first creating a flawless design."

Mr. G. reached into his cardboard box and pulled out an envelope, about six inches long, three inches across. He squeezed the envelope to open it and pulled out a green piece of plastic, approximately the same size as the envelope that contained it.

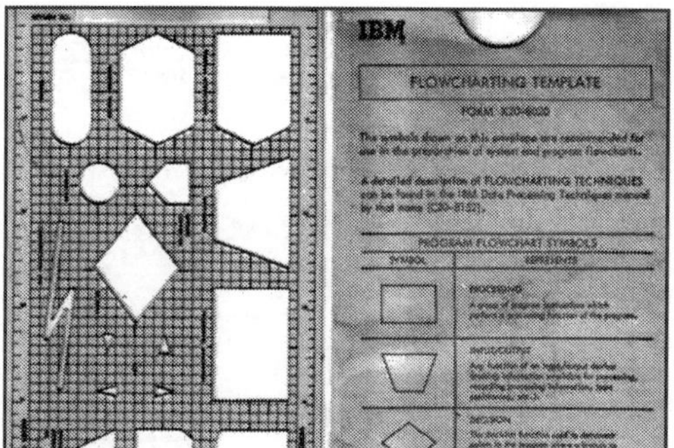

"This is the IBM Flowcharting and Diagramming Template. It is made up of circles, squares, rectangles, lines, arrows, etc. These symbols represent pieces of a program. They are the language of the system architect. This is how the architect communicates with the programmer. The more detailed the design, the less likely it is for the program to break. The more likely the program will function as the system architect's design intended. Questions?"

I never thought that piece of plastic would become my travel permit to **The Blue Highway**. A name coined by some long forgotten IBMer who flew into MSP and drove from there to visit the IBM blue buildings that made up the IBM Rochester manufacturing facility. It would become the unofficial name of the highway I commuted on from 1988 until 2000—when my wife and I moved to Arizona.

It was there, in Sedona, AZ, I found out **The Blue Highway** circles the globe. No matter where I lived, I was always on **The Blue Highway.**

August 2020

US Highway 52 (US-52), a four-lane state highway that connects Rochester, MN, to the Twin Cities of Minneapolis and St. Paul, MN. Beginning in the late 80s, my daily commute was approximately one hundred miles door to door, from my home in Plymouth, MN, to the contractor entrance at Blue Building 006 of the IBM facility in Rochester, MN. Not a bad drive since I had a music player to make it bearable, especially a multi-CD changer that played two hours or more of music. I had to have music, along with my cup of Starbucks coffee to stay awake—since I got up at 5:00 A.M. to be there by 7:00 A.M. I was usually the first one there. I could drive it in my sleep and probably did.

After exiting Interstate 494 (I-494) onto US-52 I drove past several small towns—Hampton, Cannon Falls, Zumbrota, Pine Island—all hidden from view past the frontage roads that bordered **The Blue Highway**. Traveling the ninety-minute journey on US-52 each town I passed was one step closer to my destination—**IBM**. I never thought about the entire trip, only how far it was to the next town. Thinking too far ahead lead to insanity. I had been there, done that—never again.

When I first began this commute my employer referred to me as *Ditch-Rider Dan*, and I would joke about the imaginary corn stalks sticking out of my car grill. I eventually became **DCRANK,** which was my IBM PROF's ID. Many of my clients would call me **The IBM Guy**. I assumed some people just had to give out nicknames. It's what I did as a kid growing up in the city.

By the summer of 2020, things were very different. I wasn't driving to IBM, nor was I on my way home. In fact, home was no longer in Plymouth, MN. My commute now included the entire world. Instead of one hundred miles from IBM Rochester to my home, it was more like sixteen hundred to Sedona, AZ—according to my Maps phone app.

Going home was also different now. Mary Jo, my wife of forty years, lover, best friend, partner, and traveling companion had passed away on June 24, 2020. This wasn't my first trip without her; however, it was my first trip knowing she wasn't at home waiting for me—and she was never going to be there again.

My son Matt had been staying with me at my home in Sedona, AZ. Two months earlier I called him and said, "Matt, Mom's been moved to ICU. I think you need to get down here."

I didn't have to tell him what to do next. He had learned from an expert. He hung up, booked the earliest flight on Southwest Airlines, and then told his management that his Mom was critically ill. He needed to go home.

By August, Matt had some business to take care of at his home in Crystal, MN, so I decided to travel back there with him. I had not seen any of Mary Jo's family since October of 2019. It was a short trip. We arrived in Minnesota on Wednesday, August 12, and stayed an extra day to attend an annual family get-together. The airlines were very accommodating.

As we approached the MSP International Airport, to catch our return flight home, I wondered if I would see dozens of airplanes approaching, coming in for a landing, and/or dozens more planes departing, perhaps heading for some exotic location overseas. They would have contained IBM business travelers, maybe even one or more members from my former team. Where they were going to or coming from wasn't important, if they got there and back—safely.

I am afraid those days may be over. Or, if they do return, it will not be anything like it was. The excitement that Mary Jo and I shared traveling on **The Blue Highway** could very well be coming to an end.

Prologue

I was a stone-cold killer—bug killer that is. I traveled the world cleaning up after other people's SHIT, an acronym that stands for *should have included testing*—performance testing that is. Solving performance problems was what I did for an organization known worldwide by a three-letter acronym—IBM—the world's leader in patents and acronyms.

I carried a business card which had that acronym written in **Big Blue** letters, boldly standing out to catch the eye of the individual I was handing it to. The only things that were missing on the card were the words: *Have Laptop, Will Travel* and my laptop user ID: *PaliDan*.

I wasn't the smartest guy at IBM, nor was I a lifer. I joined IBM as a professional hire at the age of forty-seven. I had over twenty-five years of IT experience, including seven years as a sub-contractor to IBM. It was how IBM came to know me, and eventually those IBM customers who all shared a common bond: at least one, very large IBM computer known as the AS/400—and it was infested with application programming performance bugs.

I had one other thing that very few of the highly intelligent lab rats—those responsible for developing, managing, and delivering the world's best kept secret—had. I was fearless. I called a spade, a spade. I kicked ass and took names, mostly program names that is. Programs that contained the algorithms that brought the biggest, largest, and mightiest AS/400s to their knees. If an AS/400 had a set of balls, then these programs kicked them dead center.

Sometimes I would take human names. Unfortunately, those individuals would be terminated with extreme kindness. I knew that because I would run into them again and again, spreading the same non-performance tested coding techniques to unprotected, naive programmers who all plied their trade using the same programming language—Report Program Generator (RPG). A language that I was an expert in.

Once I became an IBM employee, I had but one desire—to become an expert in the one thing that came free with all AS/400s—a fully integrated, state of the art, one hundred percent ANSI SQL Standard compliant, Relational Database Management System (RDBMS), known by its acronym—DB2.

Getting engaged with IBM customers was something that didn't just happen. I wasn't a free prize that came with each AS/400. No, sir, it usually required a phone call.

There's This Guy

Simi Valley, California November 1995

I was sitting in the office of Bob M., IT director for Countrywide Financial Corporation (CFC). Bob's office was located at the CFC site in Simi Valley, CA. I had been working there for about a week, reviewing application performance data. I was presenting my findings to Bob. He wasn't happy.

"Dan, I've heard all this before. It's the same old song and dance from IBM."

Bob began reading directly from my report.

"'You are not a viable candidate for OptiConnect because you have too many file open and close operations. The overhead of these would negate any performance benefit afforded to you by decoupling the application program code from the current AS/400 and isolating it to a separate AS/400.'"

Bob put the report on his desk.

"I think you must be colluding with the other performance guys. Your reports are nearly identical. It's like you take the previous report, change the date and the consultant's name, hand it over, and say, 'That will be $10,000, thank you very much.' The one thing that no one seems able to tell me is, 'how do I fix this?'"

OptiConnect was the name given to the process of connecting two, or more, AS/400s together using a high speed fiberoptic—fibers surrounding a glass core—cable.

Before I could reply, Bob's phone rang.

"This is Bob."

"Hey, Bob, **Steve Finnes [IBM]** returning your call."

I started to get up to leave. Bob motioned for me to stay.

"Steve, I've got you on speaker phone. There's somebody in the room with me. I'm going to tell you what I just finished explaining to this guy."

Bob repeated the earlier conversation he'd had with me to Steve, who listened patiently.

"To be honest, Steve, I am sick of these reports that provide all sorts of eye-popping charts and graphs, but do not tell me how to fix this problem. I am going to have to escalate this to your boss. I think we're going to need a developer from IBM Rochester to come out here and fix OptiConnect until it can manage our workloads. Do you understand what I am saying, Steve?"

Bob was speaking in a tone that did not reveal any emotion. I was sure he was angry, but I wouldn't have known it from the phone call. I could hear Steve's response loud and clear.

"Let's think this through, Bob. You have an immediate problem. Sending an OptiConnect developer out there isn't the answer. Our developers work as a team. Sending just one would not help you solve this problem in time to meet your current needs. I believe there may be a better way."

"I'm listening."

"There's this guy who's phenomenal. He has been solving these problems for several of our larger customers who, like yourself, are implementing OptiConnect and are having similar performance issues. Believe me, this guy can work miracles when it comes to making enough performance gains to buy you the breathing room you need."

"What's his name?"

"Dan Cruikshank; I don't know what he's doing right now, but I can pull some strings and get him out there ASAP."

When Steve said my name, Bob lifted his head and was staring directly at me.

"Steve, that guy is sitting across from me right now."

"Hi, Steve," I said flashing a grin at Bob.

Steve laughed. "I said ASAP, Bob. Was that fast enough?"

Thus began my long-term relationship with CFC, several of their employees, and numerous IBM colleagues.

In 1997, I shared their elation when they became an independent company—Countrywide Mortgage Investment. I was there in 2007 during the subprime mortgage crisis and saw the fear on the faces of so many people who didn't know if they still had a job. I was also there in 2008 and saw the elation on the same faces after Bank of America (BOA) purchased the company. BOA didn't know that along with the mortgage company's computer applications and existing performance issues they would also get me.

My friend and colleague, **Matt Sharron**, who was the IBM client representative for BOA explained it to them this way: "You may not appreciate this now, but Dan Cruikshank is the best bargain you're ever going to get from IBM."

I came to CFC in 1995 as an IBM sub-contractor. Three years later I would be an IBM employee. The road to IBM wasn't easy. There were several detours along the way. I am thankful that during this adventure I was clean and sober, and that I did not have to go it alone.

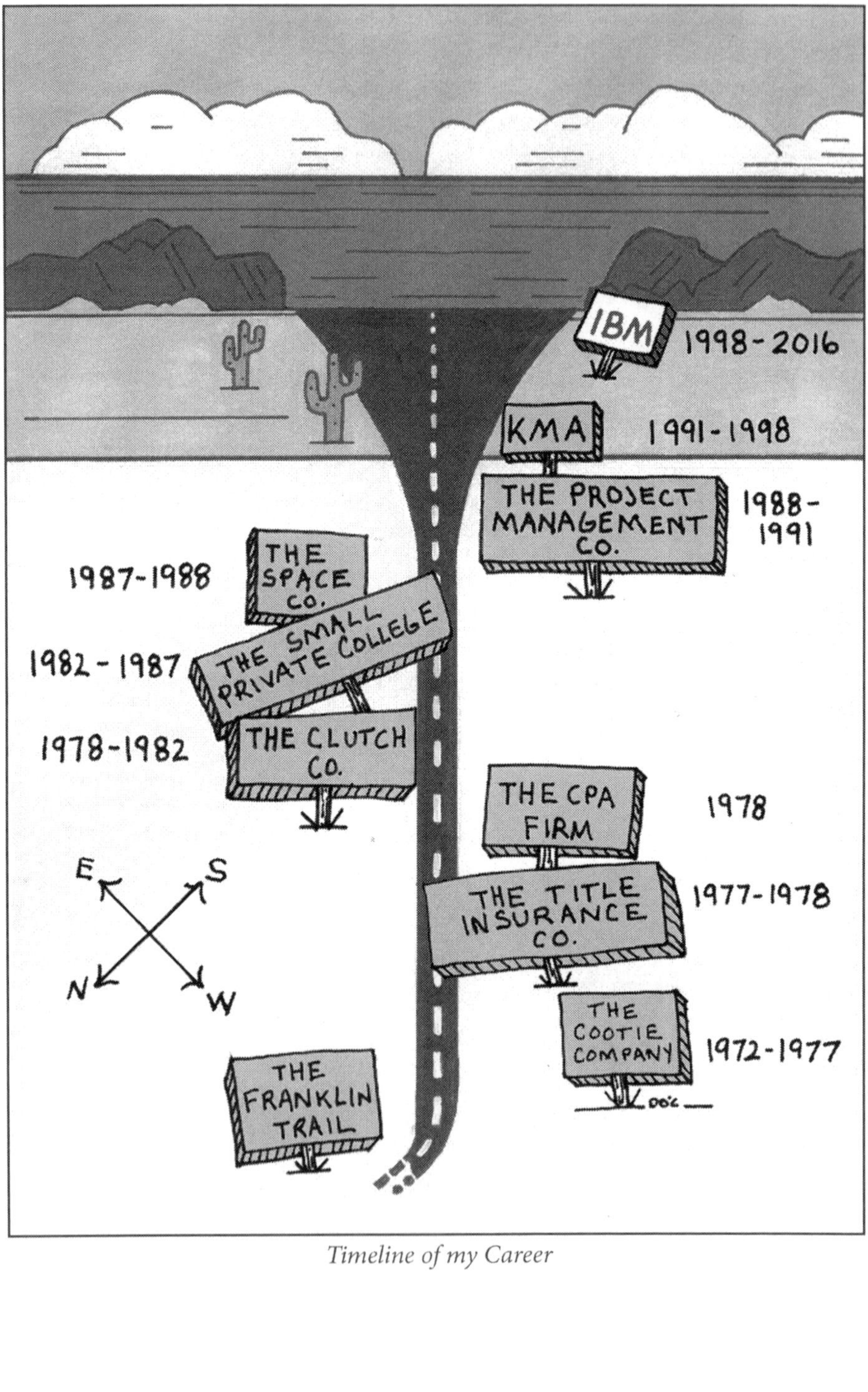

Timeline of my Career

PART ONE
WHERE I WORKED

*"God grant me Serenity to accept things I cannot change.
Courage to change things I can,
and Wisdom to know the difference."*
~The Serenity Prayer

The Serenity Prayer was inscribed on one side of the AA sobriety medallion, given to me on my sobriety anniversary date after completing another year of sobriety. That medallion was with me every day, either on my person or within my computer bag, which was always within arm's length. Every year I replaced it with the next one I received.

It was more than just a prize. Unlike the Commissioner's Trophy, awarded to the winner of the World Series, it was there to remind me of where I came from, and that I was but one step away from returning there. I wasn't going to let that happen.

The Pitch

From Out of the Blue

Space Center Inc.

St. Paul, MN March 1988

I remember sitting at my desk on that fateful day when the phone rang.

"Hello."

"Is this Dan Cruikshank?"

It was a woman.

"Yes, it is. How can I help you?"

"Well, probably in so many ways, but first let's talk about a job offer. Steve B., who recently worked with you, gave me your name. I work for a large, Boston-based firm that specializes in project management. We were just awarded a contract with a large manufacturing company in southeastern Minnesota, to manage the maintenance of operating system software. We are in the process of recruiting the best and the brightest in the System/38 world, which everyone calls S/38. Have I given you enough clues to pique your interest?"

A large manufacturing company in SE MN, operating system software. S/38? IBM?

"I may not be one of the best and brightest, but I'm interested. Is your client IBM?"

"I cannot answer that until you sign a nondisclosure statement before our initial interview. I can fax it to you, and once I receive the signed document and have it in my hot, little fingers, then we can talk about the details. What is your fax number?"

I gave her the fax number. "When will you send it?"

"It's on its way now. Oh, and just so you know, I've spoken to several people who gave me your name as a reference. A lot of people think that you are 'one of the best and brightest.'"

I slammed the phone down on the cradle and ran to the copy room. I didn't want anyone to see this. There was a document printing on the fax machine. I walked over and started to read what had been printed.

This must be it, Nondisclosure Agreement, blah, blah, blah. Hurry up, hurry up. Someone could walk in at any minute.

When it finished, I removed it from the machine and went back *to my office. I sat down and began reading it. This is an agreement between Keane, Inc. and Dan Cruikshank, and then some legal bullshit.* Before I finished reading the entire document, the phone rang.

"Hello."

"Well, that certainly wasn't any way to treat a lady."

"Sorry, I'm at work, and I didn't want anyone to read the document. I see you have my name as Dan Cruikshank. Do you need my formal name?"

"Nah, just sign it as you would normally and send it back."

"Okay if I wait until lunch time? Less chance of someone else reading it."

"No problem; here's my phone and fax numbers. Call after you send it. Any questions?"

"Yes, what is your name?"

"Stephany."

After Lunch

I faxed the signed nondisclosure agreement to the number Stephany gave me. She called me back and filled me in on the job opportunity.

"Our client is IBM, as you so cleverly solved my riddle. Specifically, IBM Rochester, MN, home of the System/3x line of IBM midrange computer systems. Believe it or not, I have hung up on one or two candidates who did not figure that out. Here's the poop: IBM will be announcing a new computer system this June. It will tentatively be named Application System 400 or AS/400. IBM has contracted with us for the next three years to support the S/38 operating system known internally as Control Program Facility [CPF]. Still with me?"

The AS/400 would be introduced on June 8, 1988. During the next twenty-six years the AS/400 would go through many name changes, the last was IBM i.

"Even more so."

"Great, because I have no idea what I'm talking about. As I said before, we are currently in the process of staffing up for this project. The ideal candidates for this phase would have leadership and managerial skills, knowledge of the S/38 operating system, experience with the S/38 High Level Language [HLL] programming and utilities—and this isn't a requirement but an advantage—experience with operating system development. How does that sound so far?"

"Except for the operating system development experience, I think I am well qualified."

"That isn't a problem. IBM will train individuals in the internal development languages, PL/MI and PL/MP, which are based on PL/1, whatever that is. Educational requirements are basic stuff, high school diploma, four-year degree. In addition..."

"Just a minute, I think there may be a showstopper here. I never went to college, nor did I finish high school. I have a GED; aka a general high-school equivalency degree."

"Hmmm, weren't you the IT director for Augsburg College in Minneapolis? How did you get that job without a college degree?"

"I put out. I'm just kidding. I used my charm and communication skills to sell myself. I beat out twenty-six other candidates for the job, all with college degrees."

"Hahahaha! I like you. Send me your resume. I think we can work something out. Oh, before I let you go, just one more thing."

"What's that?"

"Do you know RPG?"

Are you kidding me?

Schaper Manufacturing

Plymouth, MN

June 1972 to July 1977

I applied for a part-time computer operator position at Schaper Manufacturing Inc. aka The Cootie Company. I got the job. It had been nearly two years since I graduated from a Vocational-Technical school specializing in data processing, focusing on computer programming. I was now a DP Guy. I felt confident enough to quit my security/janitor job.

Six months after I started at Schaper, I was offered a full-time position as the second shift computer operator. Business was growing. They didn't have enough work to keep me busy on the computer, so they said I could spend my down time studying the computer programming manuals for RPG.

At that time, I was actively drinking to excess and experimenting with illegal drugs. Sobriety was the farthest thing from my mind. It was there, at Schaper, that I wrote my first computer programs, using an IBM proprietary programming language, developed specifically for the IBM System3/x line of computer systems. The programming language they used, which I eventually would become an expert in, was RPG—specifically RPG/II.

I have a soft spot in my heart for Schaper. Not because it was my first computer job, no sir. It was where I met Mary Jo.

Base Hit

Space, the Final Frontier

St. Paul, MN March 1988

Stephany was quiet for a moment, then she spoke.

"Dan? Hello? Are you still there?"

"I'm here, Stephany. I was just thinking about the first RPG programs that I wrote."

"So, I guess you know RPG?"

"That would be an understatement, Stephany."

"I thought so. Steve B. told me he used RPG/III at Augsburg when he did some work for you. He didn't think you would be interested in leaving there. I was surprised to find out you left Augsburg. Would you be interested in making another move at this time?"

"Yes, I would."

"I was hoping my pitch might get you to first base. You may be sliding into second."

"Stephany, I like the baseball analogies. My son Dennis is probably going to make the Metro All-Star team again this year. And I can't get over the Minnesota Twins winning the World Series last year. Are you a baseball fan?"

"Dan, I'm from Boston, I'm a huge Red Sox fan. Been watching baseball with my dad since I was a little girl. He'd let me share his coffee until I got older. Then he would share his beer. Probably why I'm such a flirt, not just with anyone, mind you."

"Only those you're trying to recruit. No need to turn on the charm, you are pitching a perfect game. You couldn't have called at a better time. I did leave Augsburg for what I thought would be an exciting opportunity—but it's going south fast."

"Was that a pun?" Stephany asked jokingly.

"Ha, ha, not intentionally, but I see the humor now."

Rochester, MN, home to IBM's midrange computer division, was approximately ninety miles southeast of St. Paul, MN.

"Well, I do need some background information. Why don't you tell me about your current job? We can work backwards from there."

"Okay, I'm currently working at Space Center Inc., in St. Paul. I was hired to replace the former IT director, who, along with most of the IT department, walked out."

"Let me guess. From what Steve said about what you did at Augsburg, you were probably thinking, *'Oh, boy, another ground floor opportunity,' right?*"

"Exactly."

"What happened?"

"Wasn't what I expected."

"Tell me about it."

The Space Company

Space Center Inc. St. Paul, MN
August 1987 thru Mid-April 1988

A pair of rather shapely legs was sticking out from underneath my desk. Nor was the body very shabby either. Overall, the entire package was a ten. I was amazed at how much she knew about computers. She was in the process of connecting my IBM Personal Computer (PC) to the company Ethernet system.

I had been at Space Center Inc., aka SpaceCenter, for several months. Getting a new PC was my first real accomplishment. This job had sounded better when the recruiter explained it to me. Not what it turned out to be—mostly a case of hurry up and wait.

Essentially, SpaceCenter had three major lines of business or LOBs—property management, office, and warehouse space. In addition, they were into radio and television, owning several stations across the nation.

I had some experience with property management, having architected the student housing application at Augsburg. I knew nothing about warehousing, and less than nothing about owning and operating radio and television stations. I was counting on IBM to have apps for that. What I wasn't counting on was a company named UNIVAC, a maker of computers that competed with IBM—and SpaceCenter's largest customer.

Politics

The CFO was in a meeting talking with a suit, a consultant from Arthur Andersen, a management consulting company. The suit had shown up an hour before. He spent some time in a conference room reviewing my report before providing the CFO with his assessment.

Strike one.

I went to get a cup of coffee. As I returned to my office, the suit was shaking hands with the CFO. I went to my desk and sat down.

Strike two.

I turned to my PC and began reviewing my resume.

"Mr. Cruikshank? Dan?" It was the suit.

"Can I come in?"

"Sure, have a seat. How can I help you?"

He closed the door behind him and sat down.

"What the fuck is going on? How did you get into the middle of this shit?"

"I presume you read my report. Did I miss anything?"

"The report is flawless, perhaps you could've added another system, say the 4300, but that would still be IBM—that's the problem."

"Because of UNIVAC?"

"Yes, they are SpaceCenter's largest client"

"That's why I included them in the comparison."

"The CFO agrees with your conclusion. IBM makes perfect sense."

"BUT a big but?"

"The president of the company does not want to ruffle any feathers. The CFO's hands are tied. He does not want to jeopardize his career."

Strike three. I'm out of here.

"Well, thanks for stopping by and filling me in."

"You're welcome. The CFO wanted me to stop by and tell you to keep us in mind should you need our services to help with the new computer system, programming, consulting, whatever."

"I will."

We shook hands and he left. As I watched him leave, I knew my time was up at SpaceCenter. Mary Jo wasn't going to be happy with me.

Just then, my phone rang. The phone call wasn't from Arthur Andersen.

Strike Outs
Don't Bet the House

March 1988

"Is this that phone call?" Stephany asked.

"Yup, couldn't have been more than ten minutes after the suit walked out."

"That's incredible."

"Happens to me more often than you would think. It seems that every time I make a poor decision, and just as the shit is about to hit the fan, something happens for the better."

"Like what?"

"Well, getting the job at Augsburg, for one. My job before that is two. There were a number of things that happened to me as a kid that I just couldn't explain."

"Well, I'm all ears. I have a lot of questions. Is it possible for you to come to our office located in downtown Rochester today for a face-to-face interview?"

"Yes, I will need to call my wife, Mary Jo, and run this by her."

"Absolutely, when you get here you can tell me about these other jobs. My calendar is clear for the rest of the day."

"Okay. I am going to take the rest of the day off and head to Rochester. I don't see any reason for staying here. Give me about an hour and a half."

I called Mary Jo, told her I had a meeting in Rochester and might be late for dinner. I stopped by the CFO's office and said I wasn't feeling well. He simply nodded as I left.

Face-to-Face Interview

Rochester, MN

Stephany's office was in downtown Rochester on the second floor of a building on 2nd St. I took the stairs which took me to an open office door. A woman about my age was sitting at a desk just inside the door. She had long, dark hair and wore glasses. She looked up as I knocked lightly on the doorframe.

"Are you Dan Cruikshank?" she asked.

"Are you Stephany?"

She nodded.

I stuck out my hand as Stephany stood up and we shook hands.

I looked around the room. "I guess I was expecting something bigger."

"This is temporary as we staff up for the CPF project. Eventually we will relocate to something larger, like the Midway Motor Lodge off Highway 52 in southwest Rochester."

She pointed to a chair opposite her desk.

"Take a seat, Dan. We'll start with some paperwork, mainly just CYA [cover your ass] stuff. I'm hoping you and Mary Jo can come down this Saturday to explore Rochester, have dinner, and stay overnight."

"Sounds like a plan. I'll run it by Mary Jo when I get home tonight."

"Go ahead and read the Keane Application for Employment document. I'm going to get some coffee. Can I get you something?"

"Coffee black, thanks."

"Okay, I'll be right back."

I had completed reviewing the application document by the time Stephany returned. She asked if I had any questions. When I shook my head, she told me to go ahead and sign it.

"Well, now we can settle down and you can tell me about your job at Augsburg."

"Okay, but I'm going to start with a couple of strike-outs."

Stephany continued with the baseball theme.

"Bottom of the ninth, two outs, and the mighty Dan steps up to plate. Strike One!"

The Title Insurance Company

The Software Analyst

Late July 1977 to July 1978

I was standing in the unemployment line. I had been collecting an unemployment check for about three weeks, since I was fired from Schaper, my first computer job. I started as a part-time computer operator and worked my way up to operations supervisor before making a lateral move to programmer.

My last project was developing interactive applications using the RPG/II programming language and an IBM developed communications tool known as Communications Control Program (CCP). I loved the work and the company until a disastrous turn of events changed my life.

After doing some serious soul searching, I determined I needed to make a change. I was unhappy in my marriage to my first wife. My boss, the man who followed his gut feeling and hired me, had been fired along with a programmer who failed to test a program change that destroyed a year's worth of sales data. There was no backup. At the farewell party held at a nearby bar and grill, The Country House, I had met someone else. Her name was Mary Jo, and I would become her lifelong partner.

In the spring of 1977, I left my wife and son. I stayed with a friend for a couple of nights. My programming team leader offered me a room in his trailer home in Shakopee, MN. That lasted for a couple of months. In June, I moved into a one-room apartment, with bath and kitchenette, located in downtown Minneapolis. I had started seeing Mary Jo on a regular basis, so I wanted a place of my own.

I collected my unemployment check. A lot less than what I had been making, but it was better than nothing. I moved to the next line to wait until it was my turn to talk with the unemployment counselor. I had expected the same old questions and answers. That time the conversation was different.

"Hello, Dan. It looks like something has come up that matches your skill set. It's Title Insurance Company [Title Inc.] in downtown Minneapolis. They are looking for a software analyst, here's the job posting. I went ahead and scheduled a job interview for you, tomorrow at 1:00 P.M. with a Mr. John G. Good luck."

"Thanks." *I guess things are starting to look up.*

The following is my best recollection of the job posting:

Software Analyst

The individual applying for this position must have in-depth knowledge of the IBM System/3 computer and the RPG/II programming language. Strong communication skills are required. The individual in this position will be responsible for the analysis of both

> in-house written applications, and third-party products. In addition, this individual will design, code, and test RPG/II programs intended for use by data processing personnel. Furthermore, this individual will be responsible for the maintenance of the Data Processing Standards and Procedures Manual...

The interview with John G. took place in a small conference room on the fourth floor of Title Inc. I met him in the lobby at precisely 1:00 P.M. I had arrived ten minutes early.

I recognized John G. the moment I saw him—tall, thin as a rail, wearing black-rimmed glasses, and dressed in a black, two-piece suit. A pocket protector filled with several pens was in the pocket of his white shirt. The smile he wore reminded me of a character I'd read about as a kid in my *Tales from the Crypt* comic books.

The interview went very well. John G. thought I was well qualified, but what he liked most was that I lived downtown. I would have no problem getting to work in snowy, blizzard-like weather, when cars wouldn't start, or the buses weren't running. I thought he was joking—he wasn't. I would soon learn John had a nonexistent sense of humor.

He offered me the job, and I accepted. I could start immediately. The job would barely last a year.

The CPA Firm

Software Developer

August 1978 thru October 1978

In July of 1978 I applied for a job as a software developer. I had been watching the want ads. The position of software developer opened at a small CPA firm, located close to the duplex Mary Jo and I shared.

The following is my best recollection of the want ad:

Software Developer

> A small, innovative Certified Public Accountant (CPA) firm, located across from Lake Calhoun, in one of the most desirable locations within the Twin Cities, has a

requirement for a software developer. The ideal candidate must have RPG/II experience. Knowledge of the IBM System/32 computer system is desirable, but not a necessity. This person will be responsible for the enhancement and maintenance of our existing accounting software and the delivery of our software to our client base. Interested parties should send their resume, job, and education history to...

That was it, the job I'd been waiting for. I mailed my credentials to the address provided. A few days later I received a call from the CPA firm. They wanted to interview me for the software developer position. We scheduled the interview for the upcoming Friday.

I left Title Inc. early on a Friday and took several buses from downtown Minneapolis to the CPA firm located at the intersections of Lake Street, Minnetonka Blvd., and Excelsior Blvd. I entered a glass-windowed building situated on a triangle of land between Minnetonka Blvd. and Excelsior Blvd.

I located the CPA firm in the directory. I took the elevator, got off on the designated floor, and entered the reception area. A man sitting behind the reception desk looked up as I walked in. "Are you Dan?"

"Yes, I'm here for an interview with a Mr. Franklin."

"That would be me," the man said, getting up to shake my hand. "Let's go into the conference room."

I followed him to a room on the lake-view side of the building—very impressive.

"I normally don't greet people, but it's Friday and you are my last meeting, so I let the employees leave early; what the heck, it's Friday. Appears to me that we are going to have some warmer than usual weather this August."

He seemed very personable. We entered the conference room, where two other men were sitting. They introduced themselves as the other two partners in the firm, Mr. N. and Mr. A. The interview went well. Mr. Franklin was extremely interested in my interactive programming experience.

"We would like to someday provide terminals to our clients, thus eliminating the need for them to acquire a System/32. They could connect directly to our computer system. Of course, it would have to be larger, probably a System/34, or maybe a big System/3. Do you think you could take us there?"

"Yes, I can, absolutely."

What's a System/32? I suppose I can learn as I go.

"Dan, we find ourselves in a rather desperate position. Our previous software developer left without notice. I think we all agree that you are the best candidate we've interviewed so far. If you can start the first Monday in August, then the job's yours."

I can't think of any reason why I shouldn't say yes.

The first Monday in August was two weeks away. Sufficient time to give notice. Mary Jo would agree. She knows how unhappy I am at Title Inc.

Downside? From what they explained it sounds like the System/32 isn't the same as a System/3 in many ways, especially size. The most important thing would be getting a larger system on order.

"Yes, I accept."

I signed a form that described the software developer position, my starting date, and salary. Not much more than what I was currently making.

The following Monday I gave John G. my notice. I was feeling very good. I was excited. On my last day, several of my coworkers gave me a farewell party. There was cake, ice cream, and coffee. I noticed some tears. I felt some emotions I hadn't felt in a long time. I fought them down.

Bases Loaded
A Clutch Hit

March 1988

"So you struck out at Title Inc., wasn't exactly the programming opportunity you expected. I could see that coming. I'm not clear as to what happened with the CPA firm."

"You could say, 'they struck me out—looking.'"

"How so?"

"I was so excited about getting a job as a programmer that I totally ignored the environment until it was too late. Something was wrong. I couldn't put my finger on it. Stephany, I need to be up front about something."

"What's that?"

"I am a recovering alcoholic. I've been clean and sober for ten years now. The atmosphere at the CPA firm seemed to me to be a threat to my sobriety, and not just the drinking."

"Well, perhaps you can share more with me, if things work out about this huge opportunity for you."

"Stephany, you don't need to sell it, I'm on board. I just didn't want my non-disclosure to come back and bite me in the ass."

"Okay, no problem. So, you're at bat, bases loaded, two outs, you got two strikes on you, no way are you letting the next pitch get by without a swing. What happened?"

"I swung with all my might. Foul ball."

"Oh, no you don't, you are not going to drag this out. What happened?"

"I hit a home-run."

"Augsburg came recruiting, tell me I'm right?"

"No, nor did anyone come recruiting. I talked to a guy at an employment agency, and something crazy happened. You won't believe it."

"Tell me, I'd believe anything right now."

"Okay, there was this sign, I'd never seen it before..."

Horton Industries

The Clutch Company

Minneapolis, MN November 1978 thru March 1982

The following is from the website for Horton Industries (Horton), my third employer since leaving Schaper Toys:

> Founded in 1951, Horton originally focused on manufacturing industrial clutches…

It's interesting to me that this company was in the same type of business as my grandfather's company; my uncles had been running his company into the ground since his death in 1966.

The Contracted Programmer

Every day I passed the employment agency that was located on the main floor of my building. One day as I was leaving work, outside the door of the agency I noticed a sandwich board sidewalk sign displaying the following words:

Job Openings

Apply Now

Some Fee Paid

Out of curiosity, I walked into the office. It was one room with a single desk, no reception area. Sitting at the desk was a guy in a suit. He looked up at me as I walked in.

"Can I help you?" he asked.

"I saw your sign. I was curious about the job openings. I want to change jobs."

"What is your profession?"

"I'm a software developer."

"Take a seat young man, you've come to the right place."

The man asked me about my educational background, my work history, and why I was looking for a new job.

"To be honest, sir, my last two jobs didn't work out. I loved being a computer programmer at the Cootie Company. I don't seem to be having luck finding that type of work."

"Dan, things are tough right now for fee-paid computer programmer positions."

"You mean there are few openings?"

"Nope, that's not it at all; the industry is screaming for computer programmers. Once an opening comes my way, I can fill it; however, none of these are *fee paid*. In addition, every potential employer wants experience; college degrees or vocational educational certificates are an additional advantage."

"Don't I have those credentials?"

"Yes, and no; right now, your credentials don't carry much weight. Let me explain. Let's start with your educational background. You did not graduate from high school. Yes, you have a GED but that doesn't come close to being a high school diploma. Second, your vo-tech certificate isn't that impressive. Mainly because ECPI went out of business. Having a certificate from Hennepin County vo-tech, Minnesota School of Business or Control Data Institute would make you far more employable."

"What about my work experience?"

"Let's see, nearly five years at Schaper Manufacturing, evidence of accomplishments, steady upward growth, i.e., started as computer operator, became operations supervisor, lateral move to computer programmer, and then you were fired. That's all a potential employer is going to see. You followed that with less than a year at Title Inc., and now, after only a few months, you're planning to leave your current job. I think if you were to engage with me, then it would be on a *fee, not paid* basis, which means you pay my fee. The only other options are to consider another line of work or go back to school."

"I appreciate your honesty. I really don't want to start a new career or go back to school. I hated school. If I agree to pay your fee, when do I do that?"

"I take 10% up front for each potential employer you interview with; the remainder is due once you are hired."

"Okay. I need to think this over. Today is Thursday. Can I call you next week?"

"No problem, please take your time. You know where to find me."

He called me first.

"Hello."

"Hi, is this Dan?"

"Yes, it is."

"We spoke earlier today about employment. Did I catch you at a good time? I hope you're not in the middle of dinner?"

"No problem, what can I do for you?"

"Damnedest thing happened—I was just closing up when I got a call from one of my regular clients, Horton Industries, a manufacturing company in Northeast Minneapolis, looking for a computer programmer. I gave them your credentials. They trust me. I've provided them with some great people over the years. Can you stop by tomorrow and talk?"

"Sure, how about if I meet you at 8:00 A.M.?"

"Sounds good. See you then."

The Next Morning

"Dan, here's the thing, my client's company is currently using an IBM System/3 Model 15D to provide their computer support. They are running *IBM Bill of Material (BOM)*, software. They need to add a job-costing component. The application has been designed; they just need an RPG/II programmer. Sound good so far?"

Although known mainly for its hardware, IBM provided several software packages that covered most major industries.

"Yes, it does. So, when do I start and how much do I owe you?"

"That's the good news, this is a *fee paid* position with a catch."

"What's the catch?"

"My client will take out a one-year loan to pay my fee. You will co-sign it. If you leave before the loan is up, then you pay the loan off in full. The ball's in your court, what do you say?"

"I agree."

"You will be meeting with Dennis W., the data processing manager, and Bruce, the system architect, next week."

The agent called me later that day. He had set up an appointment for me to meet with Dennis and Bruce at 5:00 P.M. the following Monday. I left work that day and took several buses, including one that took me past Star

Machine and Tool Company, my grandfather's business. I stayed on the bus and got off across the street from the prospective employer's location.

The interview went well. Dennis, "Please call me, Denny," and Bruce were hilarious. The meeting was held in Denny's office. He had a window that overlooked the data-entry area. There were four 3741 data-entry, single operator workstations, used to record business data onto the IBM Diskette.

I barely heard a word of what Denny and Bruce were talking about. My eyes were fixed on the white board behind, and slightly above, Denny's head. At the top of the white board were the words *Job Costing Application*. Underneath the words was a complex application flowchart. The only words I remember were from Bruce.

"We're looking for someone who can convert the flowchart to RPG/II program code."

"That would be me," I said.

"You're hired!" said Denny.

We shook hands. I left Denny's office and then the building. I caught the same bus I had taken to Horton but made a change. I took several buses until I caught a bus that dropped me off across the street from the duplex that Mary Jo and I shared.

This would not only be my commute for the next year as I fulfilled my indentured servitude, but also my commute for the next several years, with a slight change after Mary Jo and I were married and moved to our first home on Bloomington Ave. I continued to take the bus.

That time, I did not make a mistake changing jobs. I did keep a secret, though. I did not tell Mr. Franklin, the employment agent, Denny or Bruce, that I was currently attending meetings two days a week, at a center for the treatment of alcoholism—as an outpatient. As far I was concerned, it was nobody's business.

That would change.

Dry as a bone, taking it day by day. May not be enough to ride **The Blue Highway.**

The Playoffs

Keane, Inc. Rochester, MN

"I bet going to work for your grandfather's competitors did not sit well with him."

"I wouldn't know, he was long dead by then. From what I've heard, my grandfather's company wasn't keeping its competitors up at night. My uncles, who took over the company, were going nowhere—fast."

"So, it was while you were at Horton that you were able to hone your skills as a programmer, which put you in place to make the move to Augsburg as what, systems analyst, senior programmer? Steve B. is a programmer, so you were teammates, right? Am I hot or cold?"

"You're freezing, Stephany, none of the above. I applied for the job of administrative computer center manager, and I was hired."

Augsburg College

West Bank, Minneapolis, MN

March 1982 thru July 1987

I was sitting at the head of a long table with thirteen other people. There were six people on each side and one person opposite me at the other end of the table. I was there because I had responded to an ad in the Help Wanted section of the *Minneapolis Star and Tribune* newspaper. It was a small ad and I almost missed it, but something about it caught my eye. I went back and read it again:

Administrative Computer Center Manager

Augsburg College, a small private college, located near the University of Minnesota, has recently ordered a business computer. Augsburg is seeking an administrative computer center manager to assist in the conversion of Augsburg's administrative computer applications, currently in use at a service bureau, to

Augsburg's new administrative computer system. Prior conversion experience required. Knowledge of RPG/III preferred. If interested, please call personnel at...

The term RPG/III had caught my eye. It was the latest version of RPG, the programming language I had been using since 1972. This version incorporated *structured programming constructs*—used in writing programs that adhered to the current industry standard for software development. I knew this because Horton had an IBM S/38 on order, until Rich, the new data processing manager, cancelled it. It was the only computer in the world that supported RPG/III.

Besides the new version of RPG, the operating system for the IBM S/38 was written using the latest object-oriented programming (OOP) technology. In addition, the command language was *interactive*, that is, the commands could be *prompted*, and *interactive help* was provided, along with the ability to prompt for the values allowed within any of the command's *parameters*.

As if that wasn't enough, the operating system came with menus to help *navigate* the user's way thru the many commands and program products available with the new system. This included the programmer's menu, the interface used to *create, compile, test,* and *distribute* both batch programs—no user interaction—and interactive programs—user interaction involved. In addition, the System/3 CCP add-on product wasn't required. Furthermore, and this is what attracted me most to the IBM S/38, was the integrated RDBMS.

The IBM S/38 was the result of years of research and technology invented by IBM scientists during what was referred to internally by IBM as the *future systems* project. Besides an *object-oriented operating system* (OOOPS) and an RDBMS, the S/38 also came with a virtual memory system known as *single-level store*. In other words, the actual physical locations of the objects stored on the S/38 disk drives were unknown to the people using the system. It was IBM's gift to the computer industry. When my employer cancelled the order for the S/38 I began keeping my eyes and ears open, should I catch a whiff or hear a snippet of conversation about any S/38 opportunity.

I wanted the job at Augsburg more than anything else in my entire life. I believed this was the culmination of my life's path to this point. This is what my higher power had planned for me, why it had intervened so often in my life. I just had to get past this interview.

I was in a room, sitting at a table with men and women whose combined academic credentials probably dwarfed my GED and Vo-tech Computer Programming Certificate a thousand times over.

The questions that were asked were more about my experience with migrations from one computer to another. I explained my experience was limited to migrations from one release of the software to the next on the same computer system, the IBM System/3. There were a couple of migrations from a smaller model of the System/3 to a larger one, which did require the transfer of programs, data, and such.

"As you know, we are attempting to migrate from the service bureau, which is currently using a DEC Model PDP-1160. We have acquired an IBM S/38. The operating system and program products are extremely different. Do you think you have the skills and knowledge to accomplish this task?"

"I believe I have the skills. I must admit I have no knowledge of a PDP-1160. For that matter, the S/38 is quite different from a System/3. As with any project of this magnitude, I will need a plan. I have spoken with people who work for IBM. They have assured me they will provide resources to help with the planning stage. They can also provide references from other customers in the education industry who have accomplished similar migrations."

"It is our understanding that this new IBM system has an integrated RDBMS. To the best of my knowledge, the database in use on the PDP-1160 isn't relational. I am sure migrating the data from a flat-files system to an RDBMS will require a large amount of time and resources. Would you agree with that statement?"

A flat file was a term used to describe a non-relational database, i.e., flat files were simply collections of data that were used *internally* within a computer program. Relationships between files were the responsibility of the computer programmer.

A relational database required that all data be stored as *relations*, and these relations formed relationships sometimes referred to as *parent-child*. These relationships were managed by the RDBMS and were *external* to the computer programs.

The S/38 supported both types.

"Yes, I do; however, it is my understanding that everyone, even those IBM customers who are migrating from System/3s, has to deal with the same issue. The S/38 became available nearly four years ago. It is now at Version 3 of the operating system. Here in Minneapolis, there is a local user group that specializes in the S/38. My approach would be to tap this wealth of knowledge for tips and insights based on their experiences. In some situations, I will be learning as I go. It will be a learning opportunity, not just for me but for all of us."

During this time, the man seated opposite me at the table had not said a word. When it appeared that no one had any more questions, he spoke up.

"This sounds like a very big project. In your opinion, how long will this take?"

I had no clue. Most of the migrations I had done were well planned. I was given detailed instructions on what preparatory work was required before the migration was to start. I knew the skill set of the team I would be working with. The heavy lifting was carried out by either IBM or the support vendor. This was totally different. I would be starting from scratch. I played out some scenarios in my head.

"With the right team, I think I can get it done in six months."

"That's interesting, next Monday is February 24. Approximately six months from then is the start of a new semester. Do you think you could have our student information system in place to handle the enrollment process?"

"Yes, that sounds feasible."

I was making this up. I had no idea what a student information system was.

"If I were to tell you that I have scheduled courses with IBM on S/38 training beginning at IBM next Monday, would you be able to attend?"

"No, I need to talk to my wife first. If she agrees, then I still must give my current employer two weeks' notice. That's just who I am."

"Then I guess we're done here."

That was it. My dreams were shattered.

The next morning at work, my phone rang.

"Systems and Programming, this is Dan."

"Hello, Dan. This is Wayne, from Augsburg. I was the guy who asked you a couple of questions at the end of the interview."

"Hi, Wayne, how can I help you?"

"You impressed several of the people there yesterday. I talked to IBM, and the S/38 education courses are continuously being offered until the end of May. We would like to offer you the position of administrative computer center manager starting March 1, two weeks from next Monday. Are you interested?"

"Yes, I am."

"Excellent, we do have one request though. Would you be able to meet with the director of the Computer Center at our sister college in Northfield, MN, this afternoon, say 1:00 P.M.?"

"Yes, I believe I can do that."

"Good, this is just a courtesy visit. We expect that you and the director will be working closely. Our sister college was one of the beta sites for the S/38. I am also surprised that we never discussed salary requirements. We would like to offer you..."

I was shocked by the size of the amount; about 40% more than I was making.

"That is satisfactory, sir."

"Great! Welcome to Augsburg, Dan. I will send you the information about the IBM S/38 course curriculum. They are held at the IBM location in downtown Minneapolis. Please make an appointment with Jan, the personnel manager, to take care of the employment particulars."

"Thank you so very much, sir."

Before leaving the next day, I handed in my resignation, effective in two weeks. Rich congratulated me. "I knew this day was coming," he said.

Divisional Round

The Project Management Consulting Company

Keane, Inc. Rochester, MN

March 1988 to June 1991

I have become a suit.

During the previous ten years I learned to accept things I could not change. Many of these things were about who I was. Most importantly, I learned that I was a leader and that people noticed me, whether I liked it or not.

Both Mary Jo and I had accomplished several things, career wise. Personally, we had gotten our finances in order. We now lived in a new home, in a new development in one of the better areas northwest of Minneapolis—Plymouth. Matt was making new friends at his elementary school. We owned two cars. We owned a timeshare and were taking annual, two-week vacations. Life was good.

Why would I change all that?

During the next ten years I would have two employers. I would be with the first for three years and the second for seven. I would learn the main principles of consulting and project management from employer number one and apply those lessons during my time with employer number two.

Face-to-Face-to-Face Interview February 1988

Mary Jo and I drove to Rochester, MN. We found a place to park near the Keane office. I could tell Mary Jo wasn't impressed with downtown Rochester. Stephany met us as we entered the office.

"Hi, I'm Stephany, you must be Mary Jo. Dan told me many good things about you."

"Yeah, right, like what?"

Mary Jo had a way of raising the corner of her upper lip in a look of derision whenever I tried to make things look better. She wasn't quite sold on this relocation move. I was grasping for anything that might help to get her completely on board.

"Well, he mentioned that you were in charge of bringing Pound Puppies to market, and because of that you received the President's Award at Tonka."

"Did he also mention that Tonka is considering closing its doors in Minnesota? If that happens then I will be unemployed, possibly within the next few days."

"No, he didn't tell me that," Stephany replied as she turned towards me. "It's not nice to be keeping secrets from your future employer, Dan"

"Hello, Stephany, it's nice to see you again. We haven't really talked about an employment offer."

"Oh, that; we both know this is just a formality. I knew from our first conversation that I wanted you," Stephany turned to Mary Jo, "for the job, of course."

"Yeah, whatever, you can have him," Mary Jo smiled at Stephany, playing along. "Just another pain in the butt I can mark off my list."

"I like her," Stephany said to me. "Okay, so let's get down to business. You guys have a lot to do today. I have put together a map of Rochester, marking the best locations for a young family. You have two sons, right?"

"Yes, but my oldest boy lives with his mother. Our son, Matt, lives with us."

"How old is Matt?"

"Matt will be seven in November. We also have a dog, Jenny."

"Okay, I get the picture."

Stephany pointed to the map. "This area here, which is northeast of downtown, is a growing suburb. Newer homes, businesses, schools, etc., perfect for small families, with a dog, of course. This area, northwest of here, is also growing. In addition, it is very close to IBM; although, just about anywhere in Rochester is an easy commute to IBM. What I want you guys to do is spend the day scouting Rochester. Check out the neighborhoods. Locate the shopping malls, grocery stores, the basics. Look at some houses, have fun. Let's plan to meet at the Kahler, say at five. I made an early dinner reservation. Dan said you guys won't be staying overnight, correct?"

"Yes."

"We're all good then. While you guys are out running around, I will finalize the employment contract and we can discuss the terms at dinner. My goal is to get your signature on that contract before you return to Plymouth, Dan."

"Sounds like a plan."

"Mary Jo, you keep on the lookout for possible places of employment. There are not a lot of manufacturing companies in Rochester other than IBM, but you would think they would have something for a proven, international product planner, such as yourself."

"Yeah, we'll see."

Later we met Stephany at the Kahler.

"So, how was your day?" Stephany asked.

"Pretty good, actually. We found a house and we made an offer."

"You're kidding me!"

"No," Mary Jo answered. "I was getting very disappointed. You see, we just built our home in Plymouth. We haven't been there a year yet. Most of the homes in our price range were much older and did not have some of the modern features we have in our house. I almost asked Dan to drive back home."

"Oh, no, I'm so glad that didn't happen," Stephany said.

"Obviously, it didn't." I responded. "Our last neighborhood was the one located northeast. This was a new home, but it's a Victorian style, two story with a large porch and three baths. The interior is laid out like ours. The house currently has a contingency offer, but they were willing to accept another one."

"Well, that's fantastic. Let's order dinner; don't be shy, everything here is delicious. I'll cover the job offer before the food comes, and then we can discuss the details during and after we eat. The coffee and desserts are excellent. Dinner is on Keane."

The education requirements were waived in my case. Keane's salary offer was about a twenty percent increase over my current salary at the Space-Center. The package seemed reasonable. Keane would cover our current house payments for ninety days as we arranged the move to Rochester. Mary Jo had been hearing rumors that Tonka Toy Corporation (Tonka), her current employer, was working on a buyout of another toy company. If it went through, then Tonka would be leaving Minnesota. Mary Jo wasn't ready to leave Minnesota. It seemed like the timing couldn't be better.

During my first interview with Stephany, I learned that the new hires were being assigned to two groups: OS and VMC then, within the groups, teams.

The OS consisted of operating system software components that ran above the *machine interface* (MI). These components consisted of display panels the end-users used to interact with the OS and eventually launch customer or vendor provided applications. The OS programs were written in an IBM proprietary language based on PL/1—referred to as PL/MI. The screen displays were developed using the *user interface manager* (UIM).

To understand this better consider today's smart phone, a tiny computer with an OS. The screen is the user interface. The OS comes with various programs that respond to various user actions—touch, swipe, talk, butt-calls, whatever. These programs are the equivalent of PL/MI programs that responded to user actions, except the S/38 user had to use a keyboard—butts were not acceptable. Sometimes a user-action results in an external response. Connecting to Bluetooth or the internet are a couple of examples. In these cases, another part of the phone needs to get involved—the hardware.

Below the MI was the first layer of hardware software known as *vertical microcode* (VMC). Because this software was considered part of the S/38 hardware it was referred to as the *machine product* (MP). Below VMC was *horizontal microcode* (HMC). HMC was the closest software to the actual physical hardware. It was still supported by the IBM Toronto Facility. Like PL/MI, the VMC programs were written in another IBM proprietary language—PL/MP. The user interface were the dials on the S/38 console.

"Dan, we have been gradually filling up the OS component positions that, for lack of a better term, are mostly application program support. Two of the VMC positions are still open: database and communications. I understand that the S/38 is a database machine, so I assume you are well qualified. Do you have any experience with communications?"

"I am experienced with both Bisync, or Binary Synchronous Communications, and CCP."

"What is CCP?"

"An acronym."

"Ha, ha, that's funny, Seriously, I want to know what it is and how you used it."

The Cootie Company

Spring 1977

During my last year at Schaper (I didn't know it was to be my last year), I was assigned a project to implement the company's first interactive application, which made use of the *communications control program* (CCP) product. CCP was the mechanism that controlled the flow of data from a S/38 program and one or more green screen terminals.

Utilizing CCP, I wrote an interactive program in RPG/II that displayed a green screen on a *cathode ray tube* (CRT) that prompted for a customer number. After entering the number, information about the customer was displayed on the screen. Based on the number of executives gathered around the CRT, it was a big deal. When the data appeared, they clapped and cheered. Except for the office supervisor, whom we anointed Supervisor Wretched, after Nurse Ratched in *One Flew Over the Cuckoo's Nest.*

Supervisor Wretched did not care for computers, nor the people who worked with them. She was particularly bothered by computer programmers, especially us. Our team was made up of the team leader (TL) and two programmers including me. She saw us as a group of rabble-rousers, heavy drinkers, smokers, and womanizers. She especially loved walking into our programming den and chastising us for some perceived wrong.

One day she stormed in and sat down at TL's desk and said, "The CRT application isn't working."

Before TL could respond, Supervisor Wretched farted out loud. She stood up, told TL to see that the problem was fixed immediately and, with great dignity, walked out of the room.

I think the other programmer was the first to leave the room. "I better check on the computer program that's running."

"I think I should give him a hand," said TL, following him into the computer room.

I sat there for a while, trying to stifle my laughter, with little success. I thought I'd better leave, in case Supervisor Wretched returned. I went into the computer room and walked to the back, where boxes of continuous computer printer paper were stacked. It was there I discovered the team sitting on the floor, laughing their asses off. I guffawed and joined them on the floor.

Back to dinner at the Kahler

We all laughed.

"That's a funny story, Dan."

"Yup, say CCP and I remember that story. I used CCP quite a bit at Horton."

"What about Bisync?"

"Oh, yeah, but not until I was at Augsburg."

We were finishing dessert.

"This is really good coffee, Stephany. Thanks for dinner."

"Compliments of Keane, Mary Jo. Well, this brings us to the last two items on my agenda. First, Dan, can I get your magnificent signature on this employment agreement?"

Stephany passed the document to me. Mary Jo and I looked it over. Temporary housing, starting salary, everything we talked about. I looked at Mary Jo. She nodded. We held hands under the table. I signed the document.

"Great! Welcome to Keane, Dan."

We shook hands.

"I assume you will need to give the SpaceCenter a two-week notice?"

"Yes, that is what I do."

"No problem; one last thing, just for my benefit. I mentioned the two remaining areas. Given a choice, what would be your preference?"

There was no hesitation on my part, "Database, of course."

I never felt this good. Wait until I share the news with Mom and Dad. What could go wrong? Now, if only the house would sell.

Conference Championship

At Your Service

KMA and Associates

Rochester, MN/St. Louis Park, MN

April 1991 thru January 1998

I was in Rochester at the Keane offices, sitting at a table in the small conference room I was using as an office. Our house never sold. I was ready to quit Keane; however, Dan plans and my HP laughs. I commuted to Rochester daily, until Keane was able to win another project, with my help, that kept me near home until the start of 1991. By then I was one of the few Keane people left from the original CPF project. The only options left for me with Keane were managerial—not what I had in mind.

The phone rang. I was the only one there; no one else was going to answer it.

"Hello, Jim's Auto Supply."

"I'm sorry. I think the receptionist transferred the phone call incorrectly."

I recognized the voice. It belonged to Gene, one of the backroom guys.

"Hey, Gene, it's Dan, I'm just funning with you. I heard you left Keane. How's it going?"

"Great since I began working for this small services company known as KMA, located in Rochester. I've been telling my boss, Kyle N., about you. She is very progressive. She wants to move the company into the software development world. She's taken on a couple of projects and, frankly, she's in over her head and could use some help. This opportunity has Dan Cruikshank written all over it. Interested?"

"Maybe, it appears my days at Keane are numbered. I'm hoping to find an AS/400 shop needing an architect; maybe a systems and programming manager."

"I think you can name your title and price. Are you in Rochester now?"

"Yes, I am."

"Okay, I think you, Kyle, and I should meet for lunch—Red Lobster, my treat. What do you say?"

"I'll see you there."

We met at the Red Lobster in downtown Rochester. The meeting included me, Gene, Kyle, and KMA's second in command, Ann. They were all dressed for business. I was dressed according to the new IBM dress code: khakis, long sleeve buttoned shirt, and loafers—business casual.

Kyle was from St. Peter, MN. Her father was a lawyer and I believe she had a law degree, not sure. She spent time in Washington, DC, working for this congressional representative and that one before returning home to work in the IT industry. When she decided to start her own business, she took Ann with her. They were very successful.

The lunch meeting went well. I liked them both. They were easy to talk to, and I imagined myself working with them. I did have some concerns.

"So, Kyle, Gene says you are moving into software development. That sounds interesting. Are you thinking just Rochester?"

"No, Dan, we don't want to limit ourselves; this is why we have opened a branch office in the Cities."

"Really, Gene didn't mention that."

"We just opened it. Gene will be based there along with another employee."

"What part of the Cities, Minneapolis or St. Paul?"

"It's an office park, located in northeast St. Louis Park."

"Seriously? I grew up not far from there."

The area where KMA's branch office was located had at one time been mostly swamp. Today this area is known as The West End because it borders the west end of Minneapolis. Several upscale shops and restaurants now occupy the area. There is a Doubletree Hotel next to where a popular swimming hole still exists. Instead of young, bare-assed boys, the swimming hole is now populated with geese.

"Gene mentioned that you are commuting to Rochester. Should you come to work for KMA you would be based in the SLP office; however, you would need to come to the Rochester office the first two weeks to get acquainted with the staff and the current projects. Ann lives in Apple Valley. You two could carpool, should you come to work for us."

"Yes, I do have one requirement which may be a showstopper, if you can't meet it."

"What is it?"

"I believe if a company wishes to be successful in the software development business, they must have direct access to a computer they will be developing the software on. I just turned down a job offer, ground floor opportunity, for that very reason."

Kyle looked at Ann, who was smiling, and Gene, who winked at me.

"As an IBM preferred vendor, we have our very own AS/400. Is that sufficient?"

Later that week, Kyle and I came to terms concerning salary and title. I would be the Director of Software Services and have total control of all software development projects. My salary would be equivalent to my current salary; however, 20% of it would be a *draw*, that is, if I didn't contribute an equal amount by billing or assisting in the acquisition of new clients, then the draw would be forfeited. I would be with KMA for seven years. I was never underpaid.

That week I turned in my resignation to Keane. It was without ceremony. I never had the chance to say goodbye to Stephany. I think sometime during my final project with Keane, Stephany went back to Boston. I had no reason to be at the Keane office, as I had a desk at IBM. I went there directly from home in the morning and directly to home when I left for the day.

The World Series

The Request for Quotation

A Large Computer Manufacturer

February 1993

Karen, the KMA marketing rep, and I arrived at the customer location. We announced ourselves to the receptionist. We sat down in some chairs in the waiting area and discussed strategy. It was a waste of time. We thought we would be interviewing this customer about the opportunity they had sent us in a *request for quotation* or RFQ. As it turned out, they were going to interview me.

The Prior Month

I was sitting at a desk in the SLP office when Ann walked in. She came over to me, handed me a four-page document, and asked me to read through it.

"Dan, let me know if you can think of any possible candidates for this opportunity. Perhaps someone you worked with at Keane."

I read the RFQ. The first page was the cover letter addressed to Kyle. The last paragraph listed five conditions in which the contract would be awarded. The third condition caught my interest:

Analysis of presentation and technical skills/knowledge as evidenced in a mock customer review (see details below)

I reviewed page two which contained more information about the "mock" customer review:

> We will provide you with a case study that each selected candidate will need to review, determine the correct customer solution, and present that solution to a "mock" customer (made up of IBM staff). The presentation will be to help IBM assess the candidate's technical and presentation skills. The review will take place in Rochester, MN. Candidates must

be present to be considered for the available positions.

I skimmed over page three and looked at page four, Attachment A. It contained two bulleted lists of requirements:

Personal Skills Required

*Excellent speaking and writing skills
*Presentation skills
*Self-starter
*Marketing/Consulting skills
*Project Management
*Outgoing personality
*Ability to work under pressure to meet deadlines and tight schedules

Technical Skills Required

*AS/400 Operations and Programming - 2 years experience required
*PC connectivity
*Freelance
*PC Support
*Capacity / Best/1 and/or MDLSys
*Languages: CL, RPG, COBOL, OCL, C, SQL, Synon
*Application and Database expertise on the AS/400

"Ann, I can do this. It's like they wrote it just for me."

"Dan, you are the director of software services. Officers within the company don't go on contracts. Besides, this appears to be long term, three to five years. We can't have you out of pocket that long."

I reread the RFQ and found what I wanted.

"The customer is interviewing next month. I should at least give it a shot. Perhaps I won't make the cut. If I do, then, who knows, we could look for someone who could step in for me down the road."

"I'll run it by Kyle."

Rochester, MN

We were approached by a well-dressed Indian gentleman—from India, not America.

"Mr. Daniel?" he asked, in that way middle easterners and Asians whose surnames came first would ask.

"Yes, sir, that's who I am." I responded, in my best imitation of a typical American.

"Would you be so kind as to follow me, please?"

We got up.

"I am so sorry, please remain seated if you will," the man spoke to Karen. "We only require Mr. Daniel at this time. We will summon you directly."

He led me to a small room that contained a chair and table. On the table were some computer printouts and charts that I recognized as IBM AS/400 performance reports. I had reviewed a few just recently. I did not recognize the charts.

"Mr. Daniel, please, be seated," he said pointing to the chair.

"I am sorry to inform you, but our management team is most busy, with little time. They asked that I instruct you to review these documents. I will return in twenty minutes to accompany you to the conference room where they will be waiting to hear your findings. Time is very limited, so please, do not waste time taking notes. It is difficult to get so many important personages in one meeting. Of course, you understand."

I nodded and the man left. I pulled the charts closer.

The first chart was a stacked bar graph, each bar representing five minutes of clock time charged to the *central processing unit* or CPU. Each stack in a bar represented the amount of time used by the assigned OS/400 work priority.

I noticed right away that most of the time wasn't being consumed by priority-20 type work, the priority typically given to interactive applications. This was what I expected to see during daytime workloads. There were several bars grouped together, much larger than the other bars. The tops of the bars were almost touching the 100% indicator. These bars represented the time being consumed by priority-50 type work. This priority was mostly given to batch or background type work.

Across the chart was a line representing the average interactive response time. The time was in seconds, according to the legend on the right side of the chart. The average for most of the chart was sub-second. Not bad; however, the average response time during the heavy batch work was over four-seconds. That wasn't good.

I looked around the room for a clock. There wasn't one. I didn't wear a watch. I wasn't sure how much time I had left. I looked at the reports and grabbed the thickest one. It had to be the *Transition Report.* I whipped through it, looking for the section that contained the transitions—when a computer transaction would begin and end—for the time containing the heavy batch work.

I could hear footsteps approaching. The report revealed a very long transition. One of the programs in the call stack began with the letters QQ—this is most likely a query issue. The door opened.

"Mr. Daniel, please come with me."

As we walked down a hallway, he described the current situation to me.

"Everybody is very busy. The AS/400 is very slow. The people in the room are not IT personages. They are executives and they are very, very angry. Just introduce yourself and then explain what you found. Be brief. They are very busy and do not have much time for details."

We entered a conference room that was more like an auditorium. There was a stage and several chairs, stadium style. The front row was occupied by at least fifteen people. Karen was sitting in a row in the back. It appears she was invited to this rodeo.

"Good morning, my name is Dan Cruikshank and I work for KMA."

Nobody said anything so I continued.

"I understand you are upset with the response times of your AS/400. I think I know where the problem might be. It appears that you have some batch work being done during the daytime hours, when the system is being used for interactive work. This normally may not be a bad thing, except there appears to be a batch job that is doing ad hoc, query type work. At one point, this results in an object *seize* operation, which takes many system resources, resulting in the interactive applications having to stop and wait for the object *seize* operation to complete."

A man standing off to the side, who I hadn't seen when I first came in, asked, "What's an object seize operation?"

"It's a lock issued by OS/400 to update a system object or perform some other system function. It is unlike an application lock because it does not time out. Once it begins it won't let go. If it's the result of an ad hoc query then it may be creating a temporary index, which would cause a database physical file object to be seized. It appears that there are plenty of system resources available after midnight. I would suggest submitting this batch job to the overnight queue. Any more questions?"

No one responded immediately; then a woman sitting in the front row asked, "Have you ever worked for IBM?"

Where did that come from? Really? I was a VMC coder on the CPF project. I architected the Testing Support Application or TSA and led a twelve-member team to build and deliver it. I was the architect for the R1.3 release of Operational Assistant (OA). I was a turd polisher for Jay Kurtz.

I want, deep within my heart, to say yes. I can't. I did these things as an employee for Keane, a vendor IBM had contracted with. I signed a confidentiality agreement, stating I would not brag about these things outside of IBM. I don't know who these people are. They could be contractors like me—not IBMers.

"Not as an IBM employee." I waited a second, but there was nothing more.

"Thank you for allowing my firm to interview for this opportunity."

"I think it went very well, Dan," Karen said to me as we were walking to her car.

We got in the car, fastened our safety belts. I looked at her and said, "It all depends on what the hell *it* was."

It would result in my longest subcontracting contract—over five years.

It would be the last contract I would fulfill for KMA.

It would be the beginning of my career working exclusively for IBM.

Independent Contractor

The Lone Ranger

DRC, Inc. Rochester, MN

January 1998 thru April 1998

I began hearing rumors in the fall of 1997 that IBM was hiring sub-contractors. Many of the original CPF team had become IBM employees when that contract came to an end. Three members of the Rochester Consulting Services (RCS) team—the team I was on—were hired.

Eventually Kyle was approached by my current IBM manager, **Dan Heithoff**, who let her know that IBM was very interested in hiring **James Stewart**, a former IBMer working for KMA, and me. Kyle wouldn't let me go. As part of my condition of employment with KMA, I was unable to be hired by a KMA customer without Kyle's consent, while employed, and up to six months after terminating my employment. Jim was an independent contractor and had no restrictions.

By the end of December 1997, it was apparent to me that Kyle would not give in. I had three options: 1-stay with KMA and hope for the best; 2-quit, and take another job, perhaps in the Cities; or 3-quit, become an independent contractor like Jim, and then, at the end of six months, apply at IBM, and hope they were still interested.

I went with option three. My first client was KMA, who immediately put me on the IBM contract. Dan H. continued to meet with Kyle, in hopes she would relent. He kept me abreast of the situation. He also confirmed that IBM was still interested.

In March I was engaged with a software development company in Tempe, AZ. While I was in Arizona, Kyle had finally given in and consented to my interviewing with IBM. Dan H. had called and given me the news before I flew back home.

"You'll have to fill out an application and take a blood test, but it's just a formality," he explained to me. "Most people at IBM Rochester think you've always been an employee."

The Commissioner's Cup

Welcome to the Machine

IBM Rochester, MN

May 1998 thru December 2016

I believed that becoming an IBM employee would be the crowning achievement of my career. I would be vindicated for being expelled from high school and never attending college or university. I was proud that my parents were still alive and would be able to share this huge milestone with me.

Up to then, I had benefitted immensely from the graciousness of someone, or something, which had been steering my life, paying it forward, if you will. It was time for me to pay it back—in spades. I wasn't sure how to do that. The answer was the one thing I never saw coming.

I became a teacher.

Shortly After the Turn of the 21st Century

She was sitting in the back of the class. She appeared to be uncomfortable, with the look of someone who knew she was in over her head but was too shy or scared to ask a dumb question. I watched her as she squirmed in her seat. She had stopped taking notes an hour before. Occasionally she looked around the classroom, most likely wondering if anyone else was struggling as much as she was. It wasn't new to me.

I looked at my watch—a gift from Mary Jo when I went on my first IBM consulting gig. "You cannot be a bona-fide consultant without a watch," Mary Jo told me as I opened the gift.

I'd been at it for nearly three hours. Once I got started, I tended to lose all track of time. Presenting nearly five days' worth of information, with hands-on labs, gave me little time to spare. Labs, short for laboratory exercises, were tasks where the students would execute various SQL statements. During this process the students were required to answer questions about the execution of the SQL statement, based on what they had been taught during the formal class lecture.

I was also concerned that the woman in the back might cause a distraction. I decided to take some time to excuse her from the workshop before she had a breakdown.

"Let's take a break."

The young woman got up, letting the others leave ahead of her. She looked back at me, uncertain if she should ask for help, obviously struggling with what to do. I performed a preemptive strike and came to her aid.

"Pardon me, Ms. … ahhh. I'm sorry, I don't recall your name."

"Johnson."

"Ms. Johnson, I couldn't help notice that you seem to be struggling. Believe me, you are not the only one. I normally get at least one question before the first break, but as you know, I have not had any. This first day can be overwhelming for those attendees who do not have a database or SQL background."

"I'm sorry, Mr. Cruikshank. You're right. I didn't think the training would be this intense or require experience with those things you mentioned. Perhaps I made a mistake. Maybe I should rethink being here."

"That is perfectly understandable. You're not the first person attending the class to feel this way. I have done a significant amount of these workshops, and I can tell when someone may not be ready for this degree of training."

"Thank you. I do feel better. I have one question, though."

"Go ahead, shoot. I'm ready."

"When do you talk about the roles and duties of a new bank teller?"

She had inadvertently walked into the wrong classroom.

PART TWO

WHAT I DID

"The American programmer is about to share the fate of the Dodo bird."
~Edward Yourdon from
The Decline & Fall of the American Programmer 1992

Keane, Inc.

Rochester, MN 1988

I was assigned to X.25, the VMC component code. It was a communication product.

What the hell?

"Dan, I know you wanted to be part of the database team, but unfortunately there were two other applicants who had requested database before you were hired. We decided, because of your communications experience, that you were an excellent candidate for the X.25 position. The other individuals did not come close to your experience."

I had stopped by the Keane office after spending my first day in Rochester, MN, in a class on Communication Principles. I had asked Stephany why I wasn't placed on the database team, which is what I had asked for.

"I don't know about that, Stephany. I'm sure the others could learn it. I still have to go to class to learn the various protocols and such."

"That's true, Dan, but we also think that you have both problem-solving skills and the ability to learn new things, quickly I might add, as was apparent in so many of your accomplishments in your other jobs."

What Stephany had said about my accomplishments got me thinking about my past, in particular those jobs that gave me the skill set that had brought me to this waypoint on **The Blue Highway**. I didn't know it then, but everything I'd done and what I was about to do, was establishing a resume that would eventually lead to my employment with IBM.

Schaper Manufacturing

Computer Operator/Programmer

Plymouth, MN June 1973

Existing Skill Set:

He has an outgoing personality and is a self-starter.

RPG isn't a role-playing game.

Approximately one year after I started at Schaper I was asked to help out with some programming. I'd been bugging the programming manager for some time.

"Just give me a small program, anything, see what I can do."

There was a program that was run once a year. It needed to be updated with the new products that were added during the year. The programming manager said I should look at it, come up with a solution, and review it with the programmers.

I reviewed the program. It was written in RPG. I had almost quit the Vocational-Technical School because of this programming language. Originally RPG was developed to complement Common Business Oriented Language (COBOL). Compared to COBOL, which was very wordy, RPG was a much simpler language to use when creating a report program.

RPG had this notion of *indicators*, technically a switch; when ON the associated lines of code were executed, when OFF they were ignored. At that time, the RPG language provided one hundred indicators.

I reviewed the main-line code. The prior year Schaper had exactly one hundred products, including such household names as *Cootie, Tickle Bee*, etc., to name a couple. Each product was assigned an indicator. During the current year ten new products were added; unfortunately, there were no additional indicators available to assign to these products.

All the manuals I read and memorized included the latest enhancements for RPG/II, the newest version of RPG. The new RPG/II version contained many more functions that were not available to RPG. One of the new things was a *subroutine*—a set of code that could be reused.

I went to my desk and pulled out my IBM Flowcharting Template tool. I took some sheets of green bar computer paper and turned them over so I could draw on the back. I *reverse engineered* the program code into a flowchart.

Examining the flowchart, I discovered a common set of *tasks* being performed by each set of indicators. I could create a single task as a subroutine that all the products could share, then the problem would be solved. New products could be added at will, without requiring future modifications to the program.

In addition, the subroutine could store the accumulated sums for each product in a set of *arrays*. As each product is processed in product order, only one ADD instruction to the array is required. The array summaries could be printed and cleared by array element (each element represented a grouping total) when the product number changes. A rather unorthodox approach to using an array, since I wasn't using it for sorting or searching—just grouping.

I didn't bother to wait to show my solution. I copied the program, kept the program code that described the data that was read by the program, and the code that described the report to be written. I removed the existing processing code and *refactored* the program using modern RPG/II programming constructs.

I tested the new version, tweaking it here and there, and ran it with the real data. I used a similar report for comparison and verified the results of the new report program to ensure they were correct. In addition, the prior year's *Program Run Book* showed the program took four hours to complete. My version took twenty minutes.

The next day, the programming manager called me at home and asked if I could come in early to show the other programmers what I'd done. A couple of years later I was a full-time computer programmer, working days with the programming team.

I didn't realize at the time that what I did to solve that programming dilemma was based on sound principals—reverse engineering and refactoring—and that skill would help to make me an expert in application modernization.

Acquired Skills:

RPG and OCL

The Title Insurance Company
Software Analyst

Minneapolis, MN Spring 1978
Section X

On my first day I was shown to my desk in the Data Processing Department. The desk was located just outside of a room that had a door for privacy and two windows looking out into the data processing area. That was John's office.

The data processing area was a good-sized room. The room was also occupied by my coworkers, four data-entry operators, all women. John pointed out that one of my duties would be to ensure the *ladies* were kept busy. The women were all older than me. I cannot remember their names, so I will refer to them as a group, the data-entry team.

I noticed that the data-entry team was using the IBM 3742 Dual Operator Diskette data-entry machine. What this meant was that the data was recorded onto the IBM Diskette—there were no 96-column punch cards. The IBM Diskette, aka the floppy disk, was 8 inches in diameter. It was invented at the IBM Rochester, MN, facility.

The other interesting feature of the IBM 3742 was that the data-entry team members sat across from each other. It was quiet. The data-entry team was heads down, keying in data. If it wasn't for the slight noise of fingers on keyboards, I would swear you could hear a pin drop.

John turned to me and said, "Dan, I need to go to personnel to pick up your new employee packet. Go ahead and make yourself comfortable. Get acquainted. I should be back in fifteen minutes."

Five pairs of eyes, including mine, watched as John walked to the Data Processing Department door, opened it and left. I turned to look at the data-entry team.

"Is he always like that?"

It was as if I had opened the floodgates for thousands of hours of pent-up anger and frustration.

The data-entry team proceeded to describe John in an unflattering sort of way. I concluded that John might be wrapped a little too tight. At least the data-entry team was getting some laughs in. Apparently, John ran a tight ship. I could hear footsteps approaching the door.

"I think John's coming back."

The data-entry team went back to their keyboards as the door opened.

"Hello, Dan. I have your packet. Please fill out all the forms, sign each one, and return it to me when you're finished. Did I hear some laughing coming from in here?"

"Yes, you did, John. I was telling the data-entry team about my first job and how the keypunchers there called me *Dippy Dan* because I answered the phone, *DP, Dan*."

"Well, that shouldn't be a concern here, since your calls will be sent to you directly. You may answer the phone using your given name, followed by, 'How can I assist you?' It's in the Data Processing Standards and Procedures Manual. You'll need to read it at some point. I see it's almost break time. Let's go in the computer room and see if Nancy can join us for coffee."

"Sounds great, John."

I looked at the data-entry team.

"It was great meeting you all."

"It was our pleasure, Dan."

I followed John into the computer room. Just before entering, I turned to the data-entry team, crossed my eyes, and placed my tongue outside the corner of my mouth. They all put their heads down to stifle any laughter.

The computer room was about the same size as the data processing area. It held an IBM System/3, Model 12 computer system. There were several large, cabinet-like structures standing to the right of the computer. These held the disk drives that stored the data accessed by the computer programs. They were often referred to as *pizza ovens*.

The computer operator normally sat between the disk drives and the computer at a desk-like piece of furniture that was used as a console. That was where the computer operator monitored the system. Currently the computer operator's chair was empty. There was also a regular desk in the corner to the right of the door as we entered. That was where a woman, I assumed to be the computer operator, was sitting.

"Hello, Nancy. This is Dan, our new software analyst. He will be assisting me with software reviews and new software acquisitions."

Nancy got up and offered her hand to shake. "Hello, Dan. I'm Nancy."

"Hello, Nancy. It's good to meet you,

"Nancy, we're going for coffee," John said. "Why don't you come along?"

"I would like that, John."

We left the computer room and took an elevator to the basement where the cafeteria was located. After John paid for our coffees, we found a table and sat down.

We made small talk. Nancy had started at Title Inc. shortly after John. They had both risen from entry-level positions to their supervisory roles. John was single; Nancy was married with a couple of kids. They were both in their early thirties, maybe five or six years older than me. I had just turned twenty-six.

John ended the break by saying, "I have a meeting to attend. Nancy, why don't you escort Dan around the building and introduce him to some of the key players we work with on a regular basis. Don't worry about the computer, you'll be able to catch up on your duties this afternoon."

The building had several floors. Title Inc. Marketing and Sales occupied half of the floors; accounting and the customer call center were located on the first three. Nancy introduced me to various people as we walked through each area. I didn't bother to memorize names. I figured I would get to know the key players over time. We took the stairs next to the elevators and steadily moved up through the building.

Over the next few months, I would get to know Nancy and the data-entry team quite well. We would take our lunch and coffee breaks together in the cafeteria. I would soon learn about all the dirt within the company—who was screwing whom; who held this responsibility, or that duty; why this VP was called Mr. Lech, and who claimed he had groped her. To me it didn't seem that much different from The Pancake House or Schaper, my first real job and my first computer job, respectively.

My relationship with John could be called friendly at best. John was strictly business. He had very little interest in anyone's personal life. He seemed oblivious to his oppressive nature whenever he was doling out assignments to the data processing personnel. When he wasn't around, he was the butt of every joke or snide remark.

John stopped by my desk and dropped a booklet on it.

"Dan? I think I might have a project for you."

Finally, I hoped, *something exciting. Perhaps a new program or two to write.*

"I would like for you to rewrite the *Data Processing Standards and Procedures Manual*. I wrote it back when I first started here, and I believe it is time for a refresh."

I picked up the booklet and thumbed through it. I looked at the date. It was a couple of years after the glaciers had left Minnesota.

"Thanks, John. I'll get started on it right away."

The first page of the manual contained the name of the company, followed by the manual title, and the author's name. The following pages were written using an outline format style based on Roman numerals—uppercase numerals for main sections, lowercase numerals for subsections.

The Title Insurance Company

Data Processing Standards and Procedures Manual

John G.

I. Introduction...

I read through the entire report before making my first change. I replaced the author's name, *John G.*, with my own, *D. R. Cruikshank*.

The manual was very straightforward. There were several things that were no longer relevant, e.g., references to 96-column card handling and storage, the computer system model numbers, employee names, how to prepare and cook the woolly mammoth, etc.

I was getting bored to tears just reading it. I knew that I was going to be bored to death rewriting it. It was mostly minding your "Ps and Qs" stuff, things most people learned, and comprehended in kindergarten. I took out a fresh notepad of blank, lined paper and went to work.

There were ten major sections to the manual—the last two covered procedures for storing personal items and taking bathroom breaks. I thought I was going to scream. I closed my eyes for what seemed like a few seconds, thought about it, and then I finished the manual.

X. Personal Effects

Articles for personal hygiene of a female nature shall not be displayed openly on your desk. This includes feminine napkins, hair spray and brushes, make-up, etc. These items must always be properly stored within your desk.

XI. Personal Biological Needs

Please make all attempts possible to perform personal, biological functions before arriving at your desk. Once situated, remain at your workspace until the designated break times. If a personal biological function of a flatulent nature is inevitable, please follow these steps:

Stand up at your workspace and announce you are about to perform a personal biological function of a flatulent nature.

Perform the personal biological function, ensuring it is strictly flatulence.

Remove any required personal effect (i.e., air freshener, candle, etc.) from its properly stored location within your desk and use the personal effect as required.

Apologize to your fellow employees for causing a distraction from their normal duties.

Sit back down at your desk and continue performing your assigned duties as if nothing happened.

I laughed to myself, not so much because I thought it was hilarious, rather because it had been quite some time since I'd written something I thought was comical. On my way to my afternoon coffee break, I dropped off my new version of the manual with the receptionist, who also served as my department's secretary. She and I got along very well. I would always stop by to say *Hi* and share a laugh or two.

"Hi there," I said as I stopped in front of the receptionist's desk. "How's it going?"

"Great, Dan, it appears you're going for coffee?"

"Yup, did you take your break?"

"Yes, otherwise I'd join you."

"That's okay; say, could you look at this new version of the *Data Processing Standards and Procedures Manual*? John asked me to update it."

"Sure thing, Dan, just as soon as I finish this other stuff."

"Great, I'll check with you when I get back."

I went to the basement cafeteria for some hot Essence of Coffee Bean. I would swear that's about all the coffee there was in the cup of hot water they gave me. I suffered through it, dropped the empty cup off, and took the elevator to the fourth floor. As I was stepping out of the elevator, I could hear laughter. I noticed there was quite the group gathered around the receptionist.

"There he is!" The receptionist pointed me out. She had been laughing so hard, she was dabbing her eyes with a Kleenex tissue.

The others standing by her desk turned to look at me. There were a couple of people from Personnel, someone from Payroll, and two of the data-entry operators.

"Dan! This is hilarious, what a scream!" someone in the group said.

Although I enjoyed the attention, I was slightly embarrassed that the receptionist had shared my document with others. That was my bad. I didn't tell her to not share it.

"What's hilarious?" John asked.

Nobody heard him approach, no elevator dings, no door opening and closing. It was like he just suddenly appeared, as if he'd transformed into a gas form, seeped under the door, and then rematerialized next to the group.

John held out his hand to the receptionist, who glanced at me with an *I'm sorry* look as she gave the report to John who reviewed the pages, flipping through them until he reached Section X. He paused for a few moments to read through it. When he finished, he looked at me.

"Good job, Dan, I'm impressed that you got this far in just one day. I can take it from here."

John looked at the group.

"I'm sure you all have things to do or places to be."

Everyone scattered.

Acquired Skills:

Writing

Horton Industries
Programmer/Systems Architect

Minneapolis, MN Late Spring 1979

Job Costing

As Horton grew, the demand on the data-entry team to enter business data was becoming so great that they no longer had extra time to keypunch our programs. In addition, several departments were requesting interactive access to data to make better-informed business decisions. Denny, Bruce, and I were discussing this.

"So, here's the thing, the keypunchers are overloaded. The programmers are getting behind and are coming in on Saturday to keypunch their own programs. I've been checking out this interactive data-entry application by Massoglia & Associates, Inc. for entering, compiling, and testing RPG/II program code. This could take a big load of work away from the data-entry team. In addition, I think it can help the programmers learn about interactive applications that can be used by the end-users to enter data. What do you guys think?"

"You the man," replied Bruce.

"Sounds good to me," seconded Denny.

"While we're at it, I thought I could get these interactive tools, SCAN and DISK, that can help me with disk storage management and maintenance."

"Go for it," said Bruce.

"The check book is open," Denny exclaimed.

"One other thing, in preparation for the S/38, IBM is suggesting we acquire some tools that will ease the migration effort from the System/3. They are the Documentation and Conversion Aid or OCLDMA, and a complementary tool for RPG/II called Auto Report. This will allow us to create *Copybooks*, which will ease the conversion to the S/38 externally described disk-file support."

Copybooks—a term that was used by COBOL and RPG programmers when describing source code that wasn't physically part of the actual program. A /COPY statement defined the name and location of the source code to be *copied* into the source of a program prior to it being compiled.

It was typically used for reusable code routines, such as time and date arithmetic and conversion (i.e., MM/DD/YY to YY/MM/DD, etc.).

Copybooks were also used for *file description* coding specifications, referred to as FDs in COBOL and I, or O, Specs in RPG. These types of copybooks eased the conversion effort from System/3 *program described* files to S/38 externally described files. A program described file is an FD that is completely defined as part of the program source code. An *externally described* file is a file object created separately from the program but referenced as external by the program's FD. Externally described files were preferred for S/38 software development.

"The more words in the name, the better it must be," said Bruce.

"You had me at *one other thing*," Denny gushed.

A Few Months Before

Bruce's high-level system flowchart was exactly that—high-level. It was enough for me to get started. I had my flowcharting template from when I went to programming school. I asked Denny W. if he could order me a new one and, while he's at it, a HIPO Flowcharting Template. The *Hierarchical Input-Process-Output* (HIPO) template contained many of the symbols found on the flowcharting template, with some additional symbols to support programming constructs. Between the two, I detailed the various components of the Job Costing (JC) app.

I realized that to create a detailed design for each JC component and its supporting programs was going to be time consuming, especially using Number-2 pencils and erasers. I wasn't worried about how long it would take; I had the time—a year, with a huge incentive to not leave before then. However, I was eager to begin writing the programs.

After about a month of drawing the JC component flow charts—Where is the data being input from? How will it be processed? What is the output?—I started creating the program process details. It was tedious. I needed to create diagrams for both report processing (batch programs) and display (interactive programs)—a pattern emerged.

Much of the process, whether for batch or interactive programs, was the same. I do not need to create the same housekeeping process over and over for each program.

The flowchart templates each contained a symbol for a *predefined* process. I gave each unique process a name and then referenced it from other processes. I only needed to design the predefined process once. I was now able to begin writing program code that only contained the common code structures—a program shell if you will.

I coded these shells, compiled them as executable binary code (zeros and ones—the language of computers), and then ran them, or tested them, on the computer to ensure they wouldn't break. I then compiled a directory, or library, of programs, each with its own name. These templates were fully operational, just waiting to be impregnated with a unique process.

I went to Denny and Bruce and explained what I was planning to do.

"I believe that by creating these working program shells, I can complete the programming effort in half the time. IF, a big if, I have some help. I think we need to hire another programmer."

"An experienced programmer is expensive, salary, health benefits, etc."

"What if they weren't experienced? What if they took my shells and under my direction wrote the code? I could review it."

"Wouldn't an experienced programmer be able to hit the ground running?"

"Perhaps if they understood the approach I've taken. It's based on some articles I've read about structured programming and reusable modules, mainly for Assembly or COBOL programming languages, or this new object-oriented approach to program development. I can't imagine this type of thing is being taught to System/3 RPG/II programmers."

"You make a strong case. Let's run an ad for an RPG/II programmer, no experience necessary."

We hired a guy named Chris, fresh out of one of the vo-techs; he had no experience. He turned out to be a quick learner. We had the JC app in place in nine months, more than a year ahead of Denny's expectations.

Those templates, in one form or another, stayed with me for as long as I was involved in software development—basically, my entire career.

The Night Operators

We seemed to be going through nighttime computer operators like they were disposable razors, not quite one and done, but more like three to six months, the way I used my disposable razors. Then again, I had full facial hair, so my shaving was minimal.

When I started at Horton there was a nighttime operator who had been there for a while. She had a quirky sense of humor that I liked. She was fun to talk with, and if she completed what was required of her, I had no complaints. She decided to move on.

Jean R. was our next nighttime computer operator. She was a college grad who majored in Psychology. One morning I came in and Jean had left me a note. She wrote in the note that the IBM System/3 appeared to be acting strangely.

I responded, "Occasionally these things happen with older, temperamental computers, such as the System/3. They tend to become forgetful at times. Things they have been doing forever, without thought, now require some extra nudging, perhaps a good talking to, just so they get their chores done in a reasonable amount of time. I find that pointing out the system's erroneous ways can do wonders. An occasional outburst of frustration may also do the trick. I sometimes say, 'No, you are not acting rationally, you're just being obstinate,' and stamp my foot for emphasis. It will sometimes be all that is needed to get the system back on track."

The next afternoon, Jean came in early. She reported directly to Denny. They were in his office for some time. Eventually Jean came out and went into the computer room, which had windows on two sides, allowing visitors and coworkers to watch as the tapes spun around and the lights blinked.

I got up and walked by the computer windows. Jean looked out and I gave her a wave along with my patented, shit-eating grin. She laughed out loud, then turned around, probably embarrassed.

Later Denny called me into the office and showed me the note I'd written. I could see Jean watching us through the computer windows. Denny's windows were not covered.

"So, what was this all about?" said Denny, showing me the note.

"I don't know, I was just feeling silly I guess."

Denny stood up, holding the note in his hand and shaking it.

"You know I'm just putting on a show for Jean's benefit, right?"

I stood up, grabbed the note from his hand, and tore it up.

"Is she looking?" I asked, placing my hands on the desk and getting into Denny's face.

"Yes, she is. She's obviously curious about what we're saying."

"What did she tell you?"

"She wasn't sure how to respond to your note."

"What'd you tell her?"

"You were probably having a bad day."

"She didn't think it was witty?"

"She didn't say. You know she's very intelligent. When I hired her, she mentioned that she wanted to try programming."

"Really? She's perfect. Not one programming bad habit that I would need to break."

"She's getting more curious. She is looking this way all the time now. Not even trying to hide it."

I left Denny's office, walked over to the computer room, went inside, walked over to the computer printout table, looked for a program listing, found one, grabbed it, and walked out.

Jean and I would become friends. She would eventually be offered a daytime programming position. She became our best programmer. Of course, we had to hire a new nighttime operator replacement.

Cathy S. was a short, quiet woman, who'd recently graduated from a vo-tech school and was having trouble finding that elusive job in IT. *Tell me about it*. She had a slight lisp and did not speak much, but when she did her words were short—*Yes, No, Okay*. She did a good job, going out of her way at times, taking care of small problems without being asked or told. She became another programmer as Horton grew. Again, we were looking for a nighttime computer operator.

The last person we hired during my tenure was a young woman from Wisconsin. Her name was Lynn. Lynn was short and buxom with an attractive face. She would come in early in the afternoon to be trained by Sandy, our daytime operator—who would become another programmer—or by Jean or Cathy, if Sandy was busy or off for the day.

In some circumstances, I would be called upon to do the training. I had developed Denny and Bruce's habit of staying late. Sometimes, if I needed extra computer time to compile and test a program, I would leave before 5:00 P.M. to eat dinner at home with Mary Jo, and then drive back to Horton. Lynn and I would chat while I was waiting for the program to compile or complete its test run. She had a homespun way of seeing the world.

"I'm aware of my looks," she once told me. "Most men are only interested in my chest. I don't mind the stares. I like men and I'm waiting for the right one to come along. I want to get married, raise a family. If my looks are what spark the initial attraction, then I'm okay with that. I know how to weed out the wolves from the German Shepherds."

I liked that about her. I must admit, I caught myself looking, and so did she.

"Dan, I think it's time for you to go now."

Stormy Weather

Very late one night Lynn called me at home. There was a thunderstorm going on outside. There was a much bigger storm brewing at work.

"Dan, I'm so sorry to call you at home, but we had a power outage. It happened right in the middle of the report transmission to South Dakota. I IPL'ed the system and it came up okay, but there is an error message when I try to display the print-files."

"What kind of message?"

"It says, 'Print-files damaged. Call IBM for support.' I called and they haven't gotten back to me. I'm afraid we won't get the reports transmitted tonight."

"I'll come in."

I explained the situation to Mary Jo.

"I've got to go in and help. I don't know when I'll be back."

I drove to Horton. After arriving, I went right to the computer room. Lynn looked scared.

"Did you hear from IBM?"

"Yes, they are going to send someone on-site. Apparently, this storm has affected several companies. They don't know how soon they can get to us. Could be an hour, could be tomorrow sometime."

"Okay, Lynn, you're doing great. Let's look at the damage."

Lynn walked over to the computer console and brought up a list of the print-files. The error message was at the bottom of the screen. I looked at the list of print-files. There were about five listed. There were normally two-dozen reports that needed to be transmitted. The print-files were created from a batch process. I could tell from the names of the print-files which reports were missing—all the important ones.

There must be some way the computer knows how to find and display the print-file names. It must be like a directory. The directory must contain information about where the print-file data is so that it can be sent to the printer in South Dakota.

I took a seat in front of the spare terminal in the computer room that we used for testing new interactive programs. I signed in and launched the SCAN program. I entered the name of the last print-file displayed on the console into the SCAN display search field. After a couple of seconds, the data displayed. It was encoded in *EBCDIC* format.

Extended Binary Coded Decimal Interchange Code (EBCDIC) is a one-character encoding scheme invented by IBM and used on the System/360 and System/3x line of computers. It was used to translate the binary combination of eight zeroes and ones, which represented a single character, to a simpler, two-character, alphanumeric value. For example, b'1100 0001' is the eight-bit binary code representation of the letter A. In hexadecimal this would be x'C1'.

I was looking at what I would eventually come to know as a *storage dump*. I was transfixed at the terminal.

"Lynn, can you go to my desk and open the drawer? You should see some folded cards that look like envelopes. Just grab the one that is titled 'Hexadecimal Code Assignments' and bring it to me."

Lynn, sensing some urgency in my voice, ran to my desk. She quickly came back with the card that contained the EBCDIC code page layout defining the binary and hexadecimal code assignments and their human readable character equivalents. One side of the card contained special characters and keyboard functions. The other side contained the English language character set.

Using the card, I translated the last report name displayed on the operator console to its hexadecimal equivalent. I then eyeballed the display until I found it. There it was, in the upper third portion of the display. I repeated the procedure for the report directly above the one I searched for. I looked at the display. There it was, right above the other one, in the same position it appeared on the print-file display.

"Lynn, what is the name of the report that should follow the last one showing on the print-file display?"

She gave me the name instantly, like any nighttime computer operator in the world who sat in the console seat watching the lights blink and the data changing on the displays, printing or transmitting the same reports night in and night out. She knew the names by heart and could probably recite them in order—forwards and backwards.

I translated the name to its EBCDIC equivalent. We both looked at the display.

"There it is!" Lynn cried out.

I had already seen it, right where I expected, underneath the last report displayed. I looked at the data. Immediately following the reports we searched for, on the same display line, were several hexadecimal values. The report preceding the last report on the print-files display and the missing report had values. The last report only had zeros, or nulls, as they were referred to on the EBCDIC code page.

It's a linked list. The value is supposed to be a pointer to the next entry in the list—instead it is nulls. This report must have been in the process of being transmitted when the power failure occurred. The BOM data files worked the same way. The Item Master file contained a pointer to the first item in the BOM Detail file. Each BOM entry contained a pointer to the next entry. The last entry probably contained nulls. Do the print-file display entries function the same way?

At the top of the SCAN display was a field named 'ADDRESS' followed by a colon and several hexadecimal values. I used a function key to move down the lines of data displayed one line at a time. The value in 'ADDRESS' changed with each line. I kept going until the report, which contained the null values, was at the top of the display. I wrote down the value in the 'ADDRESS' field. I went down one more line and recorded the 'ADDRESS' value of the next report. I wasn't done yet.

I exited the SCAN display and loaded the DISK program. The display looked like SCAN, except for the 'ADDRESS' field, which was now followed by a blank line signifying that this field was meant for data-entry. I entered the address for the report entry with the null values.

The display changed. The lines were now double-spaced. The first line contained the data for the report name with the nulls, which I believed should contain the address of the next report. The following line was a duplicate of the first line; however, the data was highlighted and underlined. That meant I could change it.

On the highlighted line I replaced the nulls with the values I believed to be the address of the next report entry. I pressed the Enter key and held my breath. The display blinked. The lights in the room did not flicker. There was no sudden countdown, Earth exploding in 3 seconds, 2 seconds… I looked at Lynn. She smiled. We were still alive.

I exited the DISK display. I brought up the print-files display. The error message displayed; however, all the print-files were there.

I looked at Lynn, "Let's try retransmitting them."

Lynn was sitting at the console chair. She started the transmission program. The first report began transmitting. It finished. The next report began transmitting. It finished. As did the third and fourth reports. The fifth report started transmitting. I waited; I would not leave until it finished.

"It's transmitting the next report!" We both cheered.

I had probably been standing for an hour while the reports transmitted. I sat down and waited for the next report to be sent. It went, and the next. I was spent.

"Dan, it's time for you to go."

It was after 3:00 A.M. No way would I be able to sleep. I drove home. Mary Jo would need the car to get to work. I needed a shower and I had to dress for work and catch a bus.

I had stared into the abyss and it smiled back at me. Come play with me, big boy. I jumped in headfirst. I never felt so alive.

I got back to work before anyone else arrived. Lynn was still there. She stayed to ensure all the reports transmitted. She didn't have to. I told her thanks.

Later That Day

I got a call from the receptionist informing me the IBM CE had arrived. Glen E. was a customer engineer (CE) with IBM. I met him at Schaper. Glen found me at my desk. He wasn't our regular CE at Horton. We shook hands.

"Glen, good to see you. Good news, I think I fixed it, but we still have a problem that needs IBM expertise."

I explained to Glen how I had used some non-IBM tools to review the integrity of the print-file data, how I had found the null values and replaced them with the address of the next report, and how it had fixed the data integrity issue, allowing us to complete our data transmissions.

"Everything seems fine except for one thing."

"What's that?" Glen asked.

"I can't get that error message to go away. What do I need to do?"

"You tell me," Glen responded. "You seem to know more about it than I do."

Time to Man Up

It was as if they had crawled out from under the woodwork. First there was one. Then there were two. Then there were more than I could count. Consultants wearing suits and ties, the worst kind. The people in planning were not happy with the BOM product.

"It's not satisfying our needs. We want something better, more modern. More interaction with the people, less reports."

The Horton executives had reached out to their go-to consulting firm.

I was sitting in a conference room with Denny, Bruce, and a couple of suits from *Arthur Andersen.* Arthur Andersen was one of the "big five" accounting firms, leading the way in standards and accountability. During the 1970s they began moving into the highly lucrative world of computer software development and consulting. At the time they were engaged with Horton, they were also marketing a competitive product to BOM, known as MAC-PAC. In addition, they developed a methodology known as Method One.

Horton decided to go with MAC-PAC. This would replace the BOM product. The suits were explaining the process we were about to begin.

"Replacing an existing software application isn't as easy as it sounds. There is lot of work that needs to be done up front. We can't just jump in, load the new software, train the users, and leave. We need to know what other applications, in-house developed or bought from a third-party, are integrated with BOM."

"Well, we have the IBM Time and Attendance Data Collection system for labor costing and payroll," said Denny.

"Don't forget the JC app that I designed and Dan developed in-house," Bruce added, winking at me.

"We are familiar with the IBM time recording system. We already have an interface with our payroll component. Are you aware of any modifications that you, or anyone else before your tenure, might've made to the time and attendance application?"

"No, sir, we acquired the system after I was hired," responded Denny. "There have been no modifications."

"Great! So, tell us about the JC app."

Denny put out his hand like a pistol, pointing in my direction.

"Take her away, Dan."

"There are a total of 177 programs of which 55 are interactive and the rest are batch."

I knew the numbers by heart. The JC app was my baby.

"Okay, so let's say 200 programs. At one man-day per program, we are looking at 200 man-days, divided by five that is 40 man-weeks. Let's round that up to 50 man-weeks, which means one man-year, assuming the documentation is up to date. Does that sound reasonable to you?"

"No," I said. "I think three months is more like it."

The suits laughed.

"We get it. Pride of ownership and all that. Believe me, one man-year and I'm being kind. My guess is that it will take longer than that and we will have to supplement the programming work in order to get the entire project done on time."

"Three months and we will be waiting for your people to get their part of the project done on time," I retorted.

"Okay, Mr. High and Mighty. What makes you so confident that you can get it done in three months?"

"I know my team, and I know my application. I can also give you some words of advice."

"What would that be?"

"When you sit down with my team and start using terms like man-time, and such, my lead programmer, Jean, is going to rip you a new one and hand your old one to you on a plate. She'll tell you that a woman can get twice as much work done in half the time of any man. For that matter, my girlfriend would tell you the same thing. I must agree with both their assessments. To be honest, I'm happy with my old one, I don't need a new one."

We got our part of the project done well ahead of the suits.

A New Broom Sweeps Clean

I liked Denny and Bruce a lot. They were not the best management team in the world, but what they lacked in managing skills they made up for in leadership technique. Nothing seemed to bother them. They knew where they were going, and it wasn't hard to climb on board.

During my job interview, Denny let it be known that they were on IBM's list for early shipment of the S/38, IBM's latest offering in the System/3 family of computers. It had several innovative, high tech features, including a new version of RPG—RPGIII—that incorporated structured programming constructs (IF ... THEN ... ELSE ... END, DO WHILE ... ENDDOW, DO UNTIL ... ENDDOU, etc.). These new constructs would make my current coding techniques—which heavily made use of the GOTO operation—obsolete, but in a good way. I couldn't wait.

Towards the end of 1979, after I had completed my year of indentured servitude, we had a management change. First, Bruce left because he was having problems in his personal life and wanted to take some time off in hopes of getting things back on track with his wife, or, if that didn't work out, then start life anew. Denny went next. For the life of me I can't remember why. I think it was a better job offer.

The new manager's name was Rich K. He came from a big iron shop (slang for an IBM mainframe computer). He wasn't impressed with the System/3 and one of his first managerial decisions was to cancel the order for the S/38. In 1979 IBM had announced the 4300, a midrange-size computer with System/370 OS capabilities.

I was disappointed. I was so looking forward to RPG/III. I figured my days at Horton were about to end. Rich called me into his office one day, shortly after he started. We had a heart to heart.

"Dan, I want to bring in a 4300 to replace the System/3. It's not going to happen overnight. I have assessed the programming, operations, and data-entry staff and realized that everyone, except for you, isn't very experienced. I need someone to act as my second; someone who knows the crew and could help me explain my vision in System/3 lingo—someone like you. The company is growing rapidly, and as much as I want to keep my hands dirty, I know I can't manage and do programming both. I'm offering you the system architect job."

"Thanks, Rich, I accept. By the way, my fiancé, Mary Jo, and I are getting married next March. This will really help with the financial picture. It would be great to buy a home before we start a family."

When we got married at our duplex, only a few people were invited to attend. We held a wedding reception at the Calhoun Beach Club. Jean, Cathy, Sandy, and Helen (the data-entry supervisor) represented Horton. Mary Jo and I left from there for a two-week honeymoon in Ft. Meyers Beach, FL.

Three months after our wedding, the owner of the duplex on Xerxes decided he no longer wanted to rent it out. We found a small house for rent about a block south of Lake Harriet and Minnehaha Creek. We lived there for three months before buying our first home in South Minneapolis on Bloomington Ave. and 35th Street, about a block from Powderhorn Park.

Rich lived in South Minneapolis and normally took Cedar Avenue to work each day. He offered to pick me up. It was no big deal for him to go a couple of blocks out of his way. We became good friends. It was Rich who introduced me to relational database theory and RDBMS.

"You need to study up on this, Dan. It is the future. Once we get the go-ahead to order the 4300, I will make sure the latest RDBMS is ordered with it."

On November 30, 1981, our son Matt was born. I was there in the delivery room and watched as he made his exit from Mary Jo. For some reason, I felt the need to shave and cut my hair. I had a full beard, and my hair went over my ears. I told myself that I was doing it for my son and the new life he represented for us as a family. I think this thing I called a Higher Power (HP —the AA alternative term for God) had other plans in mind.

"A clean-shaven face, short hair, white shirt, and tie," they say, "is the only way to travel **The Blue Highway**."

Acquired Skills:

Project management, troubleshooting, problem solving, leadership, RDBMS theory.

Augsburg College
Administrative Computer Center Manager

The Countdown Begins

March—Six Months to Fall Registration

I began IBM S/38 training the first week of my employment at Augsburg. Training was every day, Monday thru Friday. I would catch the bus at the corner of Bloomington Ave. and E. 35th St. and take it downtown to IBM. After class, I would take the bus from the IBM facility to Augsburg. I would spend a couple of hours applying what I learned in class on my very own S/38 computer. The first week of class covered S/38 basic operations.

The director of IT at Northfield College provided the source for their payroll software application. It was on a tape. As part of my S/38 training, I learned how to mount a tape and restore the application program *source-files* to the S/38. I also learned how to display the *source-file objects* on the system and the program code in the *source-file-member*. It was my first look at RPG/III source code. I was very disappointed because it looked like RPG/II code to me.

I had found a box containing the manuals for the S/38. There were over seventy. I had time, so I started reading. I was interested in learning about how to work with source-files and the source code they contained.

As I read, I learned a source-file is a file object type whose members were strictly made up of program source code. Although each member was intended for one program only, there was no enforcement of this rule. Thus, it was possible to end up with a single source-file-member containing source code for multiple programs. Unfortunately, the compiler was only expecting one set of source code. Attempting to compile the source code would end in an error. I found this out the hard way.

I was beginning to wonder if I might have been too optimistic in my prediction.

April—Five Months to Fall Registration

I was in the office of Jan, the personnel manager. She had quizzed me on the initial phone call and persuaded Wayne to interview me. After I was hired, Jan told me she could sense a feeling of confidence coming from me as I talked to her over the phone. She was my biggest advocate. I did not want to disappoint her. She was short, petite, attractive, with red hair and a great figure, married, and tough as nails.

"Jan, I need some help. I think I can get the payroll software up and running by May 1. I just need someone part-time, a couple of hours a day, to process the payroll data, run the payroll batch programs, print, decollate, burst [separate the continuous-form paper to single sheets], and deliver the pay checks and other reports. I wonder if you could check with one of the vo-techs to see if they have any recent grads who might be interested in an entry level position?"

"Dan, that may be a problem. Our fiscal year ends May 31. I don't think anyone has any unallocated budget money so late in the year."

Jan thought about it.

"I'll be right back," she said, as she walked out of her office and was back in no time.

"Okay, here's what we can do. The Financial Aid Department has some work-study dollars available, and they are willing to use those to pay for the part-time help."

"What are work-study dollars?"

"This is money Augsburg receives through donations that isn't allocated to a specific fund. It is non-discretionary, that is, it can be spent by Augsburg in any way we desire."

"How does work-study money help me?"

"It's money that can be used to *hire* student workers to perform administrative tasks. Here's the deal: we didn't think we would hire a new ACC [administrative computer center] manager this early; thus, there is no budget set for the ACC for this fiscal year. The S/38 lease payments begin in June, the first month of the new fiscal year. Your salary is currently being absorbed by me, that is, the Personnel Department. The work-study dollars will also be absorbed by me; I will use it to pay a student to work for you as a part-time computer operator. Starting June 1, you will oversee the ACC budget that Wayne put together for your department for the new fiscal year."

"Can I see that budget? I want to ensure I have money to hire more people."

"Bring it up in the next administrative management meeting."

"When's that?"

"Next week; but, for right now, you need to find some part-time help. Better get going."

The ACC shared space with the *academic computer system* (ACS). Augsburg was in the process of building a Computer Science course for the upcoming school year. Augsburg currently offered some introductory courses on computer science topics. I thought the ACS administrator would know some students who would be interested in a job. I hit pay dirt, so to speak. The ACS administrator knew of three students, juniors, who might be able to work immediately, during the summer, and into the fall semester.

I talked with all three; two were local kids, one was from a small town. I picked him. He didn't try to impress me with computer science mumbo-jumbo stuff like the other two. He was staying with family and planned to be available all summer. He was planning to graduate from Augsburg next year. Sounded like a long-term commitment. He worked out extremely well.

May—Four Months to Fall Registration

I had the payroll application ready to go for the last payday of the current fiscal year—May 15. Augsburg paid monthly, on the fifteenth of each month, same as Northfield College, so I didn't have to mess with the RPG/III program pay tables.

I brought up my computer center budget question at the next administration management meeting. Wayne assured me that funds were available for both a full-time computer programmer and two contract programmers. I would be interviewing contractors that month, to start June 1. Wayne had some additional news.

"Dan, I've been working with the service bureau to gradually wean us off their systems. If we can get the business office applications up and running by June 1, we could save some money; money that you can use to cover your department's extra needs. Work-study, supplies, software, etc."

"Wayne, that sounds like a very optimistic goal. June 1 is just a month away."

"Dan, I spoke with several of the administration management team, and we think we can come up with some funds to cover some contract programmers this month. In addition, great news, the service bureau has agreed to provide us with the business office software. They have sent us a tape."

"How do we know if the software will even run on the S/38?"

"Even better news. It's the same system we developed here at Augsburg several years ago on our Burroughs system. It was written in RPG."

At one time RPG was offered by other vendors, besides IBM. Burroughs was one of them. By the time the System/3 was delivered, containing a new version of RPG (RPG/II), Burroughs, UNIVAC, and the other non-IBM RPG vendors had begun to abandon RPG. I worked with a Burroughs RPG programmer at Schaper. He had told me that RPG was RPG, but each vendor's version had its own idiosyncrasies.

My May calendar was filling up.

The Contractor Wars

I was sitting in Wayne's office with a representative from one of the top consulting firms in Europe. They had opened a U.S. office in Chicago and a branch office in Minneapolis. It was the second week in May. Next week a contract programmer employed with a local company known for its S/38 expertise would be starting work at Augsburg. Somehow this Minneapolis branch of the global firm had gotten that information.

"So, you see, Wayne, we know that you require contract programming. We know that you have contracted with our competitor. We think you are making a mistake. Our programmers are certified on the S/38. Our competitor has no certification offering. They advertise RPG/III programmers, but they're mostly RPG/II programmers who know how to compile programs that are nothing more than glorified RPG/II code. They compile and run, but they do not have any of the modern structured programming constructs."

"We appreciate your concern," Wayne responded, "but as far as hiring contract programmers, I am going to leave that up to Dan. He is my expert."

"Thanks, Wayne," I said. "I'm sorry, but I wish you'd been around last week before I made my decision. I feel like my hands are tied; I've decided I don't think it's good for Augsburg or me to back out of our contract. Perhaps we can do work in the future."

The representative thought about it.

"Is this a time and materials contract?"

"Yes, the contract has a week-to-week renewal."

"Our competitor's programmer will be starting next Monday?"

"Yes, and depending on the quality of the work, we will decide the following Friday if we will extend the contract."

"What if I were to offer you one of my programmers, pro bono for one week starting next week? You could then compare their work, and if our competitor's programmer is better, then we'll back off. If our programmer is better, then you cancel our competitor's contract and you grant us a six-month contract. What do you say?"

I turned to Wayne. He's not only my boss, he's also the *chief financial officer* (CFO) for Augsburg. He put his hands together in front of his lips. I could see the wheels spinning.

"A 30-day, extendable contract, with a 2-day notice."

"A 30-day, extendable contract, with a 5-day notice. We need time for planning."

Wayne looked at me. I nodded.

"Okay. It's a deal."

The Next Day

I was sitting in Wayne's office, meeting with the representative of the local contract programming company. Somehow, he had learned about our deal with the other contracting company. He was expressing his displeasure with Wayne.

"I don't see how you can put our contractor in a contest. Who's the best, winner take all? C'mon, this is outrageous. We have the best RPG/III programmers in the country, if not the world."

"So you say," Wayne replied, "and so did the other vendor. We really don't want to be in the middle of a contract negotiation war between your two firms. I have a mind to just cancel both contracts and let Dan hire a permanent programmer."

"Let's not be too hasty. What kind of deal did our competitor offer you?"

"One week, free of charge; if their programmer is better, then they get an extension."

The representative raised his eyebrows.

"Free? Tell you what, what if I make the same offer? You get my guy free of charge for one week. If he outperforms the competition, then you extend his contract for six months. What do you say?"

"We extend for thirty days, with a two-day notice."

"Thirty days, with a five-day notice," countered the rep. "We need time for planning."

"Deal."

I have acquired two programmers who will be working for free. I have a bigger problem. I had copied the source code from the tape the service bureau provided to a disk-file on the S/38. I couldn't read the code. It wasn't EBCDIC; it was in the American Standard Code for Information Interchange (ASCII) format. Fortunately, RPG/III came with a method to translate ASCII to EBCDIC.

I wrote a program to translate the data in the disk-file. Once translated, I could read the RPG code. It wasn't even close to RPG/II, let alone RPG/III. That wasn't the bad news. The data was in one big file. The source code for each program had to be in a separate source-file-member as part of a source-file. It was already 6:00 P.M. on a Friday night. I had two contract programmers starting Monday morning and I had nothing for them to do.

You have two programmers starting on Monday and you have nothing for them to do? They're RPG programmers. Have them extract, clean, copy, modify, compile, and test the programs—good thinking.

I went home for the day. I came back in on Saturday. I wanted to prove the process I had come up with was feasible for the contract programmers to accomplish the task. My first step was to create a source-file using the Create Source Physical File (CRTSRCPF) command. I used the *S/38 copy file* (CPYF) command to copy the first program from the disk-file to a source-file-member based on the starting and ending record positions of the source code. I then modified the source code, fixing any copy related errors, and/or non-IBM RPG constructs, compile errors, etc. I was finally able to successfully compile the program and create an executable program object.

Mission accomplished. I wasn't going to test it. That would be the contractors' jobs.

The Following Monday

I was sitting in my office facing the two contractors. Bob was an older gentleman, slim build, glasses, short hair, sporting a goatee, and wearing a casual shirt with solid tie. Jim, the other guy, was heavy set, short hair, glasses, clean face, kind of babyish, wearing a solid shirt with a bow tie. I have a picture of me when I was in kindergarten, wearing a white shirt and bow tie. I guess I was born to lead contract programmers.

"Okay, here's the plan. I assume you are both aware of the deal Augsburg has made with your employers."

They nodded.

"Your mission will be to transform RPG code developed on a Burroughs system, currently running on a DEC PDP-1160—don't ask me how they do that—to RPG/III. The source code is currently frozen in a chunk of cow shit, complete with straw, dung beetles, and everything else you can imagine. Still with me?"

They nodded.

"You must carefully chip the shit away from the code, transfer it to a S/38 source-file-member, where you will rigorously polish it until it is presentable to the S/38 compiler. There you will subject the code to the compilation process, correct any errors, and continue to compile until you achieve a successful compilation. At that point, you will test the shit out of the program until it is totally free of all diseases it may have acquired during its time in DEC PDP-1160 hell. Am I clear?"

"Yes, sir! Yes, sir!"

"Any questions?"

"What time are the breaks?"

"We take coffee breaks at 10 A.M. and 2:30 P.M. Anything else?"

"What are we going to do tomorrow?"

I like these guys.

A Week Later

I was sitting in Wayne's office at a small table designed for groups of four or less. Wayne and I are on one side; the employers for the contract programmers are on the other. The previous Friday, Wayne had contacted the contracting firms and arranged this meeting. We had made our decision and thought they should be there to hear it, ask questions, whatever.

"Thank you for coming. I am going to let Dan share our decision, and then we can discuss the next steps. Dan, it's all yours."

"Thanks, Wayne. I'm going to come right to the point. I would like to keep both. I think I can keep them busy for the next six months. The only thing I ask is that we can agree on a blended rate for their services."

"Yeah, but our programmer is more experienced."

"Yeah, but our programmer is just as qualified and less expensive."

"To be honest here, you both marketed your programmers as having S/38 RPG/III experience, and they very well might be the best in the field. Unfortunately, now that I have had more time to assess the situation, it appears that S/38 RPG/III experience isn't required. The program code we're working with isn't even close to being RPG/II, let alone RPG/III. I'm okay with that. Both programmers are highly skilled in RPG/II. Currently that's all we need. So, here's the deal: you agree on the same rate, ideally closer to the lower rate being charged. You will each have a programmer billing for the next six months. A coder in the bank is worth two on the bench, don't you agree?"

We agreed to a rate and the deal was done. I didn't tell anyone about my hidden agenda. I had learned at Horton that it's easier to teach someone my bad habits, rather than trying to teach an old dog new tricks. The contractors were good, but short-term only. They knew RPG/III inside and out. They knew externally described data files. They knew command language (CL); however, they didn't know relational database, nor were they interested in learning about it.

I needed someone with a fresh mind, directly out of school, votech or college, who had been exposed to new ideas and wasn't brainwashed by one product or another. Someone eager to learn, who didn't have a method or process that was superior to mine. Someone who would be open to learning a new way—Dan's way, or the highway.

I knew where to find them.

Equal Opportunities
June—Three Months to Fall Registration

"Let me see if I understand you correctly. You wish to hire, no, that's the wrong word; you wish to bring on an apprentice, a recent graduate, someone who is having trouble finding employment as a computer programmer. You will take this person under your wing for six months; train them in RPG/III and S/38 technology, with emphasis on relational database. At the end of six months, you will let them go, with a strong letter of reference from you, verifying that they have six months of on-the-job S/38 experience, including RPG/III, CL, CLP, DDS, etc. Do I have that right? Is that a good summation?"

"I couldn't have said it better myself," I grinned at the employment counselor for Hennepin Technical/Vocational Institute.

"It's insane."

"I hear that a lot."

I had been to two other vo-techs and gotten nowhere with them. They were not interested. They were having no problem placing their graduates with employers, so they claimed.

"Well, thank you very much for listening to me."

I got up to leave.

"Wait a minute, I think I know someone who might be interested. Tell me how this would work again?"

Her name was Martha, single, from New England, mid-twenties, attended college, but didn't really know what she wanted. She had moved to Minnesota, had some odd jobs, then decided to go back to school—computer programming. She'd completed the course work and was having trouble finding that first job. Not quite the pedigree employers were looking for—except for me.

The contractors had been working hard. They had almost completed extracting, fixing, and compiling the RPG programs. We reached a roadblock when we needed to know how they worked. At first, I played the middleman with the bureau. They were not very cooperative, grudgingly handing over what little documentation they had. We were able to figure out the program run sequence. The contractors were creating test data by hand, using a tool named Data File Utility (DFU).

Data Description Specifications (DDS) was the language used to define externally described data files. A file was a type of object. There were several types of files: physical (the container for actual data), logical (a virtual file typically used to order the data but could also be used to reformat the data), display (a file containing screen formats), along with a multitude of others. OOOPS system defined methods that determined how an object could be accessed. For example, a file-object could be read from, written to, copied, deleted, etc.; however, it could not be executed.

The S/38 had a tool named Screen Design Aid (SDA). It provided a visual approach to generating the DDS code used to create a *display-file* (DSPF) object—the green screen that was used to enter data and subsequently display the data. The screen communicated with an RPG/III program that could read, verify, and write data to a *physical file* (PF) object. The screen could display the data in many ways, with help from *indicators*. DDS used indicators, like RPG, as switches that could be turned on or off, to indicate a condition that influenced the way data would be displayed and, if need be, processed.

Martha and the two contractors were in my office. I looked at the two contractors.

"Which one of you knows SDA?"

They both shook their heads.

I handed the SDA manual to Martha.

"Here you go, learn something new."

Martha grabbed the manual. I addressed them all.

"Here's what we're going to do. I am going to create some HIPO charts. From these charts I am going to create some RPG/III program templates. Martha, in the charts where it shows a screen symbol, you will use SDA to design the screen. Don't worry, I will work with you. We'll learn together."

"Bob, you will be our sub-file data-entry expert. Jim will create the file maintenance programs. Questions?"

There weren't any.

"Good, then let's sling some code, partners."

One Stinking Penny

June Month End—Two Months to Fall Registration

It was a Friday. I was in Wayne's office. We were talking about the business office reporting system. Martha, Bob, and Jim worked their butts off to finish by the end of June. All the data had been entered. The first set of business reports had been printed and were ready for distribution. Except for one, the most important one. It was off by one cent, one penny, a hundredth of a dollar.

"I tell you, Wayne, I have been pulling my hair out. I've checked and rechecked the programs. I just can't find a bug. Are you sure we can't distribute the reports? That will give us time to solve the problem before the end of July."

"No can do, Dan."

I went back to my office and grabbed the computer program listing, started scanning the code.

"Goodnight, Dan."

I looked up. It was Martha. She normally left at 5:00 P.M.

"Goodnight, Martha, thanks for doing such a great job with SDA. I'll see you Monday."

"Do you and Mary Jo have any fun plans for the weekend?"

I knew Martha would be hitting the bar scene. It's what young, single people did.

"No, I'm going to be here. Wayne won't accept the general ledger report until it's right."

"Oh, okay, I will see you Monday."

I decided to call it a day. It was time to go home and tell Mary Jo I'm spending another weekend at Augsburg. Saturday morning, I was at my desk when I heard the door to the ACC open and close. It was Martha.

"I thought you might need some help."

"Thanks, Martha. You don't have to do this. It's not part of our agreement."

"Screw that. I'll just rack it up as experience."

I had shown Martha how to use Query/38, a tool for creating ad hoc reports, mostly for business analysis.

"Martha, why don't you query the data and see if you can find any discrepancies. Summarize data from different files, in ways other than how it appears on the report. I'm going to go through the data-entry program code. It's gotta be here. We'll find it."

Martha found it just after lunch.

Next Monday

I stopped by Jan's office first thing in the morning.

"Hey, Jan, got a minute?"

"The door is always open for my favorite ACC manager."

Jan and I had become close. I would go to her office and vent. Sometimes we would have laughing fits together, talking about some of the goofy things that were happening; silly things that occurred in any working environment."

"So, what can I do you for?" Jan asked.

"According to my budget, I have funds to hire another full-time programmer, correct?"

"Yes, but I thought that internship program you created, brilliant on your part I might add, would fill that need. Isn't Martha working out?"

"Yes, she is. More than I thought. I want to hire her."

Jan and I met with Martha the next day and offered her the job. She accepted.

"Do you want me to talk to the vo-tech and tell them we're cancelling the program?" Jan asked me after Martha went back to work.

"No, I'll call them and tell them we need another intern," I grinned at Jan.

I called the vo-tech and explained the situation. They were pleased with the outcome. I asked if they had others in the same situation. They did and they sent me an older woman, married, with teenage kids. She went back to school, hoping to find a career, something to get her out of the house. She lasted two days when she decided computers were not for her.

I called the vo-tech and explained the situation. They were not so pleased.

"Dan," they asked, "are you still willing to continue with the program?"

I said, "Absolutely. Send the next one."

He was a child. Well, he looked like one. Baby face, kindergarten clothes, bright colors, never had a job in his life. I couldn't believe he was twenty-one. He didn't talk much but did everything we asked of him. He never complained and stayed the full six months. On his last day, Martha and I took him to lunch. I gave him his letter of reference. I had nothing but good things to say. We said our goodbyes and good lucks. I was sure he was going to need it. He got hired right away, some insurance company. Last I heard he was still there—a big shot now.

In all I had six interns over three years. I lost one, the mom, otherwise the others were all able to find employment in the computer industry. Besides Martha, I would hire one more—to replace Martha. I knew that day would come. She was an excellent disciple in Dan's Method—Dan's way or the highway. She took the highway.

A Blast from the Past

Mid-July—One and A-Half Months to Fall Registration

Martha, Bob, Jim, and the new intern were all busy. I was having meetings with the registrar and his people. We had been meeting since April, gathering requirements for the *student information system* (SIS). We had built a *data dictionary* (DD). I was designing the new SIS relational database.

Creating the DD was the first step when designing an RDBMS from scratch. The next step was to define the *entities*, or business data objects. Relationships were then defined between the entities to build an *entity relationship diagram* (ERD) of related entities.

An entity-ID or Primary-Key (PK) constraint (an index that came with a rule—each index entry must be unique) was assigned to each entity. The data elements from the DD were then assigned to the proper entity, following the rules of *data normalization*, which resulted in a logical *data model* (LDM).

The final step was to produce a *physical data model* (PDM) that could be thought of as the final assembly, as it would be where the actual data is stored, accessed, manipulated, and presented to the end consumer.

The ACC was hopping. Wayne had stopped by.

"Dan, can I talk to you in your office?"

My office was more of an outhouse when comparing it to Wayne's. I was surprised that he wanted to talk there.

"I was walking by on my way to the business office when I remembered I haven't spoken to Dan about the accounts-receivable [AR] application."

"What AR application?"

"The one that should've been on the tape; you hadn't said anything about its progress. I just wanted to make sure that it would be ready for fall registration, like you promised."

"Wayne, we have every application created that came on that tape. There wasn't an AR application."

"Hmmmm," replied Wayne, as he put his hands together over his mouth. "You will need to follow up on that with the bureau."

Wayne left and I called my contact at the bureau. We had talked many times about the business office source code and the different applications. I found out that Wayne was one of the main contributors to the original application design. It was his baby.

"Hey, Dan, how can I help you?"

"I was talking with Wayne and he mentioned an AR application whose source code should have been included with the other RPG program source. Could you check on that for me?"

"Ha, ha, what a laugh, is he pulling that crap again?"

"What do you mean?"

"When Augsburg outsourced the administrative computer functions to us, we asked Wayne the same question. There was no AR application. We used our own proprietary software, which we happen to market. We can offer it to you at a price?"

"Is it written in RPG?"

"Are you serious?"

"Does Wayne know about this?"

"Yes, he does."

This was one of those silly, goofy things that Jan and I would vent about. I needed to confront Wayne. I was just getting up from my desk when the phone rang. I answered the phone.

"Dan, you don't know me. My name is Bill. I work for Arthur Andersen. I think you worked with one of my colleagues when we installed MAC-PAC at Horton. Is that right?"

"Yes, I remember talking with your colleague at QUSER." QUSER was the name of the local S/38 user group. I had started attending their monthly meetings.

"Yes, he mentioned that to me. You're building a S/38 empire from scratch, begging, borrowing, maybe even stealing any help you can get;

and it sounds like you're doing a fine job. BUT, and that's a big but, you have a self-imposed, impossible deadline. You need help. Did I nail it?"

"I would agree that your assessment of the situation is very close. Unfortunately for you, and me, for that matter, I have no additional funds to hire more contractors or consultants."

"Well, Arthur Andersen is always looking for opportunities, but I'm calling about something else. As you know, MAC-PAC was developed in RPG/II for the System/3x market. Customers moving to the S/38 are complaining that our product isn't taking advantage of S/38 features, mainly RPG/III. I have a proposition for you."

"I'm listening."

"What if Arthur Andersen provided you with a team of RPG/III programmers who will develop an application under your guidance. You probably have one or more that need to be written. Is that correct?"

"I can think of a couple."

"Great, so we provide the team. They take your specifications, build the application, following our Method One approach, and provide you with the finished product—and we do it free of charge. What do you say?"

"What was your name again? Is this a joke? Is this Chuck? Are you for real?"

"I am not kidding. I have cleared this with my management. There are people here who were impressed with your skills at Horton. We can start next week."

"I'll call you back."

I had to talk to Jan. After telling her about the phone call, she thought it was an incredible coincidence. She agreed with me that we should take advantage of it. I told her what the bureau guy said to me about Wayne and the AR application.

"How do I approach Wayne about this?"

"Okay, here's what you do. Tell Wayne the truth. There never was an RPG AR application. Somehow it got lost in the shuffle. The bureau, rather than getting into an argument, went ahead and used their AR application and charged Augsburg accordingly. He'll get mad, but then you play the Arthur Andersen ace in the hole card."

"How do I do that?"

"You twist the story around. You talked with this guy from Arthur Andersen at the user group. He told you about the problems they're having, not having RPG/III skills, blah, blah, blah. You then tell Wayne that you contacted Arthur Andersen and cooked up this arrangement. He'll like that. He likes you, and that is one hell of a compliment. He doesn't like many people, and nobody likes him."

The team from Arthur Andersen showed up the next week and began working on the AR application. We agreed on a six-month contract, like the intern program with the vo-tech. It lasted four months. They did complete the AR application. It was probably the only application that was built during the migration that was extremely well documented and didn't need to be rewritten.

I was going to give the AR team a new assignment when I received a call from Arthur Andersen. The woman on the other end of the line informed me that Bill had drowned in a swimming pool accident. Arthur Andersen would be recalling their programmers. She thanked me for my understanding.

In Over My Head

August—One Month to Fall Registration

I was sitting in the reception area for Wayne's office. I was nervous. I had bad news. I had taken an assessment of where we were in the conversion process. There was no way my team would have SIS ready by fall registration. The fall registration will have to be done the same as the spring registration, by way of the service bureau. Otherwise, I believe I will have everything done before Christmas.

Earlier, I had spoken with Jan. She offered to come with me. "No," I told her, "I have to do this myself."

"Dan, Wayne will see you now; good luck." Wayne's secretary, Cindy, held the door for me. She and Jan were good friends. She was also a confidante if I needed one when Jan wasn't available. I went into Wayne's office. The door was closed behind me.

"Dan, glad you are here. What do you think of this PC? I gotta have one."

"To be honest, Wayne, I haven't paid much attention to it. They've been talking about it quite a lot at the user group meetings I've been attending. They mentioned that you can connect the PC to the S/38 and download data into Lotus 123."

"Really?" Wayne stepped over to the door, opened it, and spoke to Cindy.

"Put together an order for the PC for me."

Wayne looked at me, "You want one?"

"Sure."

The folks at the user group also talked about an app called 5250 Emulation, which would allow the PC to act like a 5250 Workstation (5250-WS—the display devices that attached to the S/38). The app was part of the PC Support product.

"Make that two PCs," Wayne told Cindy as he closed the door.

"So, Dan, how can I help you?"

"Wayne, when you hired me, I said I would have the S/38 ready by fall registration and you would be able to discontinue using the service bureau. I was wrong. It's not going to happen. It is my fault and I'm sorry. I would've said anything to get this job."

Wayne looked at me in a way that made me very apprehensive. Then he smiled and laughed, and then laughed even harder. He tried to say something, but he couldn't stop laughing. The door opened and Cindy looked in.

"Wayne, is everything all right?"

Wayne waved her off.

"Leave us. Dan, you know how much we pay the service bureau per month, right?"

"Yes, I've seen the reports. It's a large amount of money to pay out."

"Dan, did Jan tell you how many people we interviewed for your job? Twenty-six, Dan, twenty-six, and you were number twenty-seven. I asked everyone we interviewed the same two questions I asked you. Do you know what they all said, the exact, same answer; three to five years, Dan, three to five years. Just do the math. You know what we pay per month, right? Multiply that result by forty-eight. That's how much money you will be saving this college."

"Thanks, Wayne, but I don't feel good about missing a deadline."

"Dan, after your interview everybody in that room, including me, didn't believe you would get it done that fast. I showed them the math and how much Augsburg would save should it take you a year, and that is an underestimate. It doesn't include the salaries for all the programmers these other applicants wanted to hire. You're doing a great job. Spring registration is soon enough."

"Thanks, Wayne."

"No, Dan, I need to thank you. There's one more thing. Think of that PC as a bonus for a job well done."

"Thanks, again."

"You're very welcome, Dan."

Not One Ounce

December 21, 1984

I was sitting at a table at the front of a large room. With me were the current members of the *Student Conduct Committee* (SCC). A female student had brought forth accusations of sexual misconduct against six males, five of which were students and part of Augsburg's athletic program.

I think it's going to be a very, very, very UN-Merry Christmas for somebody.

The Prior August

I was attending a staff meeting with Wayne and the other managers of the administrative departments for Augsburg. It was our usual monthly meeting where we discussed old and new business and brought up any issues. This meeting was business as usual, until Jan brought up a current issue.

"Next month is the start of the fall semester. It's that time again, folks. We need a representative on the SCC. Anyone wish to volunteer? If not, then Wayne will have to appoint someone."

This was the start of my third academic year at Augsburg. This subject had been brought up in the last two August administrative staff meetings. No one would volunteer so Wayne always appointed someone. So far, I had not been chosen. I was sure, at some point, it would be inevitable. There was a part of me that thought this might be a good idea.

This is a small private college, attended by kids from well-to-do families. According to Augsburg registrar records, there have been only one or two incidents of misconduct reported in the last several years that would require my presence.

I looked at Jan. "So, what's involved?"

I wasn't a stranger to sexual abuse. To the best of my knowledge, I have never been sexually abused. During treatment for addiction, I learned that I used alcohol and sex in abusive ways, either to my advantage or to be taken advantage of.

When I say I'm not a stranger to sexual abuse it's because, as a recovering alcoholic who has been through treatment centers twice, once as a concerned person and another for myself, tales of sexual abuse, incest, physical abuse, etc., are the norm. I have sat through many sessions where sex was the root cause that led many a traveler down The Franklin Trail, my euphemism for alcohol, drug, and sexual abuse.

In addition, I spent several months in a men's group that specialized in helping men diagnosed with anger or sexual dysfunctions. I sat through tales of adultery, rape, child molestation, spousal beatings, and the like. I contributed my own stories from my childhood gang activity and teenage years of alcohol, drugs, and self-abuse.

No sir, I wasn't a stranger to stories of good sex gone bad; I just couldn't believe this was happening at this college, at this time—on my watch.

The story was one that has been around since the dawn of time. There was a movie, *Where the Boys Are*, costarring Yvette Mimieux as a college coed who is gang raped by the friends of a boy she meets on Spring Break in Ft. Lauderdale, FL. Alcohol was involved in the movie, as it was in the case I and the other members of the SCC were presiding over.

As I listened to the lawyers defend their clients and victim, I noticed a slight, but familiar feeling in the pit of my stomach.

As the witnesses for the defense came forward, either to offer high praise for the accused or to offer their own tails of debauchery (in all cases involving the victim, sometimes simultaneously accommodating multiple partners)—that feeling was growing.

Witnesses for the victim spoke of instances of *date rape*, perpetrated by one or more of the defendants, or derogatory comments made by the defendants about female students, spoken within earshot of her and them, as they walked the hallowed halls of this small private college.

When I was in treatment for alcoholism, I remember the day I passed my first step of the alcoholics Anonymous Twelve Step Program. I remember the feeling of euphoria, the sense of accomplishment. It was short lived. My counselor warned me that this was probably the tip of the iceberg. There are more stories to be told; deep, dark stories, that need to be heard to be acknowledged. The following is one of those stories.

I was fifteen. I was out and about, walking the neighborhood. It was a Saturday; I was home alone, the family up north at the cabins. Dad was working, wouldn't be home until late, after midnight most likely. Earlier I had talked to my friend Jeff. "Come by the house later, I might have some Colt 45."

That's why I was out and about—I was heading for my stash.

I had several hiding places in the neighborhood, my favorite being a hill in the middle of a swamp. We called the hill Devil's Island. I had decided to hit another spot, check it out to see if the beer I'd hidden was still there. The location was a secluded trail behind the Babe Ruth ballpark, along the railroad tracks. I found my stash, still there—thank you, lord—and cool from sitting in the shade all day. I was wearing my favorite summer jacket, no shirt underneath. The jacket had two inside pockets large enough to hold one can each. I packed up and headed for home.

I came to a small clearing on the trail, just before the ballpark. There were four or five boys surrounding a girl who was on the ground. It was either a rape in progress or the aftermath of one. One of the guys called out to me, "Hey, Danny, how ya doin? You want some?"

I walked into the middle of what was going on and knelt by the girl. She wouldn't look at me. I began to get a familiar feeling. It started in my stomach. It was a growing rage that wanted to get out. My mind began to imagine who was going to get punched first, who would be kicked in the nuts, who would get an elbow to the nose. I stood up. I was no longer "Danny."

A couple of the guys witnessed the transformation and backed away. The others weren't getting away that easy. I sensed the girl moving. I turned to her and offered my hand. She took it and I helped her to her feet as the anger dissipated from my body. I was just Danny again.

None of those shit birds tried to stop me. They knew who I was. They had heard stories about me, not from the kids I beat the shit out of—they wouldn't talk—but from the witnesses who were able to walk away and spread the tales.

I asked the girl if she was okay, could she find her way home. She wouldn't talk, just stared at nothing. I took her to my house. I asked her if she wanted to use the bathroom. She did. Later, we were sitting in the living room. She didn't talk, just stared.

Jeff came by. Asked me what I intended to do with her. I said I'm going to take her home. I asked her again where she lived. In a whisper I could barely hear, she gave me her address, "Off Cedar Lake Road, close to Texas Ave."

I told Jeff he could hang out at my house until I got back. "Save a beer for me."

We left my house and took the Franklin Trail to Louisiana Ave., turned south and walked to Cedar Lake Road. I walked her home in silence. I didn't have much experience with girls. I would rather fight than date. I didn't know how to comfort her. I tried holding her hand. It was lifeless, cold as ice, so I let go. As we approached Texas Ave., she pointed to her house.

I walked her to the door. As I was about to leave, she looked at me with the "thousand-yard stare"—that look of despair, from hollow eyes, windows to a life that wasn't there.

I left her at the door to her house, walked away, and never saw her again.

For the life of me, I could not garner one speck of sympathy, empathy, or compassion for any of these students, accused or accuser—not one.

None of the students had a shred of decency, not one—not one ounce.

Of the six defendants, there wasn't one who was man enough to stand up for the victim. Not one of these smug, arrogant assholes had any sort of honor, let alone respect—with balls big enough to step in and put an end to the whole episode. Not one with any sort of dignity among the whole lot—not one ounce.

Don't get me started on the guy the girl initially went to have sex with. What sort of depraved animal would get his jollies and then throw his *girlfriend* out like a used condom to a pack of salivating dogs? No one with any shred of human kindness. Obviously, this guy had none—not one ounce.

The victim came from a good home. She was intelligent, good looking, athletic, was involved in student affairs, and sports. Yet, she totally lacked the slightest amount of common sense—or did she?

At one point in the trial, she caught my eye, and I caught hers. In the light, her eyes were clear and bright, not the eyes of an innocent, but the eyes of a willing participant. What I expected to see wasn't there, no "thousand-yard stare," not one bit.

For years I lived with the shame of being expelled from high school. I had a GED and a certificate from a fly-by-night computer-programming school. I had never been in a college classroom as a student. If this is what young adults go to college for then I guess everything I would've learned in college I had already experienced by the time I was sixteen years old.

It seems I didn't miss much. Nor would they. Not one of these students would be left unscathed. We expelled them all and I did not feel one ounce of regret.

Visual Aids

Spring 1985

Three full years had gone by since I'd started at Augsburg. We had been off the service bureau for over two years. I completed the database design for the SIS and built the database. I had one full-time programmer and one intern, and two work-study students. The contractors were long gone.

I took shortcuts when it came to developing programs for SIS. I gave the registrar and the Admissions Department access to the DFU and Query/38 tools and said, "Have at it." At some point I knew I would have to replace DFU with a more robust data-entry application. It could wait.

The ACC team's focus was creating custom reports, like class rosters and the Admissions Department's welcome letters. And don't forget the Development Department's pledge request letters, or the business office's student-loan notice letters. There were plenty of letter programs keeping us busy—way too busy.

We added an IBM Displaywriter system for handling personalized correspondence and other word processing requirements. I brought in an independent contract programmer to write an RPG/III program to communicate with the Displaywriter using *Binary Synchronous* (Bisync) communications transmission protocol. Bisync was an IBM communications protocol used to transfer data between computers or smart devices, such as word processing machines or laser printers. Utilizing this new technology allowed Augsburg to print more professional looking, upper and lower case, personalized letters to smaller groups of individuals.

The Displaywriter couldn't handle the larger volumes required for the Admissions and Development Department's correspondence. They would have to live with uppercased letters printed on continuous form letter stock. The bursting kept the work-study students busy.

I was talking to Jan about the amount of letter printing Augsburg was doing and how it was keeping my programmers from doing serious application development.

"Jan, I have found a solution, and it will only cost $60,000."

I was talking about acquiring an IBM 6670 laser printer. Jan nearly spit out her coffee.

"Are you serious? $60,000 dollars? Wayne will shit."

"Okay, let's forget about the price for now. Let's think about all those programs that still need to be created. Think about the cost of another programmer, with benefits and such. That alone would pay for the printer in two or three years."

"Nah, Wayne isn't going to buy into that argument. I understand the backlog is piling up, but Wayne would just say bring in another intern or call Arthur Andersen."

"Okay, Jan, how about we look at it a different way? What if we made the Development and Admissions Departments pay for it?"

"No, that won't fly, they don't have the money in their budgets."

"Neither do I, so we're talking June at the earliest. So, this is what I'm thinking. My departmental budget is charged the amount to buy the printer. I charge the cost of using the printer, forms, labor, computer resources, etc., back to the departments."

"How do you track the usage?"

"I acquired a tool from IBM called Job Accounting/38. It captures the computer resources used [CPU time, disk space, paper pages, etc.] by the program that created the report. I also know how to apportion the labor cost, something I learned from my prior job."

"I didn't know you could do that."

"Down to the penny. Wayne likes that. Believe me, I know."

The data provided for Job Accounting/38 looked very similar to the data that was generated by the AS/400 Performance Data Collector—data I would become very familiar with.

Later That Month

I was standing in front of the administrative department managers. They were seated in a small room—although large enough to sit twenty or more—to hear my presentation on why Augsburg should acquire a $60,000 *IBM 6670 Information Distributor, aka a laser printer.* The 6670 was larger than most industrial copiers/printers used for today's mass printing requirements.

Nobody was paying attention to me. Everyone was focused on the IBM resource who was assisting me with the technical aspects of the presentation.

Wayne liked the idea and gave the go-ahead to make the pitch to the administrative team. I believed I had all my ducks in a row, but the day before the presentation I developed cold feet. I called IBM.

"Hi, my name is Dan Cruikshank and I understand that your department oversees IBM 6670 printer sales and marketing. Is that correct?"

"Yes, that is what we do," the IBM person on the other end replied.

"Good, I am making a presentation tomorrow to a group of executives at Augsburg on why they should buy a laser printer, and I am starting to get a little nervous. Is it possible that you could provide a technical resource, just in case there are some technical questions I cannot answer, or any other question that might be more IBM related?"

"No problem, Dan, what time is the presentation?"

"It will be at 2:00 P.M. When you get here just ask the receptionist at the main building, where the meeting is being held. Oh, and come early so I can get some introductory information."

"No problem, we'll see you tomorrow."

I was in the presentation room testing some of my foils on the overhead projector.

"Are you Dan?"

I turn around and standing there was the most beautiful Asian woman in the world. She was petite, nicely proportioned, dressed in a blue suit, white blouse buttoned to her neck.

"Yes, I'm Dan, and you are?" I'm sure my words came out as, "Huh?"

"Pleased to meet you, Dan. I am from IBM and I will be acting as your technical resource. Should there be any questions that you cannot answer or are IBM explicit, then please be so kind and direct those to me. I will answer as best as I am able."

"Thank you. I am glad you are here," which likely came out as, "th-th-th-that's all folks."

My presentation took fifteen minutes. There were no questions. Augsburg ordered the laser printer the following week.

Direct Deposit

The acquisition of the laser printer freed up a good percentage of the programmers' workload. They were now focused on the SIS system, which needed smarter data-entry capabilities. I was getting numerous requests from the Development Department regarding different fundraising activities that would require additional programming. To top it off, the payroll system, acquired from our sister college in Northfield, was falling apart.

I had requested funds for an additional full-time programmer and part-time contractor. I was having coffee with Jan. "Can I transfer budget money from one line to another?"

"What do you need now?"

I explained to Jan the printing issues and a possible solution.

"There's a new software product called GradS/38. It is written specifically for the S/38; its main purpose is to track alumni and manage donations and various fundraising events. The price is less than what we allocated for the new programmer."

"Okay, I know you Dan. What else do you have up your sleeve?"

"I think we can use the money for the consultant to pay the monthly fee to outsource the payroll process. It's not the same service bureau Augsburg was using. This one is national. They will do the entire payroll process, checks, tax reporting, the whole nine yards. What's even better is that we can offer employees direct deposit of their paychecks; it will go right into their checking accounts. How great is that?"

"Are you going to get a technical expert from IBM to help you sell it?"

"Ha, ha, I have someone else in mind."

That someone was my sister, Deb.

Wayne scheduled a meeting with Augsburg executives to hear my presentation on outsourcing the payroll application. I believed my pitch was solid. There were more pluses than negatives, at least from what I could see. In my mind, the biggest selling point was direct deposit; however, there was more opposition than I expected.

I was looking at it from an ease-of-use perspective, yet many people liked getting their paycheck. They could feel it in their hands. They could stop at their neighborhood bank to deposit it and chat with the bank teller. I needed a visual aid.

My sister Deb was an artist. One of her first jobs out of college was technical illustrator for a company that produced custom designs on glassware. I had a technical document that detailed the direct deposit process. I went to Deb, with my little stick figure drawing in hand, and asked if she could use her skills to create a graphical representation of the process.

She agreed. Her rendition of the direct deposit process was perfect. I provided Mrs. Anderson with a list of high-level bullets, listing the pros and cons of outsourcing payroll, and asked her to create a Displaywriter document that I could use in my presentation. The last pro-bullet simply read: Direct Deposit. I took the document with the bullets and Deb's drawing to the copy center and reproduced the documents onto foils for the overhead projector.

The presentation went well. I walked the group through the bullets, answered a few questions. When I came to my final bullet point—Direct Deposit—I was nervous, most of the executives were not smiling. This wasn't going well.

"I will now describe the direct deposit process using a visual aid. I must warn you; the following chart is highly graphical in nature."

I displayed Deb's picture.

The frowns turned to grins, there were a few laughs. Deb had drawn a man, who looked remarkably like me, preparing the payroll tape for the fast-moving payroll tape truck, which delivered the tape to the bank. On payday a happy employee is smiling, knowing the money is already in his account.

The outsourcing of the payroll process was approved.

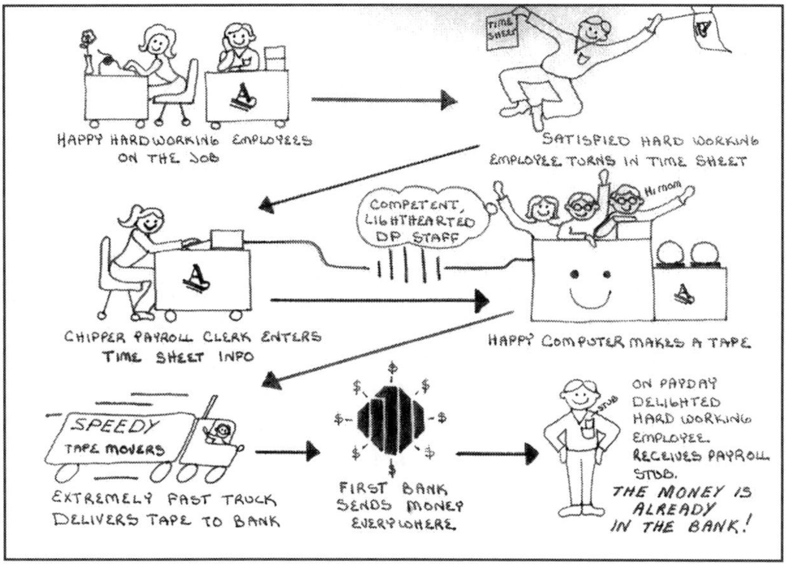

Direct Deposit Workflow

Acquired Skills:

IT management; PC/Support, RPG/III and CL, CLP, DDS; RDBMS design and implementation; public speaking, presentation and marketing; works with 3rd party software vendors and contractors; ability to work under pressure to meet deadlines and tight schedules.

Space Center Inc.
IT Director

The Cost Comparison
February 1988

I made my presentation to the CFO. I had put together a side-by-side comparison of the IBM S/38 versus UNIVAC and, for good measure, I threw in Wang, who offered a midrange line of computer systems.

All three were comparable in price, hardware wise. Once I added the cost of additional add-on products that came with the S/38 as part of the base price—RDBMS, Communications, Security, etc.—IBM blew the competition out of the water. To top it off, I added the cost of education, programming, and full-time equivalent (FTE) personnel—the competition collapsed like they were kicked in the balls.

"You see, the IBM representative is hinting about a new system that will eventually replace the midrange 3x line of computers. He claims it will come with over 10,000 applications. There should be at least one, if not more, for each LOB within your enterprise."

The CFO wasn't too impressed.

"Your bias to IBM is showing, obviously."

"No, my bias for saving time and money is showing."

"I'll need some time to think about it."

"Absolutely, let me add that the S/38 price includes an automatic upgrade to the new IBM system, which may be announced this June. If we wait until the announcement, the price of the new architecture may be much higher. Still less than the overall prices of the competition, though."

"I'll get back to you, Dan, long before then."

He never got back to me because I had taken **The Blue Highway** out of there.

Acquired Skills:

Became familiar with several third-party software applications available for S/3x and AS/400.

Keane, Inc.
Consultant
X.25

The Trailers

IBM Rochester Spring 1988

The first two weeks...

The first two weeks had flown by. The initial group of hires was put up in the trailers at IBM. These were in the southwestern corner of the IBM Rochester facility. During that time, I went to classes on PL/MP programming, X.25 essentials, S/38 architecture, and just about anything else—S/38 wise—that time permitted.

The first day I met my team leader, Ken, and two of my teammates, Allen O., and **Paul Wertzler**. Like me, Paul would eventually become an IBM employee. Tim had a separate office; Paul and Allen shared one. Coincidentally, Paul and Allen were both from St. Louis Park, MN, the same city where I grew up.

My officemate moved in a couple of days later. Her name was Debbie R. She and her husband were hired as a team. Debbie was assigned to Communications; her husband was assigned to Work Management. What I found most appealing about Debbie was, much to my good fortune, in her previous job she had been a S/38 database administrator (DBA), probably the only S/38 DBA in existence. When she found out she was assigned to Communications her first response was, "What the hell?"

When we weren't in training, finding our way around the IBM plant (it was huge), avoiding Raymonds (robots used to move supplies from one end of the plant to the other) or locating the restrooms, Debbie and I spent most of our free time discussing relational database theory and how it pertained to the S/38.

At some point **Brian R. Smith** found me and introduced himself. He was the current owner of the X.25 PL/MP code. He would be my mentor during the transition of handing over the ownership of the source code—from him to me. Brian had just returned from Japan.

Brian's first directive was, "Get a passport."

The S/38 version of the X.25 VMC code was considered *golden*, that is, it was unbreakable. During my time as owner of the code, I was involved in two *critical situation* (Crit-Sit) customer support calls. A crit-sit was the final escalation of a customer problem and usually required the developer to be brought in on the call. That was where the buck stopped at IBM. For S/38 X.25, that buck stopped with me.

During my time as owner of the code, I was involved in two *critical situation* (Crit-Sit) customer support calls. A crit-sit was the final escalation of a customer problem and usually required the developer to be brought in on the call. That was where the buck stopped at IBM. For S/38 X.25, that buck stopped with me.

Like other communication protocols, X.25 went through a series of handshakes between the sending and receiving computers. The S/38 came with tools that could trace the handshaking process. Brian II had developed a tool for analyzing X.25 communication traces. It was called VParser. He received a $10K Invention Award as a result.

In both cases the customers had provided communication traces. Using Brian's VParser tool, I was able to prove that the problem was an X.25 protocol violation. This meant the bug was in the customer's application program code.

The Happy Looper

There was trouble in paradise. The golden X.25 PL/MP code had a problem. Several IBM S/38 customers had reported a S/38 *hang*, a term for when a computer was castors up. No one could sign on to the S/38. Then suddenly, the S/38 would wake up and things appeared to be normal. The *hang* was due to a *Network Not Ready* message being sent to the S/38 System Arbiter (QSYSARB), in other words, God of all things that happen on the S/38.

Technically, a *Network Not Ready* (NNR) condition isn't a critical error. It's like not being able to connect to Wi-Fi at your favorite coffee shop. You went to settings, chose the local network, clicked OK and nothing happened—for like three minutes, which is an eternity when you need to connect.

You know what I'm saying, which is what you're probably saying to the barista who doesn't know Wi-fi from hi-five. Not only that; when you try to launch another app, nothing happens. WTF? So, the barista tells you this story that she heard from a friend of a friend (it may have lost something in translation):

"Like, there's this tiny little guy, they call him the Arbiter [QSYSARB]. He's an asshole, thinks he's God. So, he's decided that he's, like, gonna make everyone, who wants to come into the computer, wait—for like three-fucking minutes. Here's the deal, when this a-hole waits, everybody waits—for three-fucking minutes. They have to get all the big-shots to hang together and figure this thing out."

In this case X.25 wasn't the culprit. The root cause was a combination of the implementation of the error handling mechanism and the architected wait time imposed on X.25 when the NNR condition occurred.

VMC programs did not communicate directly with QSYSARB. The VMC program would simply send a code to the OS PL/MI program that was used to make X.25 active. The OS program was usually a command-processing program (CPP). The S/38 command was vary-on (VARYON). This command was used to start various devices, including those devices that support communications.

The PL/MI program received the NNR condition and sent a corresponding message to QSYSARB, which would then hand off the message to the appropriate component, in this case the QSYSOPR console display. Unfortunately, the X.25 Architecture document stated that X.25 must wait 180 seconds when the NNR occurred. This wait time was implemented in QSYSARB which, being God, when QSYSARB waited, so did everybody else. Thus, the system *hang* occurred.

"What to do, what to do?" the architects asked rhetorically.

Someone suggested changing X.25, "What if X.25 simply went into a loop when the NNR occurred? X.25 could just wait forever, until the NNR was resolved whenever that occurred, right?"

It just so happened that X.25 did not have a guaranteed response time. Unlike other synchronous protocols, X.25 was asynchronous. Once a connection was established and the data began exchanging between the two computers, X.25 did not wait for an acknowledgement.

Brian explained it to me this way:

"An X.25 packet leaves the S/38 by whatever physical communication link is being used by X.25. On its journey it may travel on other physical communication links, telephone lines, ISDN, twenty-mule team, whatever. Nobody can predict how long it will take."

A project to change the golden X.25 code was approved and the internal project code name was *The Happy Looper*, named after a popular movie and book with a slightly different name. Brian and I got together. Brian warned me that due to the importance we might be pulling an all-nighter.

With Brian's guidance I was able to change the appropriate code and test the change. The source code was stored on an IBM big iron system. This is where the code was changed and compiled. The executable object was downloaded to an IBM Series/1 system and then recorded to an 8" IBM "floppy disk." I hand carried the diskette to the communications test S/38, where I copied the code onto the computer. This process was called "Fred Flintstone," as these were "modern" conveniences the Flintstones enjoyed—manuel versions of the things we had back in the day.

Testing wasn't very easy, or quick. X.25 was mostly used for computer-to-computer communications, for example ATMs. I had a Series/1 that was connected to my S/38 using X.25. There were several automated test scripts that simulated various types of computers and other devices that could connect to the S/38. I had to run each script and ensure it was successful after I completed the first test, which happened to be the most important one. I would become very familiar with the testing process.

After loading the program code onto the S/38, I logged onto the system as QSYSOPR, by way of the operator console. I brought up the system operations menu. On the command line I entered, and prompted, the VARYON command for X.25. I filled in the necessary data and pressed the Enter key to execute the command. Nothing bad happened. Rochester, MN, still exists today.

I walked over to a table that contained several 5250 terminals. They all displayed the Sign On prompt. The next test was the most critical. Right now, the Happy Looper code fix should be doing its thing, spinning, and waiting for the network to come out and dance. That wouldn't happen until I connected the Series/1. If my sign on attempt using the terminal was successful, then I should be rewarded with the Programmer Menu. If nothing happened—the screen would be dark and no keys would work, then my code change had failed in some way. I was rewarded with the Programmer Menu.

I went to the operator's console and checked the status of X.25—ready and waiting, bring it on. I walked over to the Series/1 and entered the commands to connect to the S/38. The Series/1 connected. I went back to the operator's console and refreshed the screen. The X.25 status was now active; the fix was successful and eventually shipped to the world.

Keane, Inc. Offices

During the first three months, Mary Jo and I did our best to sell our home and relocate to Rochester. When Tonka closed its doors in Minnesota, Mary Jo applied for several jobs in Rochester, including IBM. Nothing turned up. When the initial three-month period ended, Mary Jo decided to accept an offer with Parker-Hannifin, located in Golden Valley, MN. She also made it clear that we were not relocating.

I was discussing this with Stephany.

"So, Steph, it appears that not only is it almost impossible to sell our house in Plymouth without losing our shirts; Mary Jo is also going to begin a new job. She has decided not to move to Rochester, so here," I handed Stephany my resignation letter.

"Dan, I won't take this, Keane won't take this. We can't lose you. Everybody likes you, many of the young folks think of you as a mentor. Unfortunately, per our agreement, we can't continue to cover your house payment. What are your options?"

"I've decided that if Keane is agreeable then I would like to commute."

"Don't you live a hundred miles from IBM, door to door?"

"Yes, but I've been gradually changing my driving schedule. I now come down Monday morning. I get to IBM about 7:00 A.M. I return home Wednesday night, and come back to Rochester Thursday morning. I leave Rochester at noon on Friday; I think I could handle a daily commute."

"We would be okay with that. FYI, I am aware of another project where three or four of our employees are commuting from the Twin Cities. I'll get their names.

The Commute

I drove fifty miles to Hampton, approximately halfway from my house to IBM. Hampton had a carpool parking lot where I met the other carpoolers. We took turns driving. I was driving when Eric, one of the carpoolers, came down with appendicitis. Rochester is home to the Mayo Clinic and St. Mary's Hospital. For some reason, surrounded by the world's greatest medical institutions, Eric insisted on going to his local hospital in Shakopee, MN, about a hundred miles away.

"You sure about this Eric? The Mayo is just a few minutes away. You can stick your head out the window and make siren noises."

"Shut up, Dan, and drive."

"Okay, as you wish. This will be a lousy day for a train," I muttered to myself, having never come across one—today could be the day.

Just north of Cannon Falls, a railroad track crossed Highway 52. Not the worst thing that could happen. I would have to backtrack and take a two-lane state highway to I-35. It would probably add another half hour, forty-five minutes, to the drive. I was sure Eric wouldn't complain, as the windshield held up to another barrage of kicks from Eric's feet.

We made it to the hospital in Shakopee without incident. Eric's wife was there to meet us at the Emergency entrance. Eric found his sense of humor when his wife opened the passenger door, "Hi, honey, I'm home. What's for dinner?"

I carpooled for a couple of months and then I decided to go it alone. That was when my Keane teammates dubbed me *Ditch Rider Dan*. Interestingly enough, shortly after I quit carpooling, the carpoolers hit a patch of ice and the car rolled over and went off the road into a ditch. It was a Volvo, nicest car amongst the carpoolers. It suffered the most damage. Not one of the carpoolers was hurt.

The drive along Highway 52 goes through some very rural areas. I would watch the progress of the growing corn stalks. The other things I watched for on the highway were deer, especially during the hours before dawn or after dusk. There would be dozens of them, standing in the cornfields or woods, just waiting to jump out onto the highway in front of my car. In the time I spent commuting, and all the trips I made to Rochester, MN, in the last two decades of my career on that patch of Highway 52 from I-494 to the 41st St. NW IBM exit, I never hit a deer. That happened in Plymouth, MN, a big city, less than a mile from my house. The deer totaled my car.

The Guy in the Suit

London, UK September 1990

I had been away from X.25 for almost a year, and I was no longer commuting daily to IBM Rochester. I had been assigned to a new project, which was based in Bloomington, MN, near the MSP International Airport.

A call for help had come into level-2 support and was escalated to level-3. An X.25 customer was having difficulty connecting a device to a S/38. The customer was in the UK and insisted that an IBM expert come on-site to solve the problem. I was no longer the owner of the X.25 code. I handed it off before taking on the new project. My replacement did not have a passport and the customer demanded someone immediately.

IBM decided that I could not travel alone. An IBM employee was assigned to travel with me. There would be two travel days and at least two days with the customer, based on my estimate. I was confident that it wasn't an IBM X.25 code issue.

I was right. It was more of a training effort. When we arrived at the customer location in London, I walked the customer through the process of taking an X.25 communications trace. When it was completed, we electronically sent the data to the X.25 owner in Rochester. That person used the VParser tool to identify the problem, which was a protocol violation.

This could've been done remotely; however, I remembered something that I was taught during my first two weeks in Rochester. The original group of CPF hires were gathered in an auditorium, listening to the speaker talk about customer service—IBM Rochester style.

There was a question about our status as subcontractors, not actual IBM employees: "What could we expect from IBM if we found ourselves in a situation that demanded an on-site visit?"

I'll never forget his reply.

"Our customers are our most valuable assets. They are more important to us than the president of IBM. When a customer is in trouble, whether it be castors up, knee deep in alligators, or they simply forgot where the light switch is—it doesn't matter. If they request an on-site visit, we will accommodate them. IBM Rochester doesn't care if we send the night janitor, if they're wearing a blue suit. There are six-thousand people at IBM Rochester who will back that person up."

IBM Technical Conferences

Boston, MA Fall 1989

Systems Application Architecture (SAA) was IBM's blueprint for developing modern applications, both graphic and character based. It was introduced in 1987. If you've ever wondered where the OS/2 *graphical user interface* (GUI—pronounced gooey) came from, or for that matter, the GUI for MS Windows, look no further than this document. These thoughts were going through my head as I arrived at the Hilton in downtown Boston, where the conference was being held. I arrived late and received a free upgrade to an executive room on the top floor.

Most of the presentations were held in the main ballroom. Most presenters were IBMers representing big iron topics. These guys were all dressed in customary IBM outfits—dark suits, white shirts, red tie, black shoes—except for the token presenter from IBM Rochester. He wore a light blue suit, dark shirt, and brown shoes.

I did come away with some interesting stuff. I attended a presentation where the topic was Navigation; in particular, how the function keys associated with text-based displays (i.e., green screens) were to be consistent across all platforms. I had been playing with an AS/400 back in Rochester. Like everyone coming from the System 3x world, the first thing I noticed was that F1-key is Help, not Exit, the S/3x standard.

SAA also contained a specification named Common User Access (CUA), which defined a standard interaction between the end-user and the computer. I would eventually become an SAA/CUA *lawyer,* someone at IBM who is a *subject matter expert* (SME) in a particular concept or product.

Another session that stayed with me was about a program source code generator named *cross system product* (CSP). This was IBM's latest offering in the area of HLL program code generating tools. There was a similar product for the S/38 named *display information facility* (DIF) that generated RPG code. I had just begun using this tool at Augsburg when IBM dropped support. I was very much interested in CSP until I found out that the generated program source code was COBOL. CSP wasn't popular with RPG programmers.

When it came to code generators, I was a big fan. I would spend the next decade trying to find the best one. Unfortunately, I was spoiled.

There was only one code generator that met my high-level of expectations—SDA.

SDA did something that no other tool I reviewed was capable of. Not only did it generate DDS DSPF source code from scratch; it could also import existing DDS DSPF source code and allow it to be changed. In addition, changes could be made to the generated DDS DSPF source code without using the SDA tool. SDA would learn the changes the next time the source-file-member containing the altered code was opened via SDA. These capabilities were not available in vendor-provided source code generator tools.

I would not find another tool that could do what SDA could until the next century. The year was 1989. It would be 2001, and, ironically, the company, Visible Systems Corporation, was in Boston. The tool was Visible Analyst, and I was to become an expert in *database re-engineering.*

A Template for Success

Rochester, MN Early 1989

I had plenty of free time on my hands. It was comparable to that first month I was employed at Augsburg. I had a stack of AS/400 manuals to read. One product on the AS/400 that I was most interested in learning about was the Program Development Menu (PDM).

PDM was the AS/400's answer to the S/38's Programmer Menu and the System/36 (S/36) Programmer/Operator Productivity Aid (POP). Unlike the S/36-S/38 programming tools, which were *action-object* oriented, PDM was *object-action* oriented. That is, instead of specifying an action (e.g., Edit, Copy, Delete, etc.) first, then the object (program, file, etc.) to perform the action on next, PDM provided an initial list of objects from which one or more could be chosen, and the desired action performed. In addition, the list could be filtered, positioned, and reordered.

What a great way to learn a new product, by building some menus, data-entry panels, lists (or Work With panels), and help screens, etc., that all followed CUA standards for displaying and navigating text-based (green screen) displays. I couldn't wait to get my hands on PDM and start creating some templates.

The Backroom

Keane, Inc. May 1990

I was in Rochester for some team building exercises. The team was made up of project managers and architects, like me, who were currently engaged with our main, and only, customer—IBM.

While there, I was asked to take part in a presentation on the future of the AS/400 and SQL. The presentation went well, and I received another letter of praise.

We were going through introductions and it was my turn. I had given my name and background when Stephany said, "Dan, tell them about the backroom."

"I can't, Steph, you know that is a big secret."

"Everybody here is in management and has signed an NDA [non-disclosure agreement] with IBM. Go ahead, Dan."

"Okay, listen up. There is a secured IBM facility located in an office park, just south of the Minneapolis/St. Paul International Airport, known as the *backroom*, as it is called by those who are aware of its existence and need to know about it. The backroom is a remote facility occupied by Keane employees but sanctioned by IBM Rochester. It is where the *dark* applications are developed."

I had their attention.

"Dark applications, with names referred to by acronyms only, TSA or OA, dissected, chewed and spat out by other dark applications with names like SPIES, TIPS, or SMTrace."

They were staring at me with their mouths agape; one guy had drool slithering down his cheek—I realized he was asleep.

"There will be a war sometime soon that will be fought, not by soldiers in uniforms, but by young people dressed in kindergarten clothes, sitting at PCs, armed with a headset and a keyboard."

One woman put her hand up by her mouth, perhaps silently saying a prayer.

"Got you going, didn't I?"

Minneapolis, MN

The origin of the backroom began in Minnetonka, MN, as a secured facility where new, unannounced hardware was installed and used for creating and testing typical customer applications. There were several Keane RPG/III experts who were responsible for creating these customer look-alike applications and testing them to ensure they ran without problems on the AS/400.

Since the announcement of the AS/400, the room was bound to be designated as EOL. Those Keane employees who were employed there were most likely SOL (Shit Out of Luck). They knew they had become irrelevant and were either requesting transfers to other parts of Keane or taking the highway with their newfound skill set.

IBM wanted the hardware back. Keane wanted to keep it. The problem for Keane was the contract was coming up and there weren't any projects on the visible horizon that would justify keeping the backroom operational. Keane had another problem. There were several employees, mostly recent college graduates, who were hired directly out of school by Keane to fulfill the second phase of the CPF project. Not a bad idea, according to Dan's way, but there was one fatal flaw. Rochester, MN, wasn't the type of city these young, horny, full of oats, hot to trot, money to burn, etc., recruits had in mind.

"Dan, I am hoping you can help me with a problem."

I was in a meeting with the Keane branch manager, Rick C., along with Tim and Stephany. It was a planning session ahead of a meeting scheduled with **Steve Cyr** and **Jerry Kloc** about a possible project.

"Dan, I have received a note from a Mr. Steve Cyr, here at IBM Rochester. Steve's department owns the Testing Support Application [TSA]."

Rick began reciting from the note:

"This application supports the management and reporting of test scripts, created by OS developers and used by testers, who record each test result. The application provides management with status reports, charts, and graphs. The application was developed in-house, using a code generator tool referred to as TIF."

"What's TIF?" I asked.

"The note doesn't include a definition. It says here that it runs on an IBM main-frame system. According to Steve, IBM corporate has passed down an edict to Rochester, '*Thou shalt only run in-house applications that were developed on the AS/400 using all AS/400 development tools, i.e., programming languages [RPG, COBOL, PL/1, etc.] and/or licensed program products [LPPs], such as PDM, Business Graphics Utility [BGU], SQL, Office/400, etc.*' The note also includes some example screens, menus, data-entry panels, report screens, etc., that you all can view for yourselves."

"Okay, Rick, so what does this have to do with me?"

"Dan, here's the thing, Keane needs this project. We have about a dozen employees who are ready to quit. They hate it here in Rochester. It does not have the same attractions they can find in the Twin Cities. If Keane were to land this project, we could offer these young people an opportunity to work at our remote facility in Minnetonka, MN, …"

"Wait a minute. We have a facility in Minnetonka, MN? Fifteen minutes from where I live?"

I gave Stephany the evil eye.

"That's true, Dan," she replied sheepishly. "It was in place before CPF. Please listen to some more of what Rick is saying."

"Yes," Rick continued. "What we are missing is an architect for the project. Steph tells me that you have application development and system architecting skills. Given your current situation and the stability of your component, we thought this would be a perfect fit for you. We want you to attend the meeting with Steve and Jerry. Would you be willing to help us out here?"

For several months, the three months I spent in Rochester and a few months after I started commuting, Mary Jo and I stopped having sex. I knew she was mad about almost moving to Rochester and giving up the dream house we'd just built.

"Absolutely, sounds right up my alley."

"Great! This is short notice I know, but do you think you could prepare some sample displays and programs, just to throw out some ideas of how you would accomplish this?"

"No problem, I'll whip something up."

"Okay. The meeting will be tomorrow over at the blue buildings."

Our team had moved around several times. We started in the trailers, then moved to the second floor of Blue Building 106, on the north side of the blue building campus. It was called 'the garage,' due to the sliding, aluminum door that was used to enter and exit the main area. From there we moved off-site to a set of offices that were part of the Midway Motor Lodge.

"I better get to work on those program samples," I said, giving Stephany another look. She didn't return it.

Testing Support Application (TSA)

The next day the four of us were seated in a conference room in Blue Building 004, on the east side of the cafeteria that divided the Rochester campus. The buildings west of the cafeteria were mostly manufacturing, which included some *clean* rooms—airtight rooms to prevent contamination. The AS/400 was being manufactured in these buildings. The buildings east of the cafeteria housed administrative personnel and, most importantly, software development. It was in these buildings that OS/400, SQL/400, and other software products were being developed.

Steve had restated the project particulars and then turned it over to Jerry, who provided more detail about the TSA application. Jerry was an RPG programmer that became an expert in TIF—the big iron version of DIF. The product served a single purpose—fast source code generation and quick application development. The source code generated by the TIF tool couldn't have been farther away from SAA/CUA standards—in both look and feel. The generated TIF display screens were action-object oriented.

Besides learning the nuances of the AS/400 and PDM, I was able to acquire software development related books thru Keane, by way of Stephany. I had her order James Martin's trio of books on *Information Engineering* and his book titled *Rapid Application Development* or RAD. It was like a cookbook for building applications fast, the main ingredient being templates, which I had in spades.

When Jerry finished, Rick introduced me as the system architect who would be assigned to the project should Steve decide to go with Keane.

"Steve, Dan is a very accomplished system architect, relational database administrator, and application developer. If there are no other questions, I'll turn the floor over to Dan, who will cover his approach to developing applications for the AS/400."

There were no questions, so Rick passed the baton to me, "All yours, Dan."

"Hello, Steve, Jerry. I think the best way to explain my approach is to see a demo. What I'm about to show you is an application developed on the AS/400, using the AS/400 development tool PDM and the programming language RPG/400. The displays all adhere to CUA standards for designing and navigating text-based panels, the same standards that were used for OS/400 system displays. Are we ready?"

Everyone nodded. I was seated next to a 5250 terminal, which was currently displaying the Basic Menu that appeared by default when QUSER signed on.

"Okay, let's go."

On the command line I entered the Start Menu (STRMNU) command followed by my menu name DEMO1 and pressed Enter. The display changed to the TSA DEMO menu (refer to the Addendum for examples of these screens). I had created this menu the day before. The menu looked identical to the AS/400 Basic Menu, except for the menu options and command function keys, of which there were three each.

"The first thing you should have noticed is the appearance of the menu. It is exactly like any other OS/400 system menu. I believe that by following the CUA standards those people who will be using TSA and have worked with OS/400 will not have to learn a non-intuitive user interface."

Steve and Jerry nodded.

"Let's choose a menu option."

I typed a 1 into the menu option entry field. The Work With Objects panel appeared.

"According to CUA standards, this screen is referred to as a list panel. The format is like the menu panel, in that the title and function keys are in the same location on the screen. That's where the similarity ends. Notice the center of the screen contains a list of OS/400 objects. Think of these as *test scripts*. Directly above the test scripts data is a horizontal menu of *options*. Unlike the current TSA application, the objects are listed first, and then the option or action is specified in the entry field directly to the left of the list item. Let's see how that works."

I typed a 5, which was the value assigned to *display* according to the horizontal menu. I pressed the Enter key and the screen associated with the OS/400 Display Object Description (DSPOBJD) command was displayed.

"Imagine that this is a test script. The end-user can review it and decide if they need to open it for editing."

I chose the Enter key to return to the list panel. I walked them thru several other navigation options. I had them on the ropes. I just needed the knockout blow.

"One of the most important pieces of any application is the documentation. I assume that the end-users have printed manuals at their fingertips, ready to access the page that describes what option to use in any situation or to better understand how a certain function key works. Instead of killing a hundred trees for each manual, wouldn't it be better if the manual was at their fingertips this way?"

I pressed the F1-key and brought up information about the list panel, including descriptions of the menu options and function keys and what they were supposed to do. I blew Steve and Jerry away.

"Dan, how do you intend to create the test scripts and all the screen help text?"

"My understanding is that we can use all tools available with the AS/400. Correct?"

Steve and Jerry nodded.

"Good, because I am planning to use Office/400 to create the test scripts. It has external commands that interface with actions for creating, editing, printing, whatever, for each test script document; and, according to Stephany,"—her head snapped up when she heard her name— "I can borrow one of the members of the Office/400 CPF support team, for training purposes. Right, Steph?"

"Ahhhh, yes, absolutely, that should be doable."

I may have been harboring a little bit of anger about this Minnetonka remote facility that no one told me about. Jerry had a few more questions.

"I noticed there was a function key for reordering the list. How do you intend to do that?"

"I would like to use the SQL/400 product. If that doesn't work out, I can tap into **Jon H.** who is the current owner of the OPNQRYF CPF code for some initial OPNQRYF stubs we can build from. Right, Steph?"

Stephany nodded. S/38 Open Query File (OPNQRYF) was introduced in 1985, approximately three yearsT before IBM announced the AS/400. OPNQRYF came free as part of the S/38 OS.

"I've got a question," Steve said. "How long will this take?"

"Correct me if I'm wrong, Rick, but I think I have a team of twelve, or so, RPG gurus that are ready to hit the ground running. I think we can do this in six months, eight tops."

I think Rick and Steph both wet their pants at the same time. Tim had a shit-eating grin on his face. Afterwards, we were walking the hallway from Blue Building 004 to the IBM main entrance. Rick was all grins; he was holding the signed contract in his hands.

"Dan?" asked Stephany, "Are we good?"

"Steph, do any of these unhappy youngsters, who are soon to find out that their lives are about to change, know RPG?"

"I don't think so. Is that going to be a problem?"

"Nope, that's the way I like them. I need you to order a dozen copies of Robert Cozzi's book *The Modern RPG Language*. Can you do that?"

"Glad to."

"Dan, just so you know, I don't want this to go to your head, or anything, but you knocked that one out of the park."

"Thanks, Rick."

I was highly motivated. I was going home.

Team Building

My task was to take a team of eleven young men and one woman and transform them from computer nerds to cyber killers. Insensitive to their surroundings, able to press the launch or abort button without hesitation. To be cold, not caring whether the next program they write will be a single shot, one and done, or fully automatic, executing mass instructions at the speed of light.

I had to make these people think about only one thing, the code they're currently slinging in the RPG programming language, a language as foreign to them as their college education was to me. I had to make them RPG experts like me because I told the customer, IBM, they were. I had little time to deliver tens of thousands of lines of code—less than eight months. It's what I promised. That's just who I am.

I studied the resumes Stephany provided, along with eight copies of *The Modern RPG Language*, the book I had requested. Reviewing the resumes, it appeared that my team of twelve was broken down as follows:

Eight rookies (no RPG experience whatsoever)
Four experienced
Two with RPG skills
One with COBOL skills, no RPG
One with COBOL and SQL skills, no RPG

I handed out the eight copies of Cozzi's book to the rookies. I told them they could read it at their leisure; however, the book was to be used mainly for reference. It would be the *GoTo* manual. The IBM manuals were only to be used to solve coding problems.

I divided the eight rookies into two teams. I assigned the two experienced RPG programmers, Scott and Marie, as the senior programmers for each team. Every RPG programmer was assigned a component. Each component had a set of display panels, i.e., menu, list, data-entry, and corresponding RPG processing programs. In addition, each component had a front-end command for fast path, command line execution.

The other two experienced programmers refused to learn RPG. Under normal circumstances they would be out the door; however, I did need someone with SQL experience. I also had plans to automate the process of checking in and checking out RPG program source. The SQL guy was my *GoTo* resource for SQL. The COBOL guy was tasked with creating Checkin/Checkout commands to manage the source code.

The first week wasn't too productive. It was a time for learning and getting to know each other. I did the first of what would become a weekly, Friday afternoon chat. This meeting was to explain the project, the goals, my methods, and vision for how things would work.

"My name is Dan and that's all you need to know about me. I couldn't give a shit about your personal lives, your problems with Keane management, naked pictures of your girlfriends, or boyfriends in Marie's case, or anything else you think is important within your little sphere of existence."

There were some uncomfortable laughs.

"We have a job to do and a limited timeframe. In the next six months you will learn next to nothing about RPG/400, yet I expect each of you to have generated at least 10,000 Lines of Code aka LOC, as IBM calls it. This is how they measure our project, and it is how I will measure you. You will learn a process. You will understand how to build an application, not just how to write RPG code. I have already done that for you.

I have created a pile of dog shit and you will polish it, being very careful not to get it on any of these expensive workstations our employer has provided for us."

I had their attention.

"What you are creating will be an engineering marvel. IBM calls it TSA. I call it The Savior, Amen, because I believe that this couldn't have come at a better time for all of us. Most of you were on the chopping block. Keane didn't think we were worthy. I say they're wrong and we're going to prove it."

There were some nods and an *Amen*. I thought I had them. I gave them a high-level summary of the project, the templates and the process. I showed them how to copy the templates, rename them, and build a set of program components that were bug free and integrated with each other.

I reviewed the source code with them, which consisted of the mainline source and stubs for the function and command keys, whether the component needed them or not. I knew that change would be inevitable, and if we followed CUA standards, changes would be easy and simple.

I reviewed the reusable subroutines that would be copied into the mainline code and not changed. I showed them in the mainline code where they would add custom functions, i.e., program, or subroutine, calls to other programs or routines. All custom code would be external to the templates.

"I expect you to put in a full day's work."

I heard some "Oh, shits," as expected.

"Let me explain. I believe that a workday is 80% production and 20% education. I don't expect anyone to put in more than eight hours of billable time per day. You will be heads down for six and a half hours working on your code. You will spend one and a half hours learning something new or reviewing something to get a better understanding of it. The only exception to this would be if we get overtime approval. As you know, we get paid time and one-half for all billable hours over forty hours in one week. I don't know about your finances, but I can surely use the extra pay."

Nods all around.

"I expect you to get your component finished in six months, fully polished, and working as intended. Anyone struggling will receive help from their teammates first, the senior programmers second, and lastly me. I have created this team and I will see to it that no one fails."

"What about breaks?"

"We will take daily morning and afternoon coffee breaks and one hour for lunch."

"How will you measure our production?"

"That is a good question. I will use system information to create a baseline set of program line counts, based on the cloned source. Right now, it is zero. As you check out templates that number will grow. Each week I will capture a new set of stats and compare that to the previous set. I will be able to break it down by library. You each have your own library, so I will know who the top achievers are and who is falling behind."

"How will we test our programs?"

"We are building an application that will replace IBM's current application used for verifying OS/400 code. We will use our new application to verify the process we are making, check for errors, etc. Anyone else?"

There were no more questions. My team seemed to be in place. I thought we were ready to rock and roll. I would soon run into some problems.

Outside Agitators

The first problem I met with was easily remedied.

"Steph, the guy in charge of administering the AS/400s in the backroom has to go."

I was on my weekly status update call with the Keane management team.

"I'm sorry to hear that, Dan, what's the problem? He's been there since the backroom opened. The other project didn't have a problem with him."

"I'm not the other project. He's just a poor fit. He has too much time on his hands and I think he's becoming a distraction. If you don't have someone else, then I'll administer the AS/400s myself."

"Dan, you're too valuable for that. I'll reassign him. I'll send you someone else from the Cities area."

His name was Rich. He was about my age and was experienced in managing computer centers. We had met in Rochester at a Keane workshop on hiring new workers. We were doing some role-playing. Rich was the interviewer, and I was the interviewee. I provided Rich with a phony summary of my work history that included a glaring gap of two years. Rich challenged me on it, "Dan, there's this gap here. What were you doing?"

"Time," I replied

Rich tried very hard to keep a straight face but wasn't successful.

I was glad to see him again. He not only fit in, but he also volunteered to do the Command definitions and assist in creating the online Help text. The problem was resolved.

The next problem wasn't as easy.

Mr. Bojangles

He was the project manager (PM). We called him Mr. Bojangles because his pockets were so full of change that he jangled when he walked. We could hear him coming a mile away. It was what I was listening to as he walked up behind me.

"Hey, Mr. B, what can I do for you?" I said, without looking up.

"Dan, could you come with me to my office? I need to talk with you about Marie."

I didn't like that he mentioned a member of my team, especially Marie. This sounded personal. We walked into his office and he motioned for me to sit at a chair next to a table.

"It appears that Marie will be transferred to a new project a week from next Monday. I hope that will be sufficient time for her to bring another team member up to speed. This is just an FYI; these things happen all the time."

"Did Marie request a transfer?"

"No, I don't think so. It's just that Keane has a new project ramping up and we think Marie will be a good fit."

"Why was I not informed of this before now?" I could feel the anger rising.

"I'm sure it was just an oversight. The request came from the Regional Manager and Rick and Steph approved it. My hands are tied. I'm just keeping you in the loop."

"Okay, Mr. B, is that all for now?"

"That's it, everything appears to be going well, otherwise."

I walked out of Bojangles' office and went in search of Marie. I was angry. I had been betrayed. Someone had some explaining to do. All hell was about to break loose. I found Marie at her workstation.

"Can we talk?"

"Sure."

"Let's go outside."

Marie followed me as I went out the door and down the back stairway. There was a bench near the back entrance. I motioned to it. "Let's sit down."

I expected tears. Marie was the only woman in the group. We could get raunchy at times. I thought of it as letting off steam. We were under heavy pressure to succeed. Humor was a great outlet for stress, in my opinion. I thought Marie was handling it okay—I guessed I was wrong.

"Goddamn them all to hell!"

Perhaps it is worse than I thought; maybe things have gone too far.

"Who's them?"

"Bojangles, Rick, Steph, all those fu-fu-fuckers," Marie was so angry she stammered.

"What happened?"

"They told me there was a new project starting up and they needed someone with my skills. I told them I wasn't interested. They said that's not important. This is a huge opportunity for me and Keane. You would understand, they said. I thought you knew. I've been thinking about quitting. I thought we were getting along. I love this job, especially the camaraderie within the team. I don't want to transfer."

"Don't worry Marie, you're not going anywhere."

We went back inside the building and the backroom. I walked into Bojangles' office.

"Get Rick and Steph on the phone, now!"

Bojangles looked at me, decided not to argue, and picked up the phone.

"Hey, Steph, I've got Dan in my office. He needs to talk."

Bojangles covered the mouthpiece on the phone with his hand.

"Is this about Marie?"

I nodded.

"It's about Marie's transfer. Okay, call me back when you and Rick can get together."

"Steph is going to Rick's office now. Just so you know, I didn't agree with this. I told them you would not…"

"Shut your fat mouth."

I had used my badass voice. I stared at Bojangles. We sat in silence until the phone rang.

"Hi, Steph, yup, Dan's here, I am going to put you on speaker phone. Are you still there?"

"We're here. Can you hear us?"

"Yes, we can. I think Dan has something to say."

"I am going to say this once. Marie isn't going anywhere. She will remain on my project until it has been turned over to IBM. Don't ever try to take one of my team again."

I got up and walked out. Marie remained on the team. Mr. Bojangles was replaced by Sue Kennedy, a rising star within Keane. Sue and I got along very well. What pleased me the most was that she did not attempt to manage me.

The last major problem, and how I handled it, could've easily brought an end to the entire project.

Friday Afternoon Chats

I was at the front of the conference area that was set up in the computer room, which housed two AS/400s. On Friday afternoons I would hold meetings to discuss matters of great importance.

"As you know by now, the more questions you have about matters that are of a Keane, personal, or social nature, the longer I am going to keep you here, on this gorgeous Friday afternoon. You have also come to know that I usually end these chats with a 'take the rest of the day off' announcement. The delivery of that announcement is only further delayed by your irrelevant questions. Have I made this clear?"

There were no questions. They were great disciples of Dan's way.

"Today, I have an important topic to discuss. As you know, IBM has dictated that we must only use AS/400 development tools on this project. It has come to my attention that some of our team members, who shall remain nameless, are continuing to use antiquated POS [Piece of Shit] tools, much to the disappointment of yours truly. I have concluded that friendly cajoling and reminders are simply not enough. I thought about a public flogging, but Steph and Rick informed me that this form of punishment is no longer acceptable by Keane. So, in the spirit of less cruel and usual punishment, I believe I have come up with an acceptable form of reeducation. Let's delete a licensed program product."

Scott and Marie were my top two developers in total LOC and in fewest number of bugs. Scott had a S/38 background and Marie's background was System/36. Scott loved the S/38 Programmer Menu while Marie adored the System/36 POP utility. Scott was one of the funniest people I knew. Marie was a calming influence on the younger members of the team. Being the only woman, she kept several comments and jokes from going over the top.

I liked them very much, but no matter how hard I tried, I could not break them away from these unhealthy relationships with deprecated development tools. There was no cure; however, as I learned in AA, there is a solution—complete and total abstinence.

"Gather around."

I was sitting in front of a 5250-WS used for demo purposes. I entered the GO Licensed Program Product (LPP) command. A menu was displayed, and I selected *Work with Licensed Program Products*. A list panel with that title appeared. I typed 'Program' into the *Position* to... field and pressed the Enter key. I found the S/38 *Programmer Menu* in the list of LPPs and entered a 4 into the Choice field next to the LPP. I then pressed the Enter key and the Delete Confirmation panel appeared. I pressed Enter, which returned me to list panel. The *S/38 Programmer Menu* was no longer displayed.

"Let's try that again."

I repeated the process, this time searching and finding the POP LPP. When the delete completed, I turned around and faced the team.

"Any questions?"

There were none. They were good disciples.

"In that case," I said, looking at the clock on the wall, "it's time to call it a day. You have a good weekend, see you Monday."

Everyone showed up Monday morning, including Scott and Marie.

My Way or the Highway

My team generated approximately 120-thousand lines of code in the first six months of the TSA project. We spent the next three months fine tuning Help Text and putting on demos for the end-users in Rochester.

We received high praise from Steve and Jerry and the end-users. One young user commented that she loved TSA. Keane received a letter from Steve, on IBM letterhead, praising the work our team had done and my architectural design work. Sue Kennedy supported Steve's comments.

Steve and Jerry were also impressed with the documentation. Using Office/400, we had captured screen images of each component within TSA. We included text about how this component worked, what each option and function key would do, and the expected results.

During the initial phase of the development process, I would send these documents to Jerry for approval. It was my way of keeping IBM apprised of our progress. The more information in the document, the further we were along in the project. In addition, these documents provided the text for the Help panels.

The above process is what I presented at the COMMON User Group Conference in Las Vegas, later that year. I had a handful of attendees. There were no questions. I didn't use the full amount of time. It was my first, and last, presentation at COMMON.

I was proud of what we had accomplished. I believed this might lead to other things.

Making Up Is Hard to Do

Plymouth, MN Summer 1990

Mary Jo and I were lying in bed facing each other. We were engaged in a post sex conversation.

"Dan, I was so angry with you. I thought about leaving you. I was so mad. Then I realized that I had broken one of my own personal rules about relationships."

"What was that?"

"That we would never turn our backs on each other."

"Mary Jo, it was me who turned my back on you. I was hurt and angry because you had rejected my advances again. So, you were mad?"

"Yes, I never wanted to move to Rochester. When the opportunity came up at Parker-Hannifin, I took it. I thought you would come back to your senses and stop commuting."

"Just so you know, Mary Jo, I did turn in my resignation when I realized our house wouldn't sell, but Stephany wouldn't accept it. She suggested carpooling. Then the backroom opportunity came up. I am so glad that you didn't leave me. I was so much looking forward to rediscovering you."

"You sure do know how to sweet talk a girl."

"To be honest, it's from a song by Journey, 'Faithfully.' I listened to a lot of different music the last couple of years. I've created some new CDs with different playlists."

"Actually, I'm thinking of playing with something else," Mary Jo said, as she reached for me.

It seems like most good things that happened to me began with a phone call. The phone was ringing. I picked it up.

"Dan here, what's up?"

No one outside of Keane management knew this number.

"Dan, it's Rick. You did a good job on the TSA project by the way."

"Thanks, Rick."

"Are you able to come down to Rochester tomorrow to attend a meeting at IBM?"

"Yes, what's going on?"

"We're meeting with some IBM big honchos and we may need a technical resource. You are a known commodity to IBM, due to your success with the TSA project. We don't know if there will be any technical questions, but we want to have all bases covered. Can we count on you?"

"No, problem, I'll see you tomorrow."

Things are slowing down. Now that Mary Jo and I are whole again, I hope I don't have to get back on **The Blue Highway**.

Operational Assistant (OA)

I Am Usability

Rochester, MN Fall 1990

The IBM executive team had put together a storyboard for a new application to be included with the next operating release of the AS/400 computer system. This release would be referred to as OS/400 V1R3M0. The current release was OS/400 V1R2M0.

The application was a spinoff of an OS product, currently in development, planned for V1R3M0; however, the development team would not be ready in time for the announcement, scheduled for next spring. The upper-level management folks in IBM were concerned; OS/400 was an extension of the S/38 operating system and many S/36 customers felt slighted. Some hinted that they might consider other platforms that claim to support RPG without all the latest bells and whistles RPG/400 had to offer.

The IBM executive was using the storyboard to describe the interactive displays that would be part of the new application, mainly a simpler way for S/36 customers to locate and manage the objects required to maintain and operate the AS/400. Much of the OS/400 terminology was from the S/38.

"I call this display 'Where Are My Printouts?' Notice that the display shows a list of *Spooled Files*. As you know that is the S/38 term for printouts or reports and confuses S/36 users. Next to the printouts are the various options a S/36 user is used to. For example, by placing a 6 next to the printout, a pop-up window displays asking, 'Where Do You Want to Print It?' Beneath the question there are two options, 'My Printer' or 'System Printer'; the user chooses by clicking the little circle next to the device."

Oh, boy, where did they find this guy? Does he think he's dealing with kindergartners? Come on, give me a break.

As I listened to him talk, I was already putting together a plan in my head on how to accomplish the things he was describing. I had the templates in place. My team had used them to build the TSA application in six months, generating over a hundred thousand lines of RPG/400 program code.

The templates were shells that contained the navigational code for end-users who were interacting with an RPG/400 program, executed on the AS/400. The templates conformed with SAA standards. At the time, *this encompassed mainframe* green screen terminals and IBM PS/2 personal computers. In the case of PS/2, SAA also covered conventions for graphical displays.

The shells also incorporated CUA, which defined specific actions associated with Command Function keys. Every key that caused an interaction with the computer, e.g., *Enter, Return*, etc., also had a CUA defined course of action.

These actions were not simply pulled out of thin air by a group of PhDs sitting in a *Think Tank* with nothing better to do. At IBM Rochester, there was an entire department named Usability, dedicated to understanding the impact of a human's reaction when keyboarding.

I had been given a tour of the usability lab. There were cameras positioned so they could capture the hand movements as someone pounded away on the keyboard. There were microphones positioned over the heads of the keyboarders to capture the sounds, not only of the keyboard, but also any utterances made by the person keying.

The IBM executive completed his storyboard walkthrough. **Julie Ransom** provided some additional information.

"So, what we need is a temporary solution for our S/36 customers, who are currently struggling with the native AS/400 user display. Considering what we're hearing from development, V1R3M0 may be too optimistic. This will be the last release for Version 1. Development believes V2R1, scheduled for 1992, is more reasonable. Dan, is this something you can do to help us in the interim, while Development completes the new capabilities?"

Of course, I can. I created the TSA prototype based on system information available in output file data. I know exactly where to get the information they need.

Some of the S/38 commands, namely Display Program References (DSPPGMREF), Display Object Description (DSPOBJD), and Display File Description (DSPFD) came with an option to store the command results into an output file or a report.

"Yes, this should be no problem. All the information required by the displays in the storyboard is currently available. We are also capable of providing the pop-up windows and graphics, if that is an option you wish to offer those customers who are using the 5294 color terminals."

"How soon could you have this ready?"

I have thirteen developers, all experienced in Method D (Dan's way). One of my developers had automated the Template Checkin/Checkout process. I was extremely confident.

"Three to five weeks, give or take a couple of days."

"Are you serious?"

"Yes, however, I do have a concern."

"What is it?"

"All of our templates are based on CUA standards for text-based terminals, i.e., green screens. The pictures in the storyboard do not adhere to these standards. They're more like something you would see on a PC, not an AS/400. Have you run this by Usability?"

"I am Usability," was the executive's response, "and I don't give a shit how they look if you can get them done in less than five weeks."

Programming Request for Price Quote (PRPQ)

The following Saturday, I drove to IBM Rochester and met with Julie. We spent several hours in a lab, where I showed her the different OS/400 commands that could provide the information they needed for the project. She was impressed. My company was awarded the project under the condition that my team and I would perform the work. This meant off-site, in the backroom, in Minneapolis—not Rochester.

This was also extremely important for my sex life. Mary Jo and I were now back on a regular sex schedule, after rediscovering each other when I stopped commuting. I didn't want to get back on the "blues" highway.

OA began as a PRPQ. These were typically products that were built based on a customer request, or to fit a business requirement. They were delivered As Is, which meant they might have bugs, and these bugs would not be fixed. Since PRPQs were owned by **Steve Cyr**, our IBM management team would not change.

We delivered the initial version within the timeframe I promised, even with the additional training on the packaging required for a PRPQ. Julie began demonstrating the OA PRPQ at IBM technical conferences, like COMMON and various other user groups. Julie kept me informed of her progress. As the project neared its completion date, I heard less and less from Julie.

Beware of upper management in suits showing up at noon on Friday—bearing pizzas.

Licensed Program Product (LPP)

We heard them before we smelled them.

"So, this is the infamous backroom."

The suit was one of three top dogs, two from the Rochester branch, and a guy from corporate, located in Boston. The Boston guy walked up to me and held out his hand.

"And you must be Dan. I've heard a lot about you. Your manager says there isn't anything you can't do with an AS/400."

I shook his hand.

"I haven't been able to balance one on my chin using a pencil, but I'm working on it."

The suit looked at me, obviously unsure of what I'd just said or what he'd just heard. Then he laughed. The other two suits took his cue and laughed with him.

"A techie with a sense of humor, I would've never guessed it; good one, Dan."

I glanced at the team; they were all grins. Of course, they had been putting up with my antics for several months now. Mr. Big was about to give a speech.

"Everyone, please gather around. We've ordered lunch in today. I hope everyone likes pizza. I have some great news. We've been talking with IBM all week. Apparently, this new project you've been working on, Operator Assignments, is a big success with IBM's former S/36 customers who are now on the AS/400. IBM wants to provide Operator..."

I cut him off.

"Operational Assistant, you can call it OA."

"Thanks, Dan. As I was saying, IBM wants to provide Oh Ayyy," he nodded towards me, "as an LPP. We promised IBM that you guys could have it ready by the end of the year. This means that you may have to work evenings and weekends to get it done. Oh, great, the pizzas are here."

It was early December. The end of the year was under four weeks away.

"Excuse me. What do we need to know about how to package OA as an LPP?"

"My understanding is that IBM will train you, Dan, and one other team member on the workings of LPP. You can check with Julie next week, when you're in Rochester. Training starts on Monday. Hey, guys, save a slice of sausage and pepperoni for me."

The five-week PRPQ OA project was approaching two months. Adding more bells and whistles to any project without providing a reasonable timeline or additional resources to meet an aggressive deadline is a step towards failure.

No problem, the team is hot! Bring it on. Theoretically, all we should have to do is modify the packaging. I believe the code is complete. I will also have to let Mary Jo know that I am going back onto **The Blue Highway**—temporarily, so they say.

We met our deadline. The OA saga wasn't over.

OS/400

I was sitting at a conference table in a room within the IBM blue buildings, located in Rochester, MN. I still had my contractor badge access, from when I was on the CPF support team. There were several people at the table, some I knew (i.e., Julie R. and Steve C.), some whom I would get to know—Rick Peterson and others, some who would become life-long friends—Charlie Farrell. Julie was leading the meeting.

"As you know, I've been presenting OA to several former S/36, now AS/400 customers, and the response has been overwhelmingly positive. Unfortunately, these customers are pushing back on the LPP. Many of them are willing to wait for Version 2, that's not the bad news. Development is now pushing back V2R1. It's an important release and they think there's enough in there already. Adding OA is just too big a leap for them. So, Dan, here is the $64,000 question. Do you think you and your remarkable team can modify OA enough to make the V1R3M0 release scheduled for March 1991, as part of OS/400?"

"It depends," —a term I would eventually become very familiar with at IBM—"on how many modifications we may need to make. If there are only a few, then yes, we can do it."

"That sounds wonderful, Dan. I'm going to turn this over to Charlie, who has a better handle on what might be entailed."

"Hi, Dan, Charlie Farrell, I've heard good things about you. It's great to meet you in person. Put a face to the name."

"Thanks, Charlie. So, what's involved to make OA part of the OS? Do we have to rewrite it in PL/MI and PL/MP?"

"You know how to code in IBM's proprietary languages used to develop XPF?"

Like CPF, the IBM internal code name for the S/38 OS, XPF was IBM's internal code name for the AS/400 OS.

"I was a PL/MP VMC coder when I was on the CPF support team. My product was X.25. Several of my current team members were part of the OfficeVision/400 UIM Panel development team. They know UIM and PL/MI. That said, I cannot guarantee that we would make the scheduled release date for V1R3M0 if we had to rewrite the current RPG/400 programs."

"That would be great, but it isn't the top priority."

"So, what is?"

"Performance."

Are you shitting me? Performance? I can't believe it. Our templates all take advantage of IBM's recommendations for best performance when using RPG/400. We use all of IBM's recommendations for best performance when writing custom RPG code. Perhaps Charlie can enlighten me.

"Charlie, can you be more explicit?"

"Yes, IBM has a requirement that all interactive system applications must have a response time of two-seconds, or less. We had Ed Simon, part of the RPG/400 compiler team, review your code. He said it was some of the most structured, readable RPG/400 he had ever seen. He said it appears to him that the code passes the RPG 'best practices for performance' litmus test. That said, we had Rick Peterson, who is part of the performance group, analyze the code using our internal tools, TIPS and SPIES. Unfortunately, several of the programs do not maintain a two-second response time. In some cases, it was several minutes."

I was shocked. I had prided myself, not only in the readability of my template code, but also in my efforts to ensure acceptable performance. Obviously, my standards were fine for government work, but not for IBM operating systems. Charlie probably sensed my dismay.

"Please, Dan, don't take it so hard. We think you can rectify many of the issues with some minor code changes. Thankfully, the code's modular design should minimize the changes. I'll let Rick explain his findings."

"Hi, Dan, Rick Peterson; I am with the performance team."

"Hi, Rick, it's good to meet you."

"First, I want to concur with Charlie. This may not be as horrendous as it sounds. Second, in my experience with analyzing HLL application performance data, I usually find that eighty percent of the system resources used are being consumed by twenty percent, or less, of the application programs. In your case, I have narrowed it down to a half dozen programs that need to be modified, or possibly rewritten, to meet OS/400 standards."

"Do you know the names of those programs?" I asked Rick.

"Yes, I do. They are..."

Rick gave me the names. I recognized them immediately. I knew exactly what they were doing from an application perspective. I had no clue what the performance issue might be.

"Do we need to sit down with someone who understands RPG, like Ed Simon, and perhaps a performance expert like yourself, to identify the problem?"

"Not at all, Dan," Rick said, "I can tell you exactly what the performance issue is and the line, or lines, of code in the RPG/400 program responsible."

I was amazed.

"Really? You can do that? Are you an RPG/400 guru?"

"Nope, I've never written a line of RPG/400 code in my life. Our application performance tools are the best in the world, if I do say so myself."

"So, what exactly are the performance issues?"

"More good news," replied Rick. "The main performance issue, extreme memory faulting, appears in each of the programs. The root cause is the copying of spool files, and then processing them within the RPG/400 program. It appears the OS/400 API Execute Command (QCMDEXC) is being used in all cases. Any particular reason why you're doing this?"

"Yes, I need to create the spool file, copy it to a disk-file, so I can subsequently process it by the RPG/400 program. I do this because the commands that produce the print-file do not have the output file capability."

"Can you use pointers in RPG?" Charlie asked.

A damaged pointer was the problem I fixed on that stormy night back at Horton.

"No, but I am familiar with pointers from my PL/MP coding days. I can see how pointers would allow me to access the spool file information directly, which would probably be way more efficient."

Charlie and Rick looked at each other.

"What do you think, Rick?"

"Does he, or his company, have confidentiality clearance?" Rick asked Julie.

"If not, I would be surprised, since his company is supporting both CPF and XPF."

I was watching Charlie and Rick hash this out.

"What are you guys talking about?"

Charlie looked at Rick. Rick shrugged. Charlie looked at me.

"Dan, there's something coming in a future release referred to as *controlled openness*. Have you been briefed on it?"

Application Programming Interface (API)

The controlled openness initiative began in the early 1990s, within IBM Rochester. OS/400 was considered a proprietary operating system versus the open operating systems, such as Windows. IBM, and other computer manufacturers who developed a proprietary OS, were under pressure from outside sources to move their systems to the wonderful world of Disney-Open. In other words, develop tinker toy, pre-school software that can be easily accessed and modified by the growing number of program coders who were barely out of high school, still dressed in their kindergarten clothes, and owning a PC.

IBM's approach was to create APIs, which could be used in HLL programs to access system data (e.g., spool files, messages, devices, etc.), without going through the extra layers involved when using the OS provided commands. Since OS/400 was an object-oriented OS, a malicious program cleverly disguised as a friendly file, complete with happy face emoji daring someone to click on it, could not be introduced into the system. Within OS/400 only a program object could be executed. To create a program object required access to the source language compiler and a high degree of authority. Of course, in the early 1990s, the last thing on anyone's mind was computer piracy. Except for the geniuses at IBM Rochester responsible for data integrity.

I heard something like the above at a COMMON user group conference I attended as a customer in 1991. Someone in the audience had questioned the IBM speaker as to why the AS/400 had so many hoops to jump through before someone could have access to the data.

"At IBM Rochester we believe your data is important, even if you don't," was the speaker's response.

Controlled openness was IBM's way of cautiously using their toe to test the calm, beckoning water before jumping in headfirst, not realizing there's a boulder, or a shark, hidden beneath the surface. It made perfect sense to me but, then, as a kid I ran with the rough crowd. We took advantage of people's naivety to steal cigarettes from unsecured locations within motels, food, and drug stores.

The first APIs would not be delivered until V2R1. We were targeting OA for V1R3M0. Technically, the APIs were not available to customers for another release. We were not considered customers. Virtually, my team of developers and I were part of IBM. We were given access to the APIs we needed to improve the performance, without having to replace the RPG/400 code. Problem solved—not quite.

Although the APIs eliminated the need to copy system objects (e.g., spool files) to disk, we were still required to carve out a chunk of memory within the RPG/400 program code, to hold the data returned to the RPG/400 program from the API. The release of RPG we were using was RPG/400. There was a new version of RPG in the works, and that release would be able to use pointers.

"That's perfect, Charlie, let's get it."

"Not so fast, Dan, this new version is several releases away, years probably. It is based on new technology that has not even been invented yet."

Charlie was exaggerating to make the point. I got it.

"So, does this mean that we will have to rewrite the programs after all? The release date is less than a month away."

Charlie thought about it.

"C'mon, Dan, let's take a walk."

Charlie wasn't one to use a phone when a good walk would take you to his office where you could talk face-to-face. The IBM manufacturing facility was huge. Many of the new hires would walk the halls wearing backpacks that contained fresh underwear, in case they had to spend the night in a restroom getting from one end to the other.

Charlie's office was in Blue Building 003. Our destination was Blue Building 020. The person we were off to meet was **Dick Bains**. About six hours later we arrived. Only joking, the building numbers could be misleading. It was probably about five minutes, ten tops. Dick was in.

"Hey, Dick, got a minute?"

"Hey, Charlie, I sure do. How's it going?"

"Still going, knock on wood. I want you to meet Dan Cruikshank. I am working with him and his team on the OA project. We've run into an RPG/400 programming dilemma. Thought maybe you might have a suggestion, or two."

"What's the problem?"

"I'll let Dan explain, I'm not a programmer."

I described the memory issue. Dick knew what I was talking about.

"The RPG/400 compiler allocates the entire amount of memory when the program object is activated. No way to get around that. I'm surprised you're writing it in RPG. I thought all new development was C++, because of its object-oriented capabilities?"

"We started out as a PRPQ, sir. Things have been snowballing since. We're trying to avoid a rewrite, sir."

"Call me Dick."

Dick thought about it.

"Are the variables input parameters by chance?"

"No, they're just temporary storage variables."

A parameter variable contained values that could be passed between programs. The value was stored separately from the program, allowing it to be shared between multiple programs.

"What if they were variables defined as pointer types in the calling program, written in C/400 or PL/1? They could then be defined as an input parameter in the RPG/400 program. The RPG/400 compiler is smart enough to not generate an additional memory space. Do you know C or PL/1?"

"I was a PL/MP coder."

"Ahhhh, VMC'er, I thought you had that special walk. PL/MP is a PL/1 derivative. You should be able to pick it up. Damn, I was hoping you would say no. I haven't done some meaningful code-slinging in some time."

The Handoff

I was sitting in my car. It was about 9:00 P.M. on a Saturday night. I was in front of the Country Kitchen, located in Cannon Falls, MN. The restaurant was conveniently located equidistant from the IBM Rochester facility and the backroom. It was also next to US-52—easy on, easy off **The Blue Highway.**

The highway traffic had been slowly disappearing. The traffic coming from Rochester, MN, towards the Twin Cities had been rare, if at all. When a car appeared, heading in my direction, I would move my hand to the car's light switch. If the approaching car took the frontage road exit, then I would flip the lights on and off. That was the signal.

I had tapes, music, and data—enough music to last a lifetime, much longer than the car battery. I didn't like running the car, it seemed like a waste of gas. The data tapes were not for me. They were for the person I was planning to meet.

About every twenty minutes I would start the car to charge the battery and warm up. It was cool outside; it felt like twenty below, average for March in Minnesota.

A car was approaching Cannon Falls from the direction of IBM. It appeared to be slowing down. It turned onto the frontage road and approached the Country Kitchen. I flipped the car lights on and off. The approaching car flashed its brights—that was it. I started my car.

The car pulled up next to me, driver window to driver window. I rolled my window down. The other window started to lower. The driver appeared to be holding a long cylinder like object. It was pointed right at me.

"Hey, Dan, Charlie sends his regards."

Rick pushed the cylinder my way.

"What is it?" I asked.

"It's another AS/400 poster. Charlie thought it would look great in the backroom. Brighten the place up a bit."

"Ha, ha, Charlie thinks we work in a dungeon. So, what's the verdict?"

Rick gave me a thumbs up.

"Performance is acceptable. The PL/1 frontend program interface did the trick, good job."

"Dick gets the credit. I'm just a code-slinger. Oh, this is for you."

I handed him a computer tape containing the latest copy of OA, referred to as *best so far*. Every Sunday night a refresh of the latest version of V1R3M0 was downloaded to the AS/400 test machines. During the following week, testers would launch OfficeVision/400, open their script document, and run through their tests. They recorded the results into the TSA tool. Later that day, managers reviewed the results, which had been converted to pie charts and/or bar graphs, displayed in color on their 5294 workstations, or PCs with the IBM 5250 Emulation product.

I knew this because I was the system architect for TSA. I never thought that one day that application would be used to record the results of another application that I was the system architect for; or that those testing it would find so many bugs. One hundred and eighty-seven to be precise.

Swat Week

We smelled them before we heard them. It must be a Friday because our management team had arrived, and they were armed with pizzas.

"Dan, team, what can I say? The reports from IBM are just glowing. You guys are the best. We are so close to completing on time and within budget that I can taste it," the Big Guy said, as he took a huge bite from his slice of pineapple and ham pizza. I don't know if he was trying to be a comic, but I wasn't going to laugh, nor did anyone else.

"So, here's the deal—IBM wants to do a final deep dive, sanity test. This is how it works. They bring in a team of super testers who are going to bang away on OA, six ways from Sunday. If they find a bug, and I am confident enough to think they won't, then the coder responsible for that program fixes it immediately. Let me say it again, *immediately*. Questions? Hey, has anyone tried this pineapple and ham. It's delicious."

"Question, sir."

"Go ahead and shoot, Dan."

"When you say *immediately,* how exactly does that work, when we're here in Minneapolis and they're down there, in Rochester?"

"We have the team booked in Rochester for all of next week. You guys will be on per-diem for meals. Hotel expense is covered. You can claim mileage to and from Rochester. Any more questions? No? Good, then we'll see you all on Monday in Rochester."

One hundred and eighty-seven bugs counted. The good news was that most of the bugs were DSPF related, specifically language translation. The IBM AS/400 was operating in several countries, and for many of those, English was a secondary language. Every DSPF had a bug. The most common being text, either screen titles, instructions or messages (informational or error notifications).

I took the blame. When I created my screen templates, all my applications were intended for domestic use only. At the time, I had no idea that I would be using these templates to develop software that would be used in a multinational environment.

Fortunately, the corrections were easy to make. All the messages were contained within a *message-file* (MSGF) object type. All AS/400 OS displays used MSGF objects to contain screen titles and instruction text. IBM provided a language specific MSGF object with each AS/400 sold. When an IBM screen was displayed, the OS searched the *library-list* (LIBL) object type for the MSGF object containing the screen text. The language specific MSGF was always ahead of the default English language MSGF, thus screen text language translation was dynamic. In addition, if the message wasn't found in the language specific MSGF, then the English MSGF was used.

IBM had a tool for translating messages contained within MSGF objects to the country specific language. This solved our message text language-related bugs. Unfortunately, we did not store our screen titles and instruction text in MSGF objects. They were hard coded in the screen DSPF source-file-member as individual words. The translation tool could translate the words, but it could not check that the combined words were grammatically correct, as per the language. Each screen had to be manually corrected by keying the words as a continuous text string and the DSPF object recreated. I ordered pizzas.

"Team, I know everyone was thinking that this was going to be a boondoggle. Sit around all day yakking and yukking it up, then out for dinner, having pizza and beer at one of the local establishments. Unfortunately, we must get these screens fixed before we leave on Friday. I'm not going to force you to stay and work thru the night. I just ask that you fix as much as you can before calling it a day. You know I don't drink, so spending the night consuming mass quantities of beer isn't for me. I don't mind staying later on-site and fixing as much as I can before I leave. Okay with everybody?"

They all nodded. Nobody went out for dinner, even the team members who did not own any DSPF source. By the end of the week, we had fixed all reported bugs, except one. OA was shipped with V1R3M0. There was one screen that did not translate. I never heard if there were any customer complaints.

As the OA project came to an end, so did the backroom. It was a gradual change. Several of the younger team members left Keane and found employment elsewhere in the Cities. Two members started their own business as code-slinging contractors. They even offered me a position. I turned it down.

Marie was never part of OA. She went to Rochester to support TSA. Scott stayed with Keane and took on some work in the Cities. He would eventually become a freelance consultant, with expertise in software developed by J. D. Edwards (JDE). We stayed in touch. I don't know what happened to Rick.

I would be the last one to leave the backroom. I had a meeting in Rochester that day. I stopped in and packed up my books; I had acquired quite a collection. Besides James Martin, I had *The Three Rs of Software*

Automation by Carma McClure, *The Decline & Fall of the American Programmer* by Edward Yourdon, plus a few more. I would keep these in my car, depending on where I would end up.

I left the backroom forever. Steph had informed me that they might have a new project in Rochester that fit me. The project only required one person. There was no need for my architecture skills. The work would be done in Rochester. It would be almost two decades before I would use my design skills again.

I'm going back onto **The Blue Highway**. *I couldn't wait to tell Mary Jo.*

The Turd Polisher

IBM Blue Building 005

Rochester, MN Spring 1991

When I reached the Keane office in Rochester, Steph informed me that I would meet with **Charlie Farrell** at his office in the blue buildings. *Good old Charlie*. This may be better than I thought. I still had my IBM contractor's badge which allowed me to enter Blue Building 006 through the contractor entrance. I found Charlie in his office.

"Hey, stranger, long time no see."

"Good to see you too, Charlie, but it's only been a few weeks. What's up?"

"Well, I acquired ownership of a performance report, developed /in PL/MI and PL/MP. In essence, it uses PL/MP to access performance data at the VMC level. The information is collected by the PFRTools LPP when a trace is started, via the menu option or the Start Trace (STRTRC) command. It requires some modifications to the PL/MP code. I thought of you immediately. I remember you said you were a VMC coder. Interested?"

"Yes, I am."

"Great, let's take a look."

Charlie had a sample of the report, along with several printouts of the VMC code. I recognized some of the common Macros, but others were new to me. Charlie explained the program function.

"Once a trace is started, those programs that contain performance instrumentation are enabled to dump data into a memory space object whenever the appropriate performance Macro is executed. There are some new Macros that need to be added to the program."

"That shouldn't be difficult to do," I said. I knew a Macro was like an API. The only thing I needed to test was that the Macro worked as intended when it was executed by the program. "So, it appears I'm going to be a code-slinger again."

"That was the original plan, but since I spoke with Stephany there have been some new developments."

"What are they?"

"One of the performance guys has written a new tool that deprecates this performance report. The tool is named Storage Management Trace (SMTRACE). The name of the guy who wrote it is *Jay Kurtz*. He's looking for a *turd polisher*. His term, not mine."

Storage Management Trace (SMTRace)

Each new release would introduce new Macros and other technology that would deprecate, or make obsolete, existing programs or the code said programs were currently executing. If the program was still usable, then it was simply changed or *polished* to make it more useful.

"I know exactly what he means."

"Great! Let's go for a walk."

Jay was a colorful guy. He was the first IBMer I met who didn't quite fit the mode. Like most IBMers, Jay was extremely intelligent. Unlike many others, he was direct and, in some ways, very intimidating. If he didn't like something, he would let me know right away. I learned that in our first meeting.

"I've created this turd," Jay was referring to the SMTrace tool, "and now I need someone to polish it."

"So, you created a prototype and now you need to make it presentable to ass hats who don't know shit on a shingle when they see it, even if it were handed to them on a plate."

"You got it."

"Okay, no problem. I think the best and fastest way for me to do this is to use some of my templates to create a Work with Panel based on SAA CUA conventions."

"Don't give me all that IBM acronym bullshit. What the hell did you just say?"

"Let me explain. SAA is a big bottle of Shinola that comes with instructions for shining the worst kind of turds, those that contain undigested bubble gum that seem to automatically make your foot want to step in it. CUA is the polishing cloth, especially made for getting that sticky shit off your shoes."

"Got it," Jay said, as he turned to Charlie. "I like this guy."

I spent my last few weeks as a Keane employee commuting to Rochester, meeting with Jay, and building the Work with SMTrace application. I was given some office space in Blue Building 003 close to Charlie. I enjoyed the work, and I started to get a better understanding of IBM Rochester's OS/400 performance analysis strategy.

Perhaps, someday, I would be able to use it. It may require more time on **The Blue Highway***; but that also means more time for Mary Jo and me to rediscover each other.*

March 1991

As I commuted, I started to take stock of my situation. I had completed polishing Jay's turd and was now on maintenance mode. Charlie was still my main contact at IBM. He would find some tasks to keep me busy. It would not be enough to keep me on the farm. I was becoming a hot commodity. The highway was calling.

Sue Kennedy left near the end of the OA project; another woman took her place and oversaw the dismantling of the team and the backroom. After I began commuting to Rochester, she called me.

"Hello, Dan, this is .... We worked together in the backroom for a couple of weeks."

"Oh, yes, I remember you. What's up?"

"My boyfriend, Rick B., is starting a consulting company. They are currently interviewing. I thought if you're interested, I could pass your name on. Ground floor opportunity. What do you say?"

"Go ahead."

It turns out they had opened offices in downtown Wayzata, MN, a block off Wayzata Bay. A popular place for dining and sailboat watching.

Wayzata, MN

I interviewed with Rick and two other founding members of the firm. The location was great; however, their vision wasn't quite the same as mine.

"I'm with you, Dan, but we need to crawl before we can walk, or run for that matter. What you have in mind is a couple of years away, at best. We're in no position to acquire an AS/400 for speculative purposes. If you come to work for us, you will have to take on work that may be outside your comfort zone, until we get firmly planted."

"Thanks, Rick, but I'm not interested. When your girlfriend said it was a ground floor opportunity, I didn't realize that I might literally be mopping up floors."

Rick laughed at my joke and we went our separate ways.

Mine was **The Blue Highway.** *I'm sorry, Mary Jo.*

Acquired Skills:

PL/1, PL/MP, X.25, PL/MI, RPG/400, UIM/Help, APIs, SAM (Spies), TPST (Tips), Office/400, BGU, SQL, PDM, ADM; word processing and presentation software.

KMA Associates
Director of Software Services

That's Cold

St. Louis Park, MN

The first day of my new job as director of software services I spent at the KMA SLP location. Ann met me there and introduced me to the other KMA employee sharing the office space. Gene, my colleague from Keane who had instigated my employment with KMA, would come and go, spending most of his time visiting with potential clients. During the first three months of my new job, I spent most of the rest of my time commuting to Rochester.

Rochester, MN April 1991

I met the programming staff based there, two employees and two subcontractors. One of my first requests to this group was to provide me with a list of the projects they were currently working on, along with an estimate of where they were in the project and how much they had left to do. I explained I needed this information to help me assess the current situation.

I immediately made enemies of the subcontractors. Kyle had never asked them for status reports or time estimates before. The employees had never done that before either, but they were willing to try. The first set of status reports I was given was worthless.

"Here's what I want to do," I explained in my next meeting with the team. "I want to create what is referred to as a GANTT chart. It is a document that contains a list of the projects. Under each project will be the name of the programmer or programmers assigned to it. The next twelve columns will represent months in a year. Each month will be split into two halves. The left half will contain the hours agreed to on the contract. The right side will contain the hours currently billed. This information should help Kyle to make informed decisions on which projects are going well, which are in trouble, and so on."

"I've never done this before; I don't know where to start."

"Start by making a list of the programs you are currently working on and the programs you know you need to create. Create a list of tasks, let's keep it simple; code, compile, test, debug, deliver. Assign hours to each task, e.g., code=1, compile=1, test=3, debug=2, deliver=1 for a total of eight hours, or one day. Does that help?"

The employees nodded, the subcontractors said nothing. One glared at me and immediately went to Kyle's office when the meeting was over. I needed to set an example. He was the first to go.

The other subcontractor lasted for several months. He knew he was doomed. He was a S/36 RPG/II programmer and did not want anything to do with the AS/400. It wasn't the direction I was taking my team.

Journal Scraping

St. Paul, MN

I was in a meeting at a large manufacturing company headquartered in St. Paul, MN. They were using an AS/400 to run two, third-party software applications that managed the financial and service billing data processing requirements. The software products were JDE, the industry leader in AS/400 financial software, and JDA, whose software managed shop maintenance service calls. Neither software product communicated with the other.

With me in the meeting were Kyle, Ann, a JDA representative, and two, or three, customer representatives. Kyle had a business relationship with JDA to provide sales and support of their product. She kept a copy of the software on KMA's AS/400.

The meeting was in response to a request from the customer to JDA to provide a means of integrating their product with JDE in the least intrusive means possible. The customer had started down this path on their own, but soon realized that using their known processes was too time-consuming when attempting to do it for the AS/400 applications.

The customer had identified the files in each software product that contained the required data elements, aka fields, in the JDA software and was currently attempting to cross reference the fields to the corresponding fields in the JDE software. Once this was complete, they could then begin writing the program code that would capture changes in the JDA files and then replicate the changed data to the appropriate JDE files. Currently this process was being done manually, a process that was becoming very labor intensive.

The meeting became contentious. The JDA representative had provided the database documentation that defined the fields, but did not have, or know how to extract, the data dictionary from the AS/400. The current *field reference file* (FRF) listing provided to the customer was woefully out of date, plus it did not contain any of the custom changes made for the customer.

"It's taking me several weeks to create a current data dictionary based on the provided documentation, and now I find out the documentation isn't up to date. The work I've done is worthless," complained the customer's database architect/administrator (DBA). "It will take me several more weeks to redo the work I've done, and now you tell us it may take you several weeks to update the documentation. This is a disaster."

Until then, I'd had little to offer. Suddenly the conversation had gone down this new rabbit hole, one with a neon sign flashing: *Welcome to Dan's World.*

"I think I have a simple solution."

Everyone turned to look at me.

"Who are you again?" asked the customer Chief Information Officer (CIO).

"My name is Dan Cruikshank; I am the director of software services for KMA and there is a very simple and easy solution to the data dictionary issue."

"We're all ears."

"The AS/400 comes with an integrated relational database. A base table is implemented as a physical file object that is a collection of smaller objects, one of which is referred to as the *format*. The format contains a list of the defined fields for that file. The file-format information can be displayed, printed, or captured in an output file and sent to a PC, where it could be used in a spreadsheet for external analysis, such as cross-referencing fields with another application."

"I think you just paid for your lunch," responded the CIO. He turned to look at the JDA representative, "So, now we just need to know from you: which programs access these files; which ones perform updates to the data; how long it will take to modify these programs to integrate with JDE; and how much it will cost."

"Well," responded the JDA representative, "I will need to discuss this with our application development team. We can put together a list of the programs and come up with an estimate. It will take at least two weeks to prepare the list and put together a proposal."

"Two weeks? That is bullshit. I was hoping you could provide us with one today. Didn't you come prepared?"

I politely coughed. All heads turned my way.

"There may be a simpler solution."

Everyone waited for me to continue.

"The AS/400 has another tool that can be used to build a program-to-file cross reference chart, a CRUD report, if you will, containing the 'create, read, update, and/or delete operations' a program can execute. In addition, the tool provides information about how a program opens a file, i.e., input, output, or update. This report would provide you with the information you're asking; however, I don't think you need to modify the programs."

"I disagree," responded the JDA representative. "We need to modify the programs to record the insert, update or delete transaction to a log-file that can then be processed by JDE, which already provides that batch-file processing capability."

"Yes, you will need to write some new programs to create the JDE batch-file; however, you do not need to modify your existing programs."

"Dan, I know you are new to KMA, but..." the JDA representative started.

"Shut up and let him finish," interjected the CIO. "Go ahead, Dan."

"The AS/400 comes with an auditing tool that automatically records all file change activity. This includes file opens, closes, alterations, etc., but most importantly, in this situation, the actual record inserts, updates, and deletes. In the case of updates, it records the changed data-record image and can optionally record the before image. On the AS/400 this form of transaction logging is called *journaling*. It complements the normal backup and recovery functions. In addition, the information that is recorded to the journal object is made available to an application by using the Retrieve Journal Entry [RTVJRNE] command. Once retrieved, the record image portion of the journal entry can be customized and written to the JDE batch processing disk-file."

"How long do you think this will take?" asked the CIO.

"I could work with your DBA this afternoon and show him how to extract the data. I think it will take a couple of days to create the bridge program that scrapes the journal. KMA has the programming skills to build that program. We will need to work with JDA to build the batch-file data-entry routines. I would think a couple of weeks. Does that sound right to you?" I looked at the JDA representative

"Will you be doing that up here, in the Cities?"

"No, in Rochester," I looked at Kyle. "That's where our development team is located."

"I do have a contract for KMA services with me," Kyle added.

As we left the customer location Kyle said to me, "I am so glad you're here."

Get it on the Calendar

I was at the Minnesota Department of Justice (DOJ). KMA had been awarded a project involving the synchronization of judge's calendars. Administrative assistants had become enamored with the Office/400 product, especially the calendar component. So much so that the official calendar, running on IBM big iron systems, was no longer accurate.

I was tasked with architecting a solution that would correct the current discrepancies and prevent this from happening again. I brought in one of KMA's employees, a guy experienced in coding *advanced program-to-program communication* (APPC) programs to create *a proof of technology* (POT) program that would connect and pass data between the AS/400 and the mainframe.

While he worked on that, I studied the Office/400 product documentation in hopes that there was an API for the calendar component. OS/400 now came with several APIs as part of the controlled openness initiative. Nothing jumped out at me.

KMA was growing. We had added more programmers, some of whom came from Keane, as the CPF contract ended. One of these programmers had worked on the Office/400 product. I called him and asked if he knew anything about the calendar component.

"So, as far as you know there is no API for the calendar function, is that correct?"

"Correct, Dan."

"I was hoping there would be a way to capture, or access, calendar events," I said.

"Nothing like that. I suppose you could write an RPG program to scan the file and look for new or changed entries."

"What file?" I asked.

"The calendar file, it's a physical file object."

I was incredulous. "It is? I thought it would be a space object that I would need to materialize after obtaining a space pointer. You're saying it's just a good old AS/400 physical file, complete with a format, correct?"

"That's all it is."

"Thank you so much. I owe you lunch," I said.

We had Office/400 on the KMA AS/400. I signed in and found the Office/400 program product library. I displayed a list of physical files and looked at the names, which were meaningless. I reviewed the text descriptions and found one with calendar in the text. I ran a Query/400 Run Query (RUNQRY) command to list the contents of the table. The result set looked like calendar data to me.

I attached a journal-receiver object to the calendar-file. I then started the journal process. I launched the Office/400 product, brought up the calendar application, and added two or three new events.

I exited the Office/400 calendar application and invoked the Display Journal (DSPJRN) command, entering the journal object and calendar file name. I was rewarded with a list of the journal entries, which represented the database records that were created when I added the new events.

I met with the APPC programmer and, between the two of us, we were able to complete the POT. We used the RTVJRNE command to scrape the journal and pass the calendar journal entries to an RPG program that formatted them into the format required by the mainframe calendar, and then passed those entries to the mainframe—POT accomplished.

The AS/400 journal support became the foundation for multiple data replication products offered by IBM and third-party vendors. It was also an important player in IBM's High Availability (HA) solutions. It would be a product that would play prominently in many of my future IBM client engagements.

CASEPREP

I was sitting in a lunch meeting with Kyle, Ann, and two executives—the CEO and CIO for an international corporation specializing in nutritional food additives known as FOODCORP (my acronym). It so happened that their corporate headquarters were housed in the same SLP office complex as KMA. A cold call to the CIO had prompted this meeting.

The purpose of the meeting was for Kyle to market services KMA could provide to the potential client, the most important being software engineering (SE) assistance.

"This is the main reason we created the position of director of software services within KMA and recently hired this man to fill that position and bring our current staff up to speed" Kyle pointed at me. "Let me introduce you to Dan Cruikshank."

The FOODCORP CIO, a woman recently hired, seemed to perk up.

"This sounds interesting to me. Mr. Cruikshank, how do you intend to accomplish this?"

"Please, call me Dan. My plan is to begin training the current programming staff to become more process oriented. That means to think less about coding and more about the process of application development. I have a process I call Method D, which I have used to successfully develop applications on time and within budget. While I train our staff, I will be evaluating *computer aided software engineering* (CASE) tools. My hope is to find one that would be the right fit for my process. KMA would then be able to use that to offer *rapid application development* (RAD) solutions to our clients."

"My company has acquired a CASE tool, which sits on the shelf. None of our programmers will touch it," the CIO interjected," and now we have another CASE tool vendor barking at the door."

"That is so true. I believe that most AS/400 RPG programmers are code oriented. The only SE process they know is what I refer to as the 'from napkin to code' technique, one that I used in my early days of RPG code-slinging. That was before I learned the SOYP method."

"What is SOYP?"

"Seat of your pants," I replied.

The CIO laughed.

"Code-slinging? Ha, ha, I've never heard that one either. I do agree with the 'NapCode' and SOYP processes."

"I have always enjoyed Westerns. I thought of myself as a cowboy, more of a gunslinger, a hired gun, solving problems with a flowcharting template and an RPG six shooter. I picked up on Edward Yourdon's book, *The Decline & Fall of the American Programmer,* and how he exemplified American programmers as lone-rangers and cowboys. That's how I thought of myself. I heard the term 'code-slinger' from an IBM big iron programmer describing the nature of the work he was doing with a customer I was visiting. I grabbed it and made it my own."

"So, Kyle, is training one of the services you offer?"

Kyle and Ann were quick to market.

"Yes," they replied in unison.

"I am very much interested in Dan's training program. I would also like to have Dan come in for a day and provide an assessment of FOODCORP's *code-slinging staff* and tailor a custom training class for us. Can we put together a contract?"

"I have a contract right here in my briefcase," Kyle responded.

I named it Computer Aided Software Engineering Preparation training or CASE-PREP as it would be referred to by KMA marketing. The training consisted of three workshops:

1. Relational database design methodologies—that focused on *information engineering* (IE) constructs. The outcome of this workshop would be an ERD that represented a normalized database.

2. Action diagramming—that focused on the *Warnier-Orr* methodology. This form of high-level program design fit in well with the HIPO and SDA approaches I had been using for years. The outcome of this workshop would be several AS/400 DSPFs representing menus, lists and data-entry panels.

3.Construction—taking the action diagrams and creating the RPG code templates; the programs that would interact with the various DSPFs.

The entire course would take three weeks. The workshops took three, four, and five days respectively. My first customer was FOODCORP. I was literally creating presentation material the night before the class. I used open workdays and weekends to catch up.

From Suits to Nuts

To market CASEPREP, KMA put on a two-hour seminar, with lunch, for existing clients and prospective customers. I created some introductory charts that contained quotes from books by Martin, McClure, and Yourdon. I took highlights from each workshop and did my best to technically market the product. Only one other customer would sign up for training before I moved on to a new project—which would be life changing.

In between training and marketing KMA offerings I found time to keep up on industry trends, especially if it was in the area of CASE. That is how I discovered *Adelia*. It appeared to fit my methodology very well.

Adelia was an application development tool created specifically for the IBM AS/400 platform. First, the generated DSPFs adhered to SAA CUA standards for text-based displays (i.e., 5250-WS). Second, the generated RPG code was modular. The database design tool was based on a known methodology—Merise.

I can't remember all the particulars, but eventually KMA became a partner with the French based company that had developed Adelia. KMA was given a software license to market the product and to train customers in its use. Learning to navigate the tool was easy for the KMA programming staff due to its AS/400 style displays. Understanding the Merise methodology was the biggest hurdle for programmers.

After acquiring Adelia, I made a proposal to Kyle and the KMA management team to create a *prepaid service offering*. I thought we could exploit our AS/400 by resolving customer issues electronically, thus avoiding travel costs—especially my commute to Rochester. Those customers who signed on received priority over other customers. In addition, they received a preferred hourly contract rate on those projects that required on-site assistance.

Our need for additional KMA programming expertise was growing. We had hired a few experienced people from Keane as its contracts with IBM expired. Some of these people I knew, and I was okay with their backgrounds. Others we hired out of necessity. I was becoming concerned that we may end up with too many mavericks—like myself.

"So, Kyle, what do you think about establishing an internship program for recent vo-tech computer programming graduates?"

Going Native

Shortly after the AS/400 hit the marketplace, System/36 customers were being pushed by the various AS/400 talking heads to take advantage of the new AS/400 features and functions. To do this, existing S/38 and System/36 RPG programs, running in their respective emulation environments, had to be converted to the native version of the programming language.

Several small service providers, like KMA, with backgrounds mainly on the System/36 platform, followed these industry leaders. Some had become very successful migrating their customer base to the AS/400 and were now wanting to get in on the lucrative going native opportunities. KMA was one of them.

I was in a meeting with Kyle, Ann, Karen, the IBM customer representative (IBMRep), and the CIO of a KMA client, located in Eau Claire, WI. The client was currently running their LOB software on an AS/400. The applications had been developed on a System/36 and migrated to the *AS/400 System/36 environment* (S36E). We were reviewing the proposal I had prepared for our client.

The IBMRep had contacted KMA after her customer had asked about converting from the S36E RPG/II code to RPG/400. IBM offered some tools to assist with the conversion; however, IBM did not take on the actual conversion effort. The IBMRep had worked with KMA and their relationship was on good terms, thus KMA had the first shot at the opportunity.

Using Method D, I had reviewed the clients' RPG/II program inventory and assigned a complexity factor to each program based on its total LOC. I then interviewed the current programming staff, consisting of seven people, and categorized their skill levels, i.e., rookie, experienced, or advanced. I interviewed the CIO to learn holiday and vacation schedules, which I estimated at five weeks per employee; a tough one since all employees would be taking holidays at the same time, but not everyone would be vacationing at the same time. I would build in a slush factor.

"This is outrageous! Your estimate to get this done is over a year. I can't afford this, on top of my current payroll expense."

"It is for a year and half," I replied in response to the CIO's outburst, "based on five *full-time equivalents*, or FTE, programmers, who are currently on your payroll. That leaves you with two FTE to handle ongoing maintenance of program bugs. Any enhancements to existing programs will be delayed until the programs have been converted. That way you can take advantage of new RPG functions and features, as you add new enhancements. The proposal does include *optional* KMA project management and/or programming support."

"I thought KMA would do the work. Like when you migrated us to the AS/400."

Ann spoke up, as she was the KMA S/36 to AS/400 migration expert. She was also on a first name basis with the CIO—Dave.

"That was a migration from one system to another. The programs did not require extensive testing to ensure the migration was successful. Going from RPG/II to RPG/400 and OCL to CL does require recompilation and extensive testing. As Dan stated, Dave, your people know the applications and are the best people to determine if something isn't right."

"Thanks, Ann," I said. "Dave, this estimate is what you asked for. If KMA was to do the work it would cost you more, and we wouldn't convert all the programs."

Kyle kicked me under the table.

"Dave," Kyle said, "I can have Dan add an estimate if KMA did the work."

We left the meeting and headed back to the KMA office. We had all come together in Kyle's car. It was about a forty-five-minute drive. Being together allowed us to strategize on the way there and review what happened on the way back.

"Kyle, we don't have the skill set for doing this kind of work. We would need at least three experienced System/36 programmers. Besides that, I don't think changing the RPG programs without first externally describing the file input/output definitions is the right approach. We have Adelia and CASEPREP. This is what we should focus on."

"Could we get it done sooner using Adelia?" asked Ann.

"It depends. If we simply train Dave and his people in the use of

Adelia then the burden is still on him to go native, except he's now following a more long-term strategy. If we do all the work, then the cost to Dave would be much higher. Besides the programming rate, there would be added expenses, travel to and from, lodging, etc."

"What if we worked remotely?" asked Kyle.

"That's a better option. The Rochester area would have more programmers; however, they would probably be more expensive if they live in Rochester. We would need to upgrade our AS/400 to create a serious development environment. In addition, if Dave were to agree with my approach, then he would need to acquire a DBA."

"Couldn't he use you to fill that role?"

"Yes, initially, but I would insist he hire or designate someone as a DBA, to take over once I'm gone—which would be inevitable. I still think it's problematic, trying to persuade small development shops to go this way."

"I guess it's a problem we'd like to have."

With that, Kyle ended the discussion. KMA never heard back from the client about the proposal. A couple of months later I received a call from Dave.

"Hi, Dan, I was calling to talk to you about the possibility of acquiring your services. Would you be available for some consulting work?"

"Yes, Dave, but I'm not independent. You will have to go through KMA."

"No problem, Dan, I would like to hire you to travel with me to New York. I need to meet with a consulting firm and a software development company, and I want to bring a hired gun with me. You seem the type. Interested?"

"Absolutely, what's the deal?"

Traveling Man

Dave was a die-hard. He had not given up yet on going native; however, he wanted a couple more proposals before he chose a vendor. I agreed. It was a big project and doing the due diligence was important. Dave had narrowed his search down to two providers—a consulting company and a software startup company. The former, Barsa Consulting, was named after its founder, **Al Barsa**. They were based in New Jersey. The new startup software development company was located on Staten Island, New York.

We flew from Minneapolis to New York and checked into a hotel near the airport. We had a morning meeting scheduled with Barsa, followed by a lunch meeting and tour with the startup.

The meeting with Barsa was held at his office location and was mainly presentation. Barsa had a methodology that was proven. He had several customer testimonials. Barsa Consulting provided guidance and project management support, but no programming. In that respect it wasn't much different from my approach, except it did not have the DBA role defined. Someone from Barsa would come on-site and do the estimate and project plan. If Dave agreed, then a project consultant would work with Dave's team on-site for two weeks and then provide remote status reporting.

Barsa provided us with a ballpark estimate, based on my swag of the total software inventory. We shook hands and went outside to meet our ride. The owner of the startup picked us up at Barsa's office location and took us to a fancy restaurant for lunch. There he explained his software.

"We have a tool that will convert your entire S36E software inventory to AS/400 native code, and we can do it in days instead of weeks, months, or years."

He had our attention.

"How much does this tool cost?" was my first question.

"We don't sell the tool. We provide a consultant who uses the tool on-site. We charge by the hour, which includes travel time. We usually say eighty hours as an initial estimate."

"How do you handle program described files?" I asked.

"We scan the code, create external definitions, then comment-out the original code."

A common practice when changing program code that was currently in production was to add an asterisk in the first position of the code statement. This turned the statement into a *comment*, making it non-executable without taking it physically *out* of the source code. This made it easier to identify code changes, should the change result in a bug.

It sounded too good to be true. We continued to talk and eat. After we finished lunch, our host drove us to his software development facility on Staten Island—it was his home. The AS/400 was in the living room. There were three 5250-WS devices attached to it. These were placed on the dining room table. There were two programmers, heads down, feverishly slinging code. A woman, possibly the owner's wife, was doing laundry in the next room.

The owner introduced the programmers as his top two developers. Something told me they were his only two developers. Besides that, they were both Russian immigrants who could barely speak English. They just smiled at us and went back to their work.

"Can we see a demo?" I asked, nodding towards the unused terminal.

The owner sat down, signed on, and launched some command. A display appeared. At first it was difficult to decipher, not because it was in Cyrillic (which it wasn't) but because it did not follow SAA/CUA standards. I watched the owner enter some data and the display changed. I figured the first display was a menu of some sort and this was the data-entry display. There was stuff all over the place and in different colors. I stopped paying attention when the owner failed to get anything after that to work.

We didn't have many questions after the failed demo other than when do you think this will be ready? We didn't ask for an estimate. The owner drove us to our hotel. We shook hands, said our goodbyes, and went inside. We decided to head right for the hotel restaurant.

"So, Dan, what do you think of the software tool?" Dave asked after we had ordered.

I could see he was enamored with the tool. I was sure he was thinking about the money he would save and not the fact that it was vaporware.

"Dave, bear with me, imagine you are interviewing for a job. The man who is interviewing you is well groomed, his suit coat is obviously expensive, his tie knot is a perfect Windsor. The interview is going great. You like him. The job is what you're looking for. You both stand up to shake hands and you notice that the guy isn't wearing any pants. Do you really want to work with this guy?"

"I suppose that means you aren't going to recommend him?"

I didn't answer. When we got back, I prepared my report with my analysis and recommendations. I pointed out the similarity between KMA and Barsa. Theoretically, we would both be working remotely but KMA was less than an hour away. No way in hell would I recommend the software vendor.

Dave went with the tool.

I didn't know it then, but this was to be my first of hundreds of short-term consulting contracts, the longest never exceeding two weeks. After acquiring an IBM laptop for business purposes, I would use *Palidan*, a variation of *Paladin*, as my password and the words *Have laptop, will travel* on my IBM business cards and email signature.

Acquired Skills:

Teaching, journal scraping, customer service, and consulting.

PART THREE

THE IBM SUBCONTRACTOR

Has Laptop, Will Travel

Existing Skill Set:

He has an outgoing personality, is a self-starter, has project management skills and writing skills; plus, he knows PL/1, PL/MP, X.25, PL/MI, RPG/400, UIM/Help, APIs, SAM (Spies), TPST (Tips), Office/400, BGU, SQL, PDM, ADM, OCL, CL, DDS, SQL, APIs, X.25, and PC/Support. He has a strong understanding of RDBMS design and implementation.

He is articulate, presents and markets himself well. Most importantly he has shown an ability to work under pressure, to meet deadlines and tight schedules. He has application development capabilities and is familiar with several third-party software applications, including word processing and presentation software.

He teaches a Computer Aided Software Engineering (CASE) workshop. Is familiar with journal management, replication, and tuning. Has knowledge of customer service best practices. Has performed consulting at customer locations out of state.

In addition, he has a passport and is willing to travel.

Rochester, MN

I was a performance trouble shooter, a hired gun who kicked ass and took names. I used tools that were developed internally within the IBM Rochester lab to measure OS program performance. They became available to customers by way of the Performance Tools (PFRTools) LPP, which contained the Sampled Address Monitor (SAM—originally known as SPIES). My favorite was a performance data collecting machine named Timing and Paging Statistical Tool (TPST—originally known as TIPS). This was my tool of choice. Then there were the tools that I wrote to mine the data generated by the prior tools: Analyze TPST Data (ANZTPSTDTA) and Batch Run Time Analysis (Batch/RT—pronounced Berta).

There were other tools written by my colleagues and predecessors that analyzed performance data; but those tools were intended more for generating charts and graphs, used in the high-level analysis of system performance and capacity management. They were great for impressing executives and other decision makers, but their endgame was to sell more hardware.

The tools I used and/or created were used for one purpose and one purpose only: to buy the customer more time between upgrades by modifying in-house written applications to be more efficient. It was my bread and butter, and I became recognized worldwide for my skills. I knew that because **Rick Turner**, my mentor, told me so.

"Dan, you are one of six people in IBM, and the world for that matter, that I am aware of who can do what you do, and three of those folks will be retiring from IBM within the next three years."

Interestingly, one of those IBMers would be Rick.

The Performance Guy

Rochester, MN March 1993

Since the OA project, I had developed a huge interest in performance, specifically application-related issues. I still held a fascination with relational database architecture, but that was moved to the back burner. Each new release of OS/400 brought additional performance enhancements to the Query Engine (QE), the OS component responsible for *optimizing* an

SQL, OPNQRYF command, or QUERY/400 statement before executing the request. The AS/400 integrated database was becoming self-tuning.

In addition, improvements were being made to embedded SQL, that is, SQL statements that were coded as part of the HLL program code. The SQL statements were processed by a pre-compiler and converted to SQL function calls, aka APIs (remember controlled openness), before the actual HLL code compiler was invoked. These function calls were made available to customers via the SQL call *level interface* (CLI), which follows the industry standard.

Furthermore, enhancements were being made to SQL Procedures, i.e., programs written entirely in the SQL Programming Language (SQL/PL). These procedures were translated into C code and then compiled as C program objects.

I was sure I could see the future, exactly where the AS/400 was headed. I needed to become proficient in SQL/PL and, for that matter, DB2/400, the name given to the integrated RDBMS, which, by now, could stand up to any other vendor RDBMS, including IBM big iron DB2.

I had already become recognized as an AS/400 application performance expert. I needed to become recognized as an SQL performance expert. The best way to do that was to write an application using embedded SQL. I already had the building blocks—my RPG program templates.

I was one of three new subcontractors engaged by IBM to become performance consultants. I needed to report to Rochester, MN, the first week of April to attend the performance management workshop (PMWS). The instructors included three IBM performance experts: **Larry Cravens**, Rick, and **Toby Barksdale**. Those three were present at my interview, standing off to my left, away from people who were seated. It was Rick who had asked the question about seizes during my "mock" customer interview. I would come to know that he was playing dumb.

I would also meet the other two consultants: Joe H. and Diane W. Joe was married and would commute from Maple Grove, MN, about twenty miles further northwest from where I lived. Joe's company would cover his commuting expenses. Diane lived in Rochester, so her commute was much simpler.

The class was held in downtown Rochester off the IBM campus. Mainly IBM AS/400 customers attended. The three of us were the exceptions. Each attendee was given a packet containing a set of charts and selected pages from the performance tools reports. It was the same package I reviewed during my interview, except the one given to me in the workshop was different from the interview set.

The course was four and a half days. Larry and Rick did most of the formal presentations. Emphasis was on the process for collecting and analyzing AS/400 system performance data. Toby presented on the *Best/1* tool that used performance data for capacity planning purposes. The Best/1 tool was developed by BGS Systems Inc. out of Boston.

There were also labs where attendees would reproduce reports that allowed them to drill deeper into the performance data, hoping to find the root cause. This was typically an OS/400 module that was being invoked an excessive number of times. OS modules were never called directly. They were invoked or summoned, based on an action being executed within the HLL program. Using performance reports and tools, the customers would then trace the OS/400 module back to the HLL program invoking it. I had done this in the interview, so I was ahead of the rest.

Thursday afternoon, the attendees worked heads down, preparing a summary of their findings. On Friday, they would take turns presenting these findings to Larry, Rick, and Toby.

By the end of the workshop, I knew where those charts and graphs that so impressed me during the job interview came from. I wondered who created them, and/or was responsible for maintaining them. I would soon find out—that would be me.

The Intern

The week after the workshop, Joe, Diane, and I met with our IBM management team, **Mary Sobotta**, and **Deb Navarro** in our assigned office. Mary and Deb oversaw the RCS team, which consisted of sub-contractors who specialized in AS/400 performance data analysis and capacity planning (PFRCAP) IBM customer engagements. I recognized Mary and Deb from the interview. It was their boss who had asked if I had ever worked for IBM. The RCS sub-contractors worked hand in hand with IBM subject matter experts (SMEs) and, for all practical purposes, were considered IBMers.

Mary explained that we would be interns, or trainees, for the next several months. We could share this area for a while until more office space opened. We did not have PCs, only 5250-WS devices; however, there were two IBM laptops that were signed out by consultants on travel assignments.

Before each PMWS, a *performance data collection* plan (PDCP) was sent to each customer who would be attending. The plan contained instructions for capturing performance data associated with the perceived performance problem, and for shipping it to IBM Rochester.

As interns, we would be responsible for downloading the performance data from the customer's tape to the assigned AS/400. Depending on the size of the IBM customer's AS/400, the amount of data collected might've been contained on more than one tape volume. In that case, the tape data downloading process could take several hours. In many cases, I would make a phone call to Mary Jo, letting her know I wouldn't be home for dinner.

Most of our AS/400s had the PFRTools LPP, which contained several programs that generated summary and detailed reports for analysis purposes. Some AS/400s did not contain the most recent copy of *IBMLIB*, a library of custom programs and queries for faster analysis. This included the programs Larry had written in RPG that produced the charts and graphs. Both Larry and Rick were the original contributors to IBMLIB, although, since Rick could not program, Larry created the majority, if not all, of the custom graphs. Over time every performance consultant would contribute queries that helped the team resolve various performance issues.

Once the data was fully restored to the target AS/400, we would then use a combination of these tools to generate the initial customer performance package. We would review the data, choose periods of the highest activity, and then generate additional, detailed reports and graphs. We would analyze the data, highlight specific items of interest, and note what the performance issue might be; like what I did before the interview.

In between processing customer performance data, we would attend customer conference calls. Mary or Deb moderated these calls, and several members of the RCS team would sit in and ask the customer questions about the perceived performance issue and why they contacted the RSC for assistance.

Since many of our team members were traveling it seemed that meeting all the members of the team was haphazard. We would get to meet those members who were doing the work we would eventually be doing ourselves. These people were **Leonardo Llamas**, **Anil Madan**, and **Shashi Sethi**. There were three others who were on overseas assignments and would eventually end their IBM engagement. I assumed it was those three whom we would be replacing.

Leonardo, aka Leonard, was a U.S. citizen whose family migrated to the U.S. from the Philippines. Anil and Shashi were from India and were working in the U.S. under a Green Card permit. This card allowed foreign nationals to permanently live and work in the U.S. Leonard, Anil, Shashi, and I would eventually become IBM global citizens.

Data Collection and Analysis

Besides the Performance Workshop, a PDCP was sent to those customers requesting performance consultations. In the case of workshops held at the Rochester site, it was important that the tape arrived at least two weeks before the start of the workshop the customer would be attending. Performance consulting gigs were very different. The collection of the performance data was left to the customer's discretion. In some cases, the collection had to be done at certain times of the day over the course of a week. It depended mainly on the perceived performance issue. In many cases, what the customer thought it might be turned out to be something else entirely. It wasn't uncommon to send a PDCP to a customer and never hear from them again.

Many customers collected performance data daily and used various tools to provide upper-level management with graphs showing trend information. This information was used for capacity planning purposes. It could also be used to determine the reason for an unplanned outage due to performance degradation. We would also accept this data if it wasn't massaged before being sent to us.

Some customers used third-party products that managed the collection of the data. These products would summarize the data before providing the customer with the third-party product's reports, charts, and/or graphs. This data was rarely helpful to us, as the summarized data would eliminate critical detailed information that was required to resolve performance issues, especially intermittent problems that occurred at random time intervals.

The only tool we did not use in the initial analysis was TPST. This tool was reserved for application performance engagements when an on-site visit was inevitable. It was rare that a customer would have TPST installed, as it wasn't a part of the OS/400 *complex instruction set computer* (CISC) based systems. A future version of the AS/400 would contain an entirely different OS.

For the first two, or so, years that I worked as a sub-contractor for IBM Rochester, I commuted on **The Blue Highway** every day. I would sometimes stay overnight on my own dime if a situation arose, such as bad weather, that made it difficult to drive the one-hundred miles to my home. The only other time I would not commute was when I was assigned or specifically requested to make an *on-site visit.*

On-Site Visits

Once a performance consultant analyzed the initial performance collection and determined the performance problem was most likely application related, if the consultant did not have application skills, then I would be brought in and an on-site visit was subsequently scheduled—sometimes I would leave one customer and go directly to another. I could be on the road for several weeks at a time.

I would arrive at the customer location with a tape containing IBMLIB and TPST. These tools were installed on the appropriate test AS/400 where the more intense performance data collections would be taken. This was done in a test environment to avoid the overhead these more high-powered analysis tools would add to a production system.

The biggest problem was that I assumed the customer had a test AS/400—many did not. In that case I would take the collection on the production machine. This proved to be extremely dangerous, especially when the TPST tool failed, causing a system crash. Many performance consultants were reluctant to use it—except for me.

In some cases, customers would forgo the preliminary remote performance analysis and request the services of a consultant ASAP. This wasn't recommended, as many performance issues could be resolved remotely, thus saving the customer the travel, time, and material expenses of a high dollar IBM consultant.

As I gained experience in application performance analysis, I would encourage an on-site visit. I would send a PDCP with instructions to have the data ready for me when I arrived. I usually traveled Sunday night, which allowed me to show up at the customer's door Monday morning. I would be led to the IT department where I installed my tools. I then logged into the customer's system, and, using custom queries I would quickly identify the worst problem.

I shared my findings with IT management and requested access to a test machine where I could collect detailed TPST data while someone ran the program/programs I identified. I only needed two executions of the program to verify my initial diagnosis. Inevitably I would run into backlash from the developers.

"To test those programs effectively don't you need to restore tons of data to help you find the problem?" the programmers would ask. "That's how we were taught."

"No need to do that. I just need to execute the program twice, three times at the most."

I called it the TPST *program signature*. It was a common fallacy among application developers that large quantities of data had to be processed before a performance problem would manifest itself. I only needed the program signature that TPST provided. I explained this to the programmers.

"For example, excessive activation and deactivation of a program within a single process or job is the root cause of many application performance issues. I would categorize the program causing the problem as not being *re-entrant* making it *non-reusable*. The TPST signature for this type of program would look like this."

I had noticed a flip chart and an easel at the front of the room. I strolled over to it and began writing the steps that occurred during program activation-deactivation.

"Assume Program_A, which is taking a nap, is called or executed by another program or function."

I wrote an example of the call program command on the flip chart.

"This results in OS/400 *activating* Program_A, i.e., locating the program object's physical location, bringing it into virtual memory, carving out variable storage, etc. Every action has an equal and opposite reaction. A called program must return to the caller."

I wrote the words 'Return...' at the bottom of the flip chart.

"Once activated, any files defined in Program_A will be opened."

I added the words 'Open...' to the chart.

"The program is executed," I added the appropriate words, "...and, depending on the program logic, it may close the open files; but it doesn't need to, especially if this is a program that is called repetitively within a batch process."

I wrote the words 'Close...' to the chart followed by the word, 'Why?'

"Excuse me, but shouldn't the files be closed as part of the program cleanup process? We discovered in testing that sometimes the data is still in the file buffer. We need to end the program to get that data written, correct?"

"Incorrect," I replied. "There are other, more efficient ways to flush the file buffers without ending the program; one of those being the use of *commitment control*, a journal function that ensures the integrity of data and provides the ability to *undo* a transaction. Commitment control is something that should be a part of any program that changes data in a database object."

"Dan, doesn't journaling and commitment control add more overhead to the system? How can this be a good thing?"

"Journaling and commitment control can be tuned. If you were using these and they were improperly tuned, then I would be talking about how you could tune these; however, since you are not, we will discuss program activation and deactivation instead. In fact, ensuring that your programs are re-entrant is a first step in application tuning. Anyone else?"

There were no more questions, so I continued.

"After a program is activated, it will eventually be deactivated. A file that is opened will need to be closed. An object that is created must be destroyed. All, or some of these things, occur during the life of a program. The issue isn't how often the program is activated, but when and how it deactivates."

"Doesn't returning from a called program deactivate it?"

"No, returning from a called program does not require the called program to end. Keeping the program active allows it—and the associated objects needed for the program to function—to be *reusable*, the key to achieving best programming performance and scalability."

I was usually never wrong since I was utilizing the data that TPST provided me. Unfortunately, there were things happening at IBM Rochester that would take this formidable weapon out of my hands and put it into the hands of children. IBM was about to blow the covers off the AS/400. During this evolutionary process, the AS/400 would go through several name changes. It would begin with the AS/400e. I have chosen, for consistency reasons, to stick with AS/400 as the system name going forward.

Seize the Moment

Critical Situation

Rochester, MN

As time passed, it became apparent to Mary, Deb, my teammates, and other IBMers in various areas within IBM Rochester that I had some extraordinary talents.

I was sitting with Deb in her office, waiting for the phone to ring. Deb had been contacted by the Project Office (PRJOFC), the department within IBM Rochester that handled *critical situations* (CritSits). CritSits occurred when a customer was in trouble, that is, the AS/400 or OS/400 appeared not to be working as intended. In some cases, it would be *castors up*, an expression used when the AS/400 was non-responsive. In almost all cases, an on-site visit was required.

The PRJOFC was setting up a conference call with the customer and us to get a better understanding of the problem. The customer initially called level-2 support, which required some level-3 assistance; this did not end well. The customer had now escalated the issue, which meant getting PRJOFC involved. A call to PRJOFC usually meant travel—immediately.

Ever since I began the performance gig, I was aware that travel was a requirement and, in some cases, would require hopping on the first flight out of Rochester, MN, which had an international airport facility. The major airlines always flew to Minneapolis or Chicago first. Because I commuted a hundred miles, I got into the habit of keeping a Go-bag ready. It consisted of a week's supply of clothes. In addition, I kept a sport coat on a hanger in the car. Depending on the destination, I could wear it on the plane and leave my Minnesota outerwear in the car—snowmobile suit in the winter, leather jacket with fur-lined hood in the summer.

The phone rang. Deb answered, putting the call on speaker.

"This is Deb Navarro. How can I help you?"

"Hi, Deb, it's me," the caller said. "Hold on while I connect the others."

The others consisted of a cast of thousands. I knew this because the person from the PRJOFC introduced each one after connecting. Three days later, Deb and I were able to introduce ourselves.

"On the call, besides me, is Deb Navarro, who manages our team of performance experts. Deb, is anyone with you?"

"Good morning, with me is Dan Cruikshank, one of our performance consultants."

I was impatient.

"Hello," I said. "Can you explain the problem you're currently having with your third-party provided software?"

"Hello, Dan. This is the president of the company that provides the software. We believe there is a bug in the OS. The processing of our overnight batch programs is taking forever. It started slowing gradually but is getting worse each day. What usually takes a short time is now taking several hours. Nobody from our company, or our clients, can figure it out. It isn't our software issue, in my opinion, nor do we think it is a lack of system resources. We can only assume it is an OS problem. We contacted IBM support and they couldn't help, so they passed us on to the Project Office, and now here we are, another phone call and no relief."

Several other people began talking at once. I looked at Deb.

"Sounds like an object seize to me. I…"

I didn't get another word out because Deb had quickly pushed the mute button on the phone. She looked at me and made a *zip your lip* motion with her hand, while angrily shaking her head and giving me the evil eye. Meanwhile there wasn't a peep coming from the other end of the phone connection. After what seemed like hours, but was probably only seconds, a voice came through the phone.

"What's an object seize?"

Deb unmuted the phone, keeping her eyes on me.

"Hi, Deb here; as Dan was going to say he can make travel arrangements and…, excuse me a second."

Deb muted the phone because I was vigorously shaking my head, while doing my best to keep my mouth closed.

"What?" Deb asked me.

"It doesn't require an on-site visit. If they can capture some performance data and send it overnight, I can verify it is an object seize and provide a solution. Save them mucho dinero."

"Dan, I understand English. My family has been in this country for generations. I can speak English better than you can. We do not give away the store here. Are we clear?"

"Yes, amiga, errr, Deb, I mean," I joked, sharing my shit-eating grin.

She did not smile when she looked at me, while unmuting the phone, and making the zip-it motion again.

"Hi, Deb here, sorry about that; Dan, and I needed some private time. Dan thinks that he can assess the situation from here. He does not feel an on-site visit is warranted at this time. Dan does require the collection of performance data. He will contact the appropriate member of the customer's IT department and provide them with performance data collection instructions over the phone. I will send the customer an hourly contract for the analysis of the performance data. The clock will start when we receive the tape. Are there any questions?"

"Are you going to answer the question about the object seize?"

Deb looked at me, with one finger on her lips.

"No, he is not. Once you sign the contract and return it, you can then talk to Dan about seizes, grasps, clutches, whatever. Anyone else?"

No one else dared ask a question.

"No? Okay then, I will hang up and begin work on the contract right away. I will need to have it signed and returned to me before Dan can begin analysis. The sooner you get it back to me, the sooner we can resolve your problem. Thank you for providing us with this opportunity to serve you. With that I will say goodbye."

Deb hung up the phone and looked at me, shaking her head.

"Coffee?" I asked

"Si," she replied and smiled at me.

The Next Day

After receiving the tape and signed contract, sent by overnight courier, I walked to the computer lab where several IBM AS/400s, provided by IBM for the sole purpose of processing IBM customer performance data, awaited me. I had asked the customer to collect the following:

1. A performance trace of the batch job using the Start Performance Trace (STRPFRTRC) command

2. An output file from the Display Program References (DSPPGM-REF) command for each program in the batch process

3. An output file from the Display Physical File Description (DSPFD) command for each file referenced.

After downloading the tape data to a library I had created for this customer, I ensured that everything I asked for had been collected. It had. My first step was to run the Print Lock Report (PRTLCKRPT) command. Besides locks, this report included seizes, also known as waits. The information included the name of the object being locked, or seized, and the amount of time that another program waited for the lock, or seize, to be released.

The main difference between a lock and an object seize is: a) the former is customer application initiated and has a specified time-out value; b) the latter is initiated on behalf of a customer application and there isn't a specific time-out value. A seized object can take forever before the object seize is released—and sometimes it did.

Database indexes were one of the most common objects to be seized. Prior to 1999, this would happen during index maintenance, as rows were added and/or deleted. In 1999 index maintenance was improved by only seizing the portions of the index impacted by a CRUD event—not the entire index. Another, much longer seize could occur when the table was held while a new or temporary index was created. In this customer situation, index seizes were not the issue—it was worse than that.

I was right, the count and durations for seizes were off the charts—literally; the durations were printed as all 9's. The PRTLCKRPT also contained the name of the holding program that initiated the object seize or lock. In IBMLIB there was an AS/400 query that was used to query this data and provide a list of the holding programs. I ran that query and then compared the holding program names to the names of the programs provided by the customer.

The program responsible for obtaining the most seizes was in the customer's program list. There was a custom query or program that displayed the names of the HLL program accounting for the object seize and the next three programs in the program call stack. I expected to see a program beginning with QQ, which are the first two letters of the OS/400 query component. I assumed the object seize was caused by an ad hoc query, perhaps building a temporary index—I was wrong. The initial letters of the OS module that jumped out at me were QDB—the OS/400 database component. It was time to roll up my sleeves—I had some work to do.

I had created a custom query that joined the files referenced by the program to the files contained in the PRTLCKRPT data, and the files contained within the output file created by the DSPFD command. I prompted the query and modified the filtering criteria to only return the data that contained the file name with the longest object seize hold time. The result was returned immediately.

Reviewing the file information, I noticed the file was extremely large. I multiplied the file record size by the number of active rows. It did not account for the file size. There was only one other data item to check that might explain this extraordinary file size—the number of deleted rows. There it was— the deleted row count was several times more than the number of active rows.

Unfortunately for this customer, index maintenance seizes were not the issue. Database indexes, like book indexes, do not reference things that no longer exist. It was a different type of seize. The deleted record spaces were not being re-used—the file needed to be changed.

Time to share the bad news. Under the current release of OS/400, the file could not be changed. The AS/400 contained two methods of defining externally described physical file objects: DDS or SQL. DDS was a carryover from the S/38. Physical file objects were created using the Create Physical File (CRTPF) command, which read the DDS source and created the PF object. This command consisted of several parameters, the defaults of which were still the same as the S/38 defaults. One of those was the Reuse Deleted Record Space default of *NO, which was how the customer's file had been created. I put this information in the following note and sent it to the customer:

> The root cause is too many deleted records in the file... because the file has been defined with the reuse of deleted records value set to *NO.
>
> There are only two ways to correct the deleted record space value. Recreate the file and specify Reuse Deleted Record Space (* YES). Or reorganize the physical file Member via the RGZPFM command to remove the deleted record spaces.

I asked Deb to inform PRJOFC that I had identified the problem and was ready to discuss next steps. This time the call did not contain as many people. After minimal introductions, I provided my findings and was offering my solutions.

"I don't understand the deleted record issue. Why are they being read by the program? It's using a logical file. That doesn't make any sense. This sounds like an OS bug to me," complained the software provider.

"Unfortunately, sir, the OS is working as intended. The deleted records are not being read by the program; they are not a part of the logical file access path. All physical data, including deleted records, must be brought into main memory, where only the rows matching the logical file selection criteria, if any, are then placed in the Open Data Path, or ODP, before it even reaches your program. The data exists in auxiliary storage in 4K memory page pieces. These pieces are currently being processed by the Retrieve Data Space Entry [*RETDSEN] MI instruction which is called on behalf of the OS/400 module Get Sequential Data [QDBGETSQ], which is invoked, based on the READ operation in your HLL program. The 4K memory page contains both active and deleted records, the majority being predominately deleted records, thus the object seize placed on the file is being held much longer than necessary."

"Why's the object seize being placed on the file?"

"Because the program is opening the file for update intent. I did see the OS/400 Database Update, Delete or Release (QDBUDR) module being invoked, so I assume this program is responsible for deleting the records. Unfortunately, the deleted records are not being purged. Over time it has become the root cause of your problem. So, it comes down to two options. Recreating the physical file is my recommendation. It will be the most time consuming, but it only needs to be done once. After that, the OS will write new records to the deleted spaces. It is the best long-term solution."

"It sounds to me like the second option would be simpler?"

"Simpler, yes, but reorganizing the file will be time consuming the first time; after that, if you reorganize daily, you should barely notice it; however, I suggest that you designate someone in Operations to be responsible for database maintenance. The new database maintenance person could also review why so many deletes are occurring daily. Perhaps some process re-engineering is in order. So, it's up to you. Keep us posted with what you choose. We can answer any other questions you might have now or later. Thank you for allowing us this opportunity to serve you."

The customer chose option two. I would make several on-site visits over the next three or so years, doing mostly performance analysis and some database support. The customer refused to create a new database administrator position.

"The AS/400 does not need a DBA," they would recite record and verse from AS/400 marketing literature.

Reorganizing tables to recover deleted record space is a DBA activity. It seemed crazy to me that IBM Marketing didn't think the AS/400 needed a DBA.

Palidan

September 1993 thru April 1995

I was on my own. I was given an IBM Think Pad running OS/2. I was familiar with OS/2 because I had an IBM PS2 at home. I used the dual boot feature to use Microsoft products (i.e., Power Point, Excel, MSWord, etc.). IBM would acquire Lotus in 1995. In 1993, Lotus products were provided on IBM Laptops running OS/2. Now I would have to learn Lotus products like Freelance and Word Pro—I already knew Lotus 1-2-3.

Over the next several years I would travel to various major cities and dozens of smaller cities in the U.S.: Newark, Chicago, Indianapolis, Philadelphia, and New York, to name a few. I would also make several international trips: Great Britain, France, Honduras, New Zealand, etc.

My reputation as a lone practitioner problem solver was growing. In addition, I was raising eyebrows with my reporting style, mainly by providing detailed RPG coding recommendations that would reduce and/or eliminate inefficiency—and they worked.

I was in Rick's office. Larry was also there. Rick was talking.

"Larry, I've never seen an application analysis report that looked like this, have you?"

"Can't say that I have," replied Larry.

"Did I do something wrong?" I asked.

"No, not at all," replied Rick. "We normally don't provide charts and graphs within a report. They are usually part of the executive summary presentation during an on-site visit after the initial performance analysis has been completed."

"Oh, well, in this case, I did the summary overview during the on-site visit before I left. It was an overnight batch problem. The executives wanted to hear my findings and recommendations. I didn't think I was going back."

"You're recommending the use of a *join logica*l file [JLF]. We normally don't do that. They tend to be more problematic than using traditional techniques."

"Unfortunately, those traditional techniques are the ones that are showing up as problems. For example, every time they do a READE to

FILEA, they immediately follow that with a CHAIN to FILEB. This results in two calls to the OS module Random_Read_By_Key (QDBGETKY), followed by two executions of the Unblocked_Database_Read (*RETD-SEN) MI complex instruction. In addition, these operations are being done in batch, millions of times in a single process."

"Why not just change the blocking factor for FILEA by using a READ instead of READE?"

"Because the CHAIN operation will still slow it down, resulting in IO pending faults. By using a READ operation to a JLF, the calls to the QDBGETKY and *RETDSEN modules are replaced by calls to the Sequential_Reads_Using_Blocking(QDBGETM) and Blocked_Database_Read (*RETSDSE) MI complex instruction. I think making a change that results in blocking, especially in batch, is a good recommendation. Besides, I used JLFs on the S/38 all the time, without any problems."

"Larry, what do you think?" asked Rick.

"I think we taught him too well, Rick."

Rick would co-author a Redbook, *Application and Program Performance Analysis Using PEX Statistics on IBM i5/OS*, along with **Deborah (Debbie) Hatt** and **Jim Cook**. The book was a rewrite of another Redbook, but the premise was the same—collecting and analyzing application performance data and identifying the root cause. The modules and MI instructions I mentioned above were listed in Appendix E. I would be acknowledged in the new book as a contributor.

The Deposition

New Jersey

September thru October 1993

I was standing in front of the Board of Directors for a midsize company. This was my first on-site visit as a performance consultant. I was there representing IBM. For all intents and purposes, I was an IBMer. I didn't realize the people seated at a conference table staring at me were the Board of Directors—at first.

I had arrived at the customer location early, around 8:00 A.M., according to the clock in my Hertz rental car. I looked at the new watch Mary Jo had bought me, in honor of my first gig.

"A consultant in a suit isn't completely dressed unless he has an impressive watch," Mary Jo had to explain to me.

My new watch read 7:00 A.M. I forgot I was on Eastern Time. Things don't happen until 9:00 A.M. around here. I sat in the car and reviewed the materials I had prepared for my interview with the IT director. I had requested that we meet in a room with an overhead projector, as I had several foils that I planned to present.

At precisely 9:00 A.M., I entered the front door, gave my name to the receptionist, and sat down in one of the chairs in the lobby. The receptionist approached me about five minutes later.

"They are ready for you now, Mr. Cruikshank. I will escort you."

They? I thought I would be meeting with the IT director and no one else.

I followed the receptionist to a door that had the words Board Room on it. She opened the door and I walked in. There were several people sitting around an oval conference table, all dressed in suits and ties. They were not dressed like programming staff.

"Please take a chair in the front, Mr. Cruikshank, next to the overhead projector."

I walked up to the projector and introduced myself.

"My name is Dan Cruikshank, and I am a performance consultant with IBM. I have conducted a review of your AS/400 performance data and prepared a summary of my findings. When I return to IBM Rochester, I will complete a report containing more detailed information along with a list of recommendations."

"I didn't know IBM had a facility in Rochester, NY," interrupted the man sitting second on my left. He was wearing a suit and tie and sported a ponytail.

"Rochester, MN, where they build the AS/400s."

"I didn't know they had one there either," spoke Ponytail.

This brought on some laughs from several others, seated at the table. There's always one clown in every IT organization. Some had more than one.

"Please proceed, Mr. Cruikshank," said an older man seated in the first seat to my left.

"Thank you."

I put up my first foil, which contained the title *Performance Review for...* followed by my name so everybody would know how to spell it. That was followed by the day's date. I then put up my second slide, which was the standard IBM list of disclaimers. This is where I would try to lighten up the crowd with a joke.

"This is our standard list of disclaimers, just in case there are any lawyers in the room," I said, with my patented shit-eating grin.

I started to remove the slide when someone said, "Just a minute, I haven't finished reading it yet."

It was Ponytail being the clown again. In that sense, I was wrong. He wasn't a programmer after all. He was the corporate attorney. This wasn't the audience I expected; however, they were expecting me.

As I presented my foils, Ponytail grilled me on each one. Mostly irrelevant questions, "Why did you choose that color? What does that line running through those bars mean?"

I assumed some people just needed to hear their own voice. It was getting close to an hour and I hadn't gotten to the meat of my presentation—yet.

"So, why is the response time so bad?"

Finally, a real question.

"I'll show you," I said.

I skipped about three foils and put up a pie chart titled *Components of Response Time.*

"This chart is based on average response time during peak performance intervals, which are five minutes in length. In all cases the CPU utilization for each interval was at 100%. The pie chart shows the system components—CPU, DISK, and OTHER—that make up response time. Most of the time is in CPU, then OTHER, followed by DISK. Your CPU is overloaded. The AS/400 cannot handle the amount of work you're throwing at it."

"What can we do?"

"I have compiled a list of programs which can be modified in such a way that their demands for CPU may be reduced. Unfortunately, this is only a stop-gap measure. At best, these programs may reduce the amount of OTHER time, which I think is CPU queuing."

"We're not rocket scientists," said the guy with the ponytail. "What does that mean?"

"It means there are several transactions waiting in the CPU queue for their chance to be processed. I believe many of these transactions have a low CPU requirement. I base this on the fact that the average CPU per transaction is under fifty milliseconds, with minimal disk activity. Every now and then a longer running transaction is processed, causing the queue to back up. Then the average response time goes up."

"I didn't understand a word," said Ponytail, throwing his hands up in the air.

"It's my Scottish/Scandinavian accent, sir, with a touch of Minnesotan, don't ya know."

There was some laughter. The man in the first chair on my right identified himself as the former CIO, now serving on the board of directors.

"If we change the programs you identified, that will solve this problem?"

"No, sir, it is only the first step. If the CPU usage isn't reduced, then you must change the next ten programs that are the highest in CPU usage and continue this process until we can capture a peak period at, or below, 95% CPU utilization."

"What will you do with that?"

"We will use that to do a capacity planning exercise, to determine the amount of memory you might need to accommodate the current workload, and to estimate how long that memory upgrade will last. Most likely, memory isn't going to be enough. You are probably going to require a system upgrade."

"How much will that cost?"

"I have no idea, sir. I am not a sales representative. I am just a performance consultant who is providing you with recommendations that may solve your current problem."

"This is exactly what I expected!" cried out Ponytail. "We had a capacity plan done for us last year. The consultant who did it told us it would last for five years. This is bullshit!"

"Forgive my ignorance, but I wasn't aware that IBM did a capacity planning exercise. Do you know the IBM consultant's name?"

"It wasn't done by IBM," replied the former CIO. "It was our IBM Business Partner."

"Then I can only speculate that someone made a mistake. Either the performance data wasn't representative of a peak period or the projections were understated."

This is exactly what I told the IBM lawyers who took my deposition about a year later when the customer filed a lawsuit naming the IBM Business Partner and IBM. I was being deposed because my name was on the Performance Review report I left with the customer.

Later I learned from the IBM client representative that the original capacity planning report did contain a recommendation for a much larger AS/400. The customer took advantage of a midnight Christmas sale and bought a smaller system. That did not lessen the embarrassment I felt that my first solo gig ended in a lawsuit against IBM.

I wasn't the only one. Diane was also deposed when another customer filed a lawsuit against IBM. Diane had chosen capacity planning as her niche. She became an expert in the Best/1 tool. We both believed our careers as IBM performance consultants were to be short lived. That wasn't to be the case.

The Industrial Supply Company

Chicago, IL 1993

My next travel gig wasn't the type of engagement that the RCS team normally took on. It would be a thirty-day assignment throughout November. It was the outcome of an Application Performance Review conducted at the customer location. It involved three members of the team—Leonardo, Joe, and me. In addition, we added **Ed Simon** for his RPG skills.

The customer was approaching their peak season and a capacity planning report indicated, based on the customer's growth assumptions, that the AS/400 would run out of gas about a week into the season. To meet the customer's objectives, the report had recommended memory and disk upgrades. Unfortunately, the customer did not have enough money in their budget to make the purchase that year. They asked for application assistance from the RCS.

Leonardo was the original performance consultant for the gig. He had identified dozens of programs that if properly modified could free up a substantial amount of computer resources, enough to allow the customer to limp through the peak season. Most of the programs were written in RPG; however, there were a few COBOL programs. The RPG programs were divided between Ed and me. Leonardo had the most COBOL experience, so he took responsibility for those programs. Joe had no programming background, so he was anointed the PM.

Joe made all the travel arrangements. He booked a Residence Inn near the customer for November. We would fly to O'Hare International on Sunday night and be at the customer location by 8:00 Monday morning. We would put in nine-hour days, Monday thru Thursday, and fly back home Friday afternoon. The project budget allowed for us to return home three out of four Fridays. We would take turns staying the weekend.

When my weekend stay came up, I convinced Mary Jo that our son, Matt, could fly out and spend the weekend with me. It sounded like a good idea. Matt had flown to visit Mary Jo's sister (who lived in Dallas) by himself a couple of times. Dan plans and my HP laughs.

We did not have cell phones. Once I left for the airport to pick up Matt I was out of communication. There was a flight delay. Mary Jo could not reach me. Matt would be flying blind, so to speak, not knowing for sure if he would be met. Everything worked out okay, but Mary Jo was a wreck. Once Matt arrived and we were on our way to baggage, I stopped at a public phone and called Mary Jo, hoping she was at home. She answered the phone immediately.

Her first words were, "I'm never doing this again."

That would change, with the exception that Mary Jo would be leaving Matt at home, as she flew to meet me in some exciting place around the world.

The project was a success; however, our group would never take on application programming projects again. There was another department for that known as the CTC—Custom Technology Center.

Hollidazzle

Indianapolis, IN, and Minneapolis, MN

December 23, 1993

I was at a customer location in downtown Indianapolis putting the final touches on my report. The prior month I had nearly spent Thanksgiving in Chicago. I couldn't bear the thought of spending Christmas in Indianapolis.

This was my second trip to the customer. The customer was using SQL and was having performance issues. The original call came through the CTC. When the customer said *performance*, the call was instantly transferred to RCS. I happened to be the only consultant available, so I sat in on the call with Mary. They wanted someone on-site yesterday. Mary looked at me.

"Have you ever done an SQL engagement before?"

"No, I need to find out what type of performance data to collect. Is anyone still around?"

"C'mon," Mary said, as she got up and walked out of her office.

Mary's office was on the second level of the middle white building, which was about two blocks north of the IBM blue building campus. The white buildings were used for customer education, internal training, and were home to some of the more notable people who represented IBM Rochester at AS/400 conferences worldwide. We stopped at the office of one the most prestigious IBMers at that time, at least to me—John Sears.

"John," Mary said, as she knocked on his doorframe, "do you have a minute?"

"Sure, Mary, how can I help you?"

"I want to introduce you to Dan Cruikshank, one of our new performance consultants."

We exchanged introductions.

Mary explained the reason for our visit.

"John, Dan is about to go on a performance assignment at a customer location in Indianapolis. It is his first SQL engagement. He's not sure what type of data to collect. I thought if anyone knew, it would be you."

John looked at me.

"You can use the performance tools trace function. Are you familiar with trace?"

"Yes, I am, sir. Okay, that sounds easy enough. Are there any specific OS/400 components I should be looking for in the Transition Report?"

"Have you ever worked with OPNQRYF performance issues?"

"Yes, I have." OPNQRYF was the function responsible for the object seize I found in my job interview.

"Good, SQL uses the same QQ components for optimizing the SQL plan. You should see object seizes associated with temporary index creates, assuming that's the issue, which is most likely."

"Thank you for your time, sir."

"Call me John. I think we will see each other some more."

Two days before I was scheduled to leave, I received a call from **Ed Simon.**

"Dan, I heard you're going on an SQL performance assignment. Can I tag along?"

"Sure, Ed, if it were up to me, but I am not in control of the project, Mary is."

"Okay, I will call her. Thanks."

About an hour later, Mary came to my office.

"Dan, got a minute?"

"Yes."

"I just got done talking with CTC. Apparently, they have a new tool that they want you to try out. Ed will be joining you on the Indianapolis trip."

The tool was called EXPLAIN. It existed in a library with the same name. He explained EXPLAIN to me while we were on the plane.

"The tool dumps the query access plan from the query object and then prints the plan, using messages that describe the steps the query optimizer is taking."

"Are these messages the same as the ones that get printed when you run a query with the Debug function turned on?"

"No, they have different message IDs, the text is similar, if not the same."

"Do we need to read a large report?"

"No, Dan, my plan is, while you are talking with the customer, I will be writing an RPG program to pull out the messages that contain index recommendations. These are the temporary indexes that are created to assist the query. Once we have those messages, we can recommend which ones should be created permanently."

"Sounds like fun."

Ed had a tape that he used to install the tool on the customer's system. The tool worked wonders. We provided immediate relief while on-site. The customer was extremely happy, based on the satisfied grins all around. I made a mental note that whenever I made an on-site visit, I would always provide at least one solution before I left.

The customer extended the contract to allow me to return the week of December 21, to review performance data and make any other recommendations. I spent all day Monday with the customer. After work I walked the deserted streets of downtown Indianapolis looking for an open restaurant. I struck out. Fortunately, my hotel had an open restaurant, but the menu was limited.

I was able to leave on Wednesday, December 23, the day before Christmas Eve. Mary Jo told me to meet her, Matt, and some friends, downtown for dinner. I arrived at the MSP International Airport about 5:00 P.M. It was dark and cold. I drove downtown, parked the car, and found Mary Jo and the others on a skyway overlooking Nicollet Mall. There were lights everywhere. The buildings and streets were adorned with Christmas decorations. As I looked down from the skyway at the street below, I watched as a marching band passed underneath. I was home for Christmas.

They Call Me 'Crash' Shank

London, UK, and Lille, France June 1994

It was Sunday. I was walking the streets of Lille. I had no map or GPS. The first, I didn't think to bring; the latter, well, it was 1994. I had been walking for about three hours. It was noon, time to head back to the hotel.

I came to Lille from a town west of London, situated near the River Thames. This is my first international trip as an IBM performance consultant. I stayed at the Holiday Inn in London and took a train to and from the customer location. The customer was experiencing poor interactive response times on their 5250-WS devices attached to the AS/400 via a communication link. They were also concerned about the increasing length of their overnight batch process.

I was walking to clear my head before starting my next gig. I had just crashed the previous customer's AS/400. I couldn't let that happen to this one.

Benchmark Center Rochester, MN 1994

I would sometimes be involved assisting with a customer benchmark, a process used to test the performance or scalability of a customer's application, in between preparing for performance workshops, quick turnarounds of capacity planning reviews, or being mentored by Larry and Rick, etc. In this case, it was a large customer doing a scale up exercise, something commonly done in benchmarks.

The capacity for the latest versions of the AS/400 was incredible. The customer wanted to see how much growth the new AS/400 could handle. The customers would capture workloads (performance data) from their systems and bring the data to Rochester. An IBM expert in the use of a simulation tool would use the customer's data and a PC attached to an AS/400 to test the workload. Normally the Benchmark Center would use system performance data to evaluate the effect the test had on system resources. A performance expert, like myself, would be brought in when TPST data might be required.

Recently in the field, one of the team was using TPST at a customer site and brought the system down. That wasn't good. A TPST developer reviewed the storage management dump and determined that a variable in the TPST program was too small. The program was changed, and a Program Temporary Fix (PTF) was created and made available to the field.

I was in the Benchmark Center reviewing the standard performance reports, based on the data collected from the last simulation run of the customer's application at 100% growth. The number of transactions processed during the test were less than expected. The performance data indicated an excessive number of sync IO operations due to memory faulting, most likely due to excessive file open and close operations. No more memory could be added to the AS/400.

I was there to collect and analyze TPST data. Using that data, I would identify the customer programs with the most file open and close activity and assist the customer with the program changes that might be required to reduce those operations.

Let me try to explain the open and close problem using a coffee shop experience as an analogy:

You are at your favorite coffee shop and you order your favorite espresso drink. The barista opens the empty cup dispenser (the file, if you will) and removes a cup (creates an Open Data Path [ODP] for input and output purposes). Using the coffee dispenser (the program) the Barista fills the cup (or writes to the file) and gives the cup to the consumer (Interactive Display) who then consumes the drink (reads from the file) and throws the cup away (hard closes the file). The barista continues this process for each consumer using a new cup, the old cup being discarded into the garbage pile (aka non-reusable ODP). Eventually this becomes a landfill (memory) issue.

Once I'd identified the programs with the most open and close activity, I would then identify the cause—the most common being the program is coded to be non-re-entrant. When the program ends, all files are closed. The next time the program is activated, the files must be reopened. Besides statistical data, TPST provided program information that allowed me to determine the cause, without needing to review the program code.

TPST captures the following information about programs: their name, how many times they are invoked (activated), how many times they end (deactivated), how many files are opened by the program (calls made to OS/400 module QDMCOPEN), and how many times each file is opened and closed. This includes HLL programs, OS/400 modules, and

MI programs. Theoretically, if the number of program invocations is equal to the number of deactivations, then the program isn't re-entrant. The only way to make a program re-entrant is to change the program—I knew what changes had to be made.

I was aware of the recent customer system crash. Before I started TPST, I checked the PTF levels. The PTF for TPST had been installed. I started TPST and signaled the simulation tool driver with a thumbs up. He started the tool. It took about two minutes for the system to crash.

London, Just for Fun June 1994

On the flight over, I had reviewed the latest *Performance Capabilities* manual for tips and techniques. It was one of many manuals I had brought with me. When I arrived at the customer site, I met with the management team and explained what I needed to do.

"In some cases, I may need to collect TPST data. I have brought the tool with me and would appreciate it if someone could load it on the test system."

"We do not have a test system. Is that a problem?"

"No, I am surprised that you do not have a test system. You seem like a large organization. Do you develop your own software?"

"Yes, we do."

"How do you test?"

"We use separate library lists for test and production data. When we test, we change the library list." I knew it. Shit.

The use of library lists was a S/38 innovative solution for testing. A production library was created to disallow updates to production data, unless the person running the application had the Update-in-production (*UPPROD) job preference setting set to *YES while running in debug mode. Otherwise, testing was done in test libraries, usually one per developer. It was rare for any customer to have more than one S/38; however, the larger AS/400 customers were acquiring multiple AS/400s for testing and backup.

"What if someone is testing and forgets to change the library list?"

"Worst case, we might have to restore from backup, but that has never happened."

"If I need to run TPST then it will be in production. Did you load the latest PTFs?"

"Yes, we did, according to your instructions."

"Good, then let's get started."

The interactive response time issue was caused by some inefficient settings in the communication link configuration. I had been there three days and provided some relief. If this had been a domestic engagement, I would probably be changing travel arrangements to go home. Unfortunately for me, I had to be in Lille, France, the following week. I would be visiting another customer having AS/400 performance issues.

During the daily status meeting, I reported that I believed I had completed the contract requirements; however, I did have some time to kill.

"Are there other application issues that I could look at while I'm here?"

"Now that you mention it, we are experiencing periodic slowdowns in our overnight batch process. Could you look at it?"

"No problem; that is my forte."

A couple of London IBMers decided to stop by after hearing an IBM performance expert from the States was on-site.

"Hello. Are you the bloke from the U.S.?"

"Yes, and you are?"

"My name is Debbie Hatt."

"Pleased to meet you, Debbie."

We would become good friends. I explained to them that I was going to collect some data from the nightly batch process later that evening. They were welcome to stick around and watch.

When the batch process was about to begin, we verified that the latest PTFs were installed. A couple of minutes before the batch job was submitted, I started TPST. About fifteen minutes into the run the system crashed.

We contacted Level-2 support in Rochester and learned that another bug was found in TPST and it was now part of the latest Cumulative PTF package, which wasn't installed on the customer's system. My GoTo bug-killing machine was bug-ridden.

The Designated Driver June 1994

I took a flight from London to Paris. In Paris I connected with a high-speed train going to Lille. I watched as the countryside passed us by. I fantasized that Lille was a quaint, little village. When the train stopped, I would get off, collect my bags, and walk across the street to the hotel. I was in for a surprise; Lille was the third largest city in France.

I got my luggage, crossed the street, and then realized I had no clue where to go. I pulled out my travel documents and found the information about my hotel in Lille. I saw the street address and read the extra information—Hotel Belle Vue was located just two blocks from the train depot.

The next morning, I took a taxi to the customer, a large manufacturer and distributor of cosmetics founded by a businesswoman in America. It was there I met several English consultants, who were also staying at my hotel. One of the consultants had brought his Jaguar across the English Channel, so he would drive us to and from the customer.

My last night there, we went out to dinner at a Chinois restaurant. By then, my English colleagues knew I did not drink alcohol, so they made me the designated driver. There I was behind the steering wheel, wrong side of the car I must add, driving through the streets of Lille in a Jaguar. That was the only time I ever drove while traveling overseas.

I left the IBM customer, after spending most of the time reviewing standard performance data. I provided some helpful suggestions on when to collect the data, what to look for, basic performance settings, etc. I did not have a need to use TPST.

I left Lille on the train to Paris and eventually found my way to the Paris Charles de Gaulle airport, where I caught a flight home.

The Crypt

Simi Valley, California November 1995

I was standing with Bob M. in the basement of the Countrywide Simi Valley location, in a room known as The Crypt. Bob, Mac (the AS/400 system administrator), and I were holding flashlights under our chins. We were discussing the latest earthquake and how it brought down not only the lights, but also the production AS/400 and the high availability backup AS/400.

A Week Before

I had been at Countrywide for about three weeks. After the phone conversation with Steve Finnes, I agreed to stay until Thanksgiving and change the top-ten programs using the most CPU.

I had been modifying RPG programs to remove instances of where the LR—Last Record—indicator was being set to ON, and, if necessary, adding the RETURN operation at the end of the mainline code. This would make the program re-entrant. Eliminating the LR indicator was much easier said than done.

With me was **Christine Lamorte,** the equivalent of a CE. She did not know programming; however, she was an excellent note taker. After successfully reducing the CPU consumption by about twenty per-cent, I would use Christine's notes as the details in my executive findings and recommendation report.

"You can't just disable it?" asked Christine.

"Nope, you see, Christine, the LR indicator is an RPG Programmer's best friend. It eliminates many of the housekeeping chores."

"How is that?"

"When an RPG program is invoked, it must first open the files, then initialize the indicators to OFF, and temporary storage to zeros or blanks, depending on the variable's definition. Removing the LR indicator results in the prior work not being done."

"Isn't that the goal? Make it happen only once."

"Yes, however, when the program exits, whatever the indicator settings are, and whatever values were in the variables, remain as is. This can result in the RPG program performing computations assuming the variables are zero or blank. Best case, the program fails. Worst case, the program produces erroneous results. Most RPG programmers use the LR indicator as a housekeeping device. Unfortunately, although they are excellent cleaners, IBM is the world's most expensive housekeeper."

"So, that's why you created that new data structure?"

"Exactly, and why I am using the CLEAR and RESET functions to re-initialize the indicators and temporary variables to their original state. But this isn't where we make the most CPU gains."

"I don't get it. You are making many code changes. Isn't this reducing the CPU cost?"

"Nope, they are just necessary evils. When an RPG program returns with LR ON, then all open files are closed. This action, and the subsequent action to re-open the files when the program is called again—and it will be thousands of times—are where the biggest gains are made."

"And that is all done by OS/400?"

"Normal MO; however, there is still another important thing to validate."

"Which is?"

"I must ensure the file cursor is repositioned at the beginning of the file. This is only required if the file is opened for sequential processing—in other words, the data is processed from beginning to end. After the first execution of the program, these files would be at the end, thus I need to use a SET operation to return the cursor to the beginning of the file."

"Wow, that is a lot of work."

"It is. I am so glad you are here to document this for me."

I would also use Christine's notes as the basis for the article, *The Case of Leaving Las Vegas With LR Off,* which I published in November of 1997, about two years later.

Back to the Crypt

Bob and I had taken an elevator two miles (not really, more like two floors) underground to the Crypt facility. It was called the Crypt because it was below ground, and someone had named all the AS/400s after monsters made famous in Universal Studio horror movies. There was the Mummy, Wolfman, Dracula, and Frankenstein, oh my; plus, several other computers with movie-monster names. In addition, there were the two workhorse AS/400s that were responsible for running the mortgage software. They were named Hansel and Gretel—go figure.

"Dan, these are the big guns. Gretel runs 24x7. During the daytime hours she is busy processing loans, applying payments, producing notices, etc. At night she is processing other data in batch. She is one busy gal. Hansel is just laid back, watching the blinking lights and recording Gretel's changes into a duplicate database. Should Gretel ever go down, Hansel jumps into action. In the blink of an eye, all communications are switched to Hansel. It's business as usual. No one is any the wiser."

"Cool," I was picking up some California lingo. "How are you replicating the data?"

"We are using a journal scraping product from a company based in Minnesota. They were not able to keep up for a while and then IBM helped them with performance and things became more manageable. Maybe you've heard of them."

I had, but I didn't tell Bob that. In fact, I was the guy that helped that company out. One of my first engagements as an IBM sub-contractor. Christine had heard about it when we first met in Rochester. She knew I was the guy.

"So, what happens if you should have a power outage?"

"Got it covered, Dan, we have redundant *uninterruptible power supply* [UPS] systems. When the power goes down, the first UPS kicks in. If that UPS fails, the second one kicks in. Hansel and Gretel don't skip a beat."

I suddenly felt nauseous, almost like a vertigo episode. The lights flickered for an instant. I heard the sound big computers make when they're shutting down. The first UPS turned on. The lights flickered again as the first UPS shut down. I heard the second UPS turn on and immediately shut down. It was pitch black in the Crypt.

"Mac! Are you in here?" Bob yelled.

"Over here, Bob; I'm looking for some flashlights. Found 'em."

Mac turned on a flashlight and used it to find us. He had an additional two and gave one to each of us. We turned them on and held them under our chins to light up our faces.

"Mac, you've met Dan, right?"

"Yes, I have."

"Hey, Mac, nice to see you again."

"Mac, what happened?"

"Not sure, Bob; I called Sparks as soon as the lights flickered. He said, 'earthquake' before he was cut off."

"Well, Dan, welcome to California."

"Thanks, Bob; did I tell you they call me Crash?"

Bunches of Bananas

Honduras, Central America April 1995

It was dark. It was our last night in Honduras. We had a plane to catch the next day. We had stayed at the compound longer than we should have. We had been warned not to be out after dark. It was dangerous, especially for Norte Americanos.

We had been in Honduras since Monday. Each morning, we would be picked up in a company van, along with several others staying at the hotel who had business with the customer. The van would drop us off at the customer compound, which was fenced and guarded by armed, company-employed security teams. At 5:00 P.M., the van would return and drive us back to the hotel, before dark.

"It is not safe, Señor. Mucho bandidos," the driver responded to my question about why we couldn't drive ourselves. Thus, this was our routine until Thursday.

My colleague, an employee of the customer who came to Honduras regularly, had decided to rent a car. This allowed us to stay at the hotel a little longer for a more leisurely breakfast, a way of celebrating a successful trip.

The Previous Day

I had come to Honduras at the request of my client, IBM, to assist their customer—a large grower and distributer of bananas—with their overnight batch processing. Gradually, the batch process was taking increasingly more time to complete, to where it was infringing on the daytime processing. This meant the daytime employees were sitting around with nothing to do until the batch process finished.

The preliminary performance data analysis had uncovered many *IO pending waits* (IOPEND), an indication that the CPU was waiting for *async disk IO* operations to be processed. To understand this, imagine you have acquired a turntable that can play 45 RPM records with the aid of a spindle, which allows the 45s to be stacked. When a 45 completes, the turntable arm lifts and separates away from the record just played. At the same time, or *asynchronously*, a catch in the spindle allows the next 45 to drop onto the platter. The record arm returns to the platter and magically begins playing the next record.

But *wait*, it just played that record.

You then notice the record that should be playing is resting on the turntable arm and you watch in horror, as your favorite record is snapped in two by a turntable arm gone crazy. This happened because the speed at which the turntable arm lifts, separates, and returns to play the next 45 is faster than the speed of the spindle mechanism—they are out of sync.

A smart turntable arm, like a CPU, would wait for the next 45 to be properly seated. If it is collecting performance metrics like an AS/400, it would then record the event as an IOPEND wait.

There were two possibilities for this condition: one, a lack of memory, or two, the application programs were written as 45s. The latter being most likely since the customer had plenty of memory. The CPU was now meant for digital music.

It wasn't because the batch programs were sloppy or chock full of bugs. They were simply written for a different age, when batch processing was the only processing, mainly done using punched cards or diskettes. When IBM introduced the RPG/III language, it included a whole new set of operations intended for interactive program development.

The talking heads declared batch was dead. Batch wasn't dead. RPG/III was introduced in 1978. Here it was 1995, almost twenty years later, and I was making a living resolving batch processing performance issues.

Application development was continuously evolving towards more ways for end-users to interact with data. Clunky, green screen CRTs were being replaced with PCs. Client/server and distributed computing were the latest fad. Time to move off batch. The push was coming to shove. IBM was the pusher, and I was the hired gun who did the shoving.

I was presenting my findings and recommendations to the customer management team. The customer's corporate headquarters in the U.S. had provided me with a translator, a young woman from the States, whose family came to the U.S. from Cuba. I had shown a graph to the team depicting CPU utilization, i.e., the percentage of CPU used during a specific 5-minute interval. The chart represented a 24-hour period. Every interval beginning at 6:00 P.M. and ending the following morning at 8:00 A.M. was at a hundred percent. The percentage gradually decreased to a low of twenty percent by noon, then gradually climbed to a hundred percent by early evening.

"As you can see, there is plenty of CPU resource available during the day."

I paused to let the translator repeat what I'd said in Spanish. I noticed some nods from the management team members.

"The work being done overnight involves the processing of database changes which occurred during the interactive daytime work."

Pause. More nods as the translator repeated what I'd said in Spanish.

"My first recommendation is to process the database changes as part of the interactive transaction that incurred the database change."

No nods. Several team members began speaking. Voices were rising. I looked at the interpreter and raised my hands as if to say, "What's going on?"

"Señor, they insist they cannot do this thing. It would be extremely expensive and time consuming. They do not have the budget for new programming. It is impossible. The recommendation is unacceptable."

She was translating several conversations at once, but I got the message. This recommendation wasn't going to happen in my lifetime.

"Okay. Then the only other option is to change the batch programs to be more efficient."

Pause while the translation was done, then some more outbursts.

"Señor, it is the same problem. They do not have resources to accomplish this thing. It would take forever to change all the batch programs."

"They do not have to change every program, only a dozen or so for now. Then some more later, when the workload increases."

There was some more discussion between the managers, then more questions.

"Señor, how can they do this thing?"

"They must use a separate, output-only file for RPG WRITE operations. They must replace the RPG READE operation with the READ operation. They then must increase the blocking factor for these files to 128K, which is 32 times the current blocking factor."

The customer team was having trouble understanding the recommendation to modify the programs to stop doing record-at-a-time read and write operations, thus allowing them to take advantage of blocking. I thought something was being lost in the translation. An idea came to me.

I moved to the white board and picked up a colored marker. I drew a single banana on the white board. Next to that I drew a bunch of bananas. I then posed the question, "What would be the best way to ship bananas to the U.S.? One at a time or in bunches?"

The translator laughed as she repeated the questions. Soon the members of the management team were laughing with her.

"Si, blocking, si, si."

Back to the Compound

Unfortunately, we had stayed too late at the compound so my colleague could finish some last-minute work items. He completed his work and said it was time to go. We were the only ones left in the office.

The road from the compound to the hotel was very primitive. No lights to illuminate our way back. It wasn't only dark, but I remembered seeing huge potholes in the road on the ride to the compound. We took it slow.

We passed several vehicles coming from the other direction. We stayed as close to the right shoulder of the road as was physically possible. There were no markings in the road separating the right lane from the left.

Regular cars coming at us were the least of our worries. I was more concerned about the pickup trucks filled with people in the back, driving with their headlights off. Having our headlights on was probably a dead giveaway that we were not local—easy pickings.

We made it back to the hotel in one piece. We parked the car and paid a young man a few dollars to stand by the car throughout the night. He was a member of a local gang and his presence was a warning to others that our car was protected.

We entered the hotel and headed for the bar/dining room. My colleague ordered a stiff drink. I ordered a coffee. We clicked our drinks.

"We made it," my colleague said in a congratulatory way.

Willing to Take Risks

The Performance Explorer

The previous story was just one of many that were nearly identical. The customers most unwilling to rewrite their applications were either very small, with limited resources, or they were part of a larger organization and the AS/400 wasn't getting the attention it deserved.

For me it was frustrating because I loved programming, and performance improvements were not enough to persuade these customers to rewrite. I concluded that it would take something big—not new, yet available to most AS/400 customers.

The answer was there right in front of me.

Structured Query Language (SQL)—it was the future.

RISC Based Systems 1995 Onward

Everything changed with the delivery of the AS/400e—the first AS/400 models to use 64-bit Reduced Instruction Set Computer (RISC) processors. Besides the new processors, these new systems also came with a new OS—OS/400 4.1 (OS/400 3.6 for non-RISC AS/400s). The most remarkable thing about the CISC to RISC migration was that existing programs did not have to be changed—not one line of code.

That didn't matter to me; what did matter was, in order to take advantage of new performance enhancements (especially the Integrated Language Environment or ILE), programs did have to be changed—but not every program. Not only did ILE allow RPG, COBOL, or C modules (MOD) to be combined into a single program (PGM), it would eventually do away with the practice of using copybooks, which contained common code functions—typically copied into programs as procedures (PRC).

In addition, a PRC could be created as a service program (SRVPGM) that could be accessed by many programs regardless of program language. I couldn't wait to find the time to rewrite my templates.

The new OS had two new tools that would become indispensable to me. One was the Database Monitor (DBMon), and the other was the Performance Explorer (PEX). PEX contained three essential tools for the application performance expert: Profile, Stats, and Trace.

PEX Trace, formerly SMTRace, Jay's tool, was now packaged with PEX. In other words, it was part of the OS available on every AS/400e, or AS/400 running OS/3.6 or above. PEX Profile, formerly SAM, was also part of the PEX package; however, the original version was still available as part of the PFRTools LPP. PEX Stats, formerly TPST (my bug killing machine), was also packaged as part of PEX. Not only were all known bugs corrected, PEX Stats contained some much-needed improvements. These included the ability to:

1. Start, Stop, and Resume PEX.

2. Collect for single jobs, all jobs, or a generic set of jobs.

3. Collect in Cumulative or Hierarchal mode (Invoking and invoked programs).

4. Collect application performance data at the PGM/MOD/PRC levels.

This became my performance data collection tool of choice.

Tooling Around

Besides the PFRTools LPP, and the custom tools that were part of IBMLIB, I would eventually create a few of my own. The main purpose for these tools was to teach myself SQL. The secondary purpose was to fill a gap—provide a tool that would reduce the analysis time, which was mostly mining performance data for the golden nuggets of inefficiency. The tertiary purpose was because I wanted to program, and I could.

I needed to recreate my templates. I no longer had access to the original code; however, I did have my original flowcharts, and they weren't on paper. During the TSA project I had access to an IBM personal computer. Besides technical books, Stephany could order PC software. I had her purchase a software tool named PC Flowcharter. I used this to create the TSA program template flowcharts. It was an automated version of my plastic flowcharting template. I saved the data files to a diskette before the backroom was dismantled.

In 1992, I bought a used IBM PS/2 for about $1000. It was for personal use. It had dual boot capability, so I used both OS/2 and MS/DOS. I acquired PC Flowcharter and proceeded to recover my template flowcharts. I printed them out and brought them to IBM. I used these to create my new program code templates.

The Batch R/T tool was a combined effort with Diane W. I enlisted Diane's aid because of her knowledge of Best/1 and her ability to project future run times by reducing CPU cost and disk IO. Batch R/T was based on system performance data and was not impacted by PEX.

The ANZTPSTDTA tool became obsolete with the introduction of the PEX tools. I began working on a new version for PEX. I named it PEX Data Query (PDQ). I created it using techniques described in a document I read about n-tier architecture. I created three tiers: 1-database, 2-application, and 3-user interface (UI).

I designed the database using the techniques I learned during my tenure at Augsburg, and as the database architect for TSA. Initially, I followed the current best practices for AS/400 applications. I later enhanced my database with features and functions that were beyond the norm—the most important being the use of constraints—primary, unique, and foreign keys (PK, UK and FK)—aka referential integrity (RI).

A PK was used to define the unique ID of a parent table in a relationship. A UK was used to define an alternate unique ID for any table. An FK represented the value of a PK or UK contained within another table. The FK-PK (or FK-UK) combination defined the relationships between two or more tables. RI was the rule that defined the actions that took place when a CRUD event occurred against a table in a defined relationship.

For example, when a table named Dan was created, his *unpublished* DNA became the PK. His *published* phone number became his UK—another way in which information about Dan could be found. When Dan met Mary Jo, they established a relationship table named Marriage. They still retained their own unique DNA-PK; until one day a dependent table was created named Matt. Matt had his own unique DNA. In addition, he had both Dan's and Mary Jo's DNA which were FKs. An RI rule was created to ensure that when a DELETE event occurred on one of the Dan or Mary Jo tables, or both, Matt would not be deleted.

The application layer was written in RPG/ILE (RPG/IV). All data access was done using SQL data-manipulation statements and performed against SQL views, a virtual table built over the actual base table or tables (JOINs). This type of application development was referred to as *data cen-*

tric. Using it when I did was very *bleeding-edge.*

I created my UI using the User Interface Manager (UIM). This was the tool used to define AS/400 OS Panel Groups—the green screen displays. The panels were described using a tag language—like languages used for web development. I thought this would make it possible to convert the UI to a Web browser somewhere down the road. UIM was now available to customers, made possible by APIs as part of the controlled openness initiative.

John Sears and I were talking. John had stopped by our shared office shortly after the first RISC systems were being rolled out to needy customers. Diane and I had been discussing changes that needed to be made to Batch R/T.

During lunch several days before, I was sitting with Rick and Larry when John joined us. We were discussing PEX and what would be required to collect performance data from customers who started using ILE concepts, such as SRVPGMs, local PRCs, integrated languages in the same PGM, etc.

John had made the comment that modular techniques didn't make sense to him. He would like to meet a programmer who was using them. I raised my hand.

"I'll stop by and see you, Dan, when I get some extra time."

So, here I am, having a conversation with one of my idols. The conversation became contentious. John's point-of view was that procedure calls versus sub-routines would be less efficient. My argument was that using procedures would simplify development, reduce the cost of testing and speed up the time to market.

Diane witnessed the argument.

"That was scary, Dan. I thought you guys were going to start fighting."

"No worries, Diane. We were just tooling around."

Executive Briefing, User Group, or Technical Conference

Data Mining

The process of analyzing performance data did not change greatly for me with the move to RISC and PEX. I still used the Performance Tools data as the first step in performance problem resolution. When analyzing batch-processing data, I used two tools, PDQ and Batch/RT. These were not IBM standard performance data analysis tools. They were used specifically to solve batch performance problems.

The next step was to use the PDQ tool to transform the PEX data into SQL tables for the purposes of Online Analytical Processing (OLAP). The PDQ tool was an interactive, or online, application that provided access to summarized views of the PEX data, using dynamic, embedded SQL, the industry standard for accessing data stored in relational databases. In addition, the PDQ tool provided some additional capabilities or functions not provided in the AS/400 current version of SQL.

The final step was to use Batch/RT to create a timeline of the batch process. The data generated by Batch/RT was subsequently used as input into a graphing tool. The data was presented as a bar chart, each bar representing a time interval, typically minutes, depending on the duration of the batch process. Each bar contained two data elements: 1-the amount of clock time used by the CPU, and 2-the amount of time the computer spent Waiting to do work.

Don't feel bad if the last three paragraphs confused you. You weren't the only one. I discovered this when I first began presenting my findings to executives and members of upper management.

Somewhere in the World

I would present my findings from various performance gigs at user groups where I was a guest speaker, or to IBM customers at technical conferences. I would present my topic and then ask for questions. The following was a typical presentation:

"To help you to understand *CPU* time and Wait time, I will use the following analogy:

Assume you are a *CPU*, and you need to get from your house to your favorite coffee shop, three blocks away. To get there you are going to take advantage of two auxiliary devices called legs, which will allow you to walk from your house to the coffee shop. As you walk, you move your arms (another pair of auxiliary devices) and, if the four devices are working in unison with you, the CPU, you arrive at the coffee shop in five minutes flat.

"Now imagine that each intersection you cross is controlled by traffic lights. If the light is green, you keep walking, your arms keep moving, and you, the CPU, are being utilized at one-hundred-percent capacity. Congratulate yourself; you are probably very healthy. Oh, and as you are congratulating yourself, you unconsciously slow down, just enough that you didn't make the green light on the second intersection. You now must wait. Good news, no need to be embarrassed, all *CPUs* wait at the same speed.

"In addition, after you can walk again, just before you reach the coffee shop, you're inclined to pick your nose. You have now lost the coordination required to keep a steady gait. Since you can't walk and pick your nose at the same time, you must stop and wait until this IO or Input/Output operation is completed—more wait time. You arrive at the coffee shop, glance at your watch, and say to yourself, 'My walk took fifteen minutes today, normally it only takes five minutes. WTF?' Then you notice the line of CPUs ahead of you, waiting to put in their coffee orders. Don't get me started on Queueing Theory."

About this time, I might get a question. "Why the wait?"

"That is a good question. When reviewing collected performance data, my first step is to determine where CPU is being underutilized and find out why. In most cases the main reason is due to the CPU waiting for more work. This is normal for online, interactive workloads. The CPU can take a break during end-user key-think time. It is very rare for me to find an AS/400 that does not have enough CPU for interactive work.

"As you can see from the chart, CPU usage by Batch Jobs is gradually increasing until it hits one-hundred percent during overnight hours. A breakdown of the CPU time shows that CPU-Wait is occurring, in other words the CPU is getting ahead of the async IO operations. Because the data isn't in the reserved memory location, the CPU must wait for the data, like waiting for the cable guy who said he would be there between two and four, and now it is five and where the heck is he?

"In computer performance lingo, we refer to this as an *IO-Pending fault;* however, it isn't recorded as a memory page fault, thus making it difficult for the system operators to understand whose fault it is—they're trained to find fault with everything.

"Additional analysis would usually indicate that during each five-minute time interval in which a batch job was running, there would be millions of IO operations to the auxiliary storage devices, disk drives in this case, not your nose. These disk IO operations are divided into two types: synchronous [sync] and asynchronous [async]."

Sync and async disk IO operations are like good and bad cholesterol. The last thing you want to hear from your doctor is that you have a high count of bad cholesterol. It literally may be the last thing you hear from your doctor. Like cholesterol, sync and async IO operations are a necessary part of an efficiently operating computer system.

"A sync IO operation occurs when the data being requested by the application is currently not present in virtual memory. High counts of sync IO operations would be considered normal in a highly interactive computer application where end-users are constantly requesting random bits of information. The likelihood of the information being in memory is low. Thus, the CPU must wait while the data is retrieved from its physical location on the disk and brought into memory—that's okay.

"Most humans couldn't process the data if it were fed to them directly by the CPU, so it's slowed down to human readable form by going through a communication device, such as a 5250-WS, or a PC acting like one. This is also good because if your eyes attempted to read data directly from the CPU, they would probably melt, and everyone would laugh at you. These communication operations show up in performance data as wait time.

"An async IO operation occurs in tandem with a sync IO operation. To help understand this, imagine again that you are a CPU, and you are about to enter a race. You are poised at the starting block, waiting to make your first step towards the finish line, several yards, or meters, away.

"The starting gun is fired, you make your first stride, or sync IO, because you were waiting. With each subsequent stride, you move faster towards your goal, the ground seems to move in unison with you, like it was anticipating your next step. This is how async IO works.

"In other words, sync IO is like a leisurely walk to the coffee shop, with occasional stops along the way—no hurry. Async IO is like a race, the faster the better. No time to smell the coffee and drink the roses. In the case of the banana customer, I told you about, they had a bad case of high cholesterol, too much sync IO. In addition, the async IO operations were being forced to wait. They were becoming synchronous. Thus, they would show up in performance data as IO-Pending waits.

"As I said earlier, a high occurrence of sync IO within an interactive environment isn't an immediate cause for alarm; however, at some point this will lead to reduced performance and should be investigated. A high occurrence of sync IO in batch applications should be resolved immediately. In either case, the cause is most likely application related.

"In the banana customer case, the batch application was developed in-house, thus the customer can only find fault with themselves. The application was written in RPG/400, the programming language of choice for most AS/400 programmers.

"Like the S/38, the AS/400 includes a native virtual memory management system, referred to as Single Level Store. Every object is assigned a virtual memory address. The number of addresses capable of being assigned exceeds no bounds. Well, there are more virtual addresses available than the amount of memory that can be physically installed.

"When an application request is made for a particular object, the OS/400 data management system checks to see if the object is located at its virtual memory address. If not, then the object is faulted into memory, which results in a sync IO—thus the CPU waits. Questions?"

I would use my remote clicker to bring up the next chart. I wasn't a stand-in-one-place presenter; thus, the remote clicker was a godsend. I would move around the room, keeping the action going. I would go and stand by someone who asked a question to ensure that others nearby would hear me—even if I were wired up.

"This chart should answer any root cause questions. The most likely application programming causes for excessive sync IO operations, in order of appearance, are... Drum-roll please."

I would use the built-in pointer on my remote clicker to highlight the numbered items on the chart.

1. Minimal use of blocking techniques.
2. Lack of memory available to the batch application.
3. Excessive file open and close operations.

By then, I had made a chart of the banana solution. After walking thru each bullet point, I would bring up the banana chart.

I used the banana engagement as the basis for the article *The Case of Creeping Batch CPU and Runtimes*, published in June 1997.

I would use the coffee analogies later when I taught database optimization. They worked to explain the concepts of Re-usable ODPs and Set-at-a-time versus Record-at-a-time when explaining SQL IO methods.

I used them when teaching SQL concepts to one of my largest customers—Starbucks.

The Lone Practitioner

Up until then I was The Lone Ranger, Paladin, Kit Carson, or any other notable personage who could and would work with little or no supervision. I was a team player, if being a part of a greater team made sense. I would attend team meetings and contribute my two cents worth. I partook in company outings; however, I would not stay long. That would change.

About a year after I started the IBM gig Joe H. left the group. There was an opening for another consultant. IBM contacted KMA to see if they had another Dan. KMA found someone better.

Jim Stewart quit IBM shortly after **Rick Turner** retired. Jim wasn't happy that he wasn't offered a retirement package like Rick's. He was familiar with Kyle and Ann and heard they were looking for someone to fill a request from IBM.

Jim and I had never met, but we hit it off immediately. Jim had great leadership skills and had worked with several IBM customers at the Executive Briefing Center in Rochester, MN. Jim did not have a programming background, but he had done something that I hadn't; and truth be told, that I never knew I wanted to do—Jim was a published author.

Jim had co-authored a book—along with Rick and a few non-IBM industry experts—that described AS/400 performance basics and the art of performance analysis.

Jim and I would become a team. We were referred to as the *performance detectives.* We traveled together to several IBM customers who were suffering from performance-related issues. Most of these customers were large, like CFC, or household names—like Costco.

Although the issues might be slightly different, in most cases, the outcome was always the same—giveback—in the form of reduced consumption of computer resources. For the customers, this meant more room for necessary upgrades to meet the growing demands of the business.

Many of the IBM AS/400 customers we serviced had started out as mom-and-pop shops, or were small businesses servicing a niche market. These customers were growing substantially, and the small AS/400s they were using could not keep up.

Big IBM wanted to sell them big iron. These customers did not want to give up their beloved AS/400s. There was only one solution—Jim and Dan to the rescue.

The Case of the Optical Illusion

Rochester, MN Fall 1994

There was trouble in River City. Specifically, a city built next to the Zumbro River in southeastern Minnesota. The next release of OS/400—V3R6 as it was known to existing customers, V4R1 as it would be delivered to new customers—was behind schedule. This was a big release. Not only did it include many new features and functions, but it also involved the rewrite of the OS architecture from CISC to RISC.

IBM development had come across a few obstacles delaying the announcement and scheduled delivery of the new OS. This wasn't the main concern. Several of IBM Rochester's largest customers were growing by leaps and bounds. The AS/400 was always there to vertically meet its customers' growing system needs; that is, scale up by adding additional hardware, i.e., memory, CPU, and disks. A computer shutdown, by even the smallest of these customers, could result in huge, negative ramifications, not only for the customer, but for IBM Rochester as well.

The latest fad in the computer industry was known as client-server. The concept seemed simple enough. Several clients, i.e., PC or smart terminals, would be able to connect to a larger system, typically a repurposed PC known as the server, which would primarily provide data access. Other than the OS, the server would theoretically not have any application software. As the data storage requirements for a client-server environment grew, the customer would simply add more servers, referred to as server farms, providing nonintrusive horizontal growth for the business.

This solution to handle the growing requirements for more data storage, especially the needs of small businesses with even smaller computer budgets, was highly touted by Microsoft. Microsoft (MS) had become the world leader in OS software for personal computers. The marketing people at MS were obviously salivating over the perceived revenues to be had by breaking into the small to medium-sized business market, currently occupied by IBM and its System/3x class of computers.

It was a target-rich environment. The people at IBM Rochester understood this. Their efforts to persuade the remaining System/3x customer base to migrate to the AS/400 wasn't going well. IBM hoped that the latest version of RPG, known as RPG IV, would bring this remaining group of customers on board; however, these customers were also growing. If push came to shove, the ability to grow the business would supersede upgrading RPG. Besides, MS was hinting that by using PCs a business might not need to employ computer programmers. The management of the PCs could be outsourced to service bureaus. The industry had come full circle—enter OptiConnect.

I was sitting with Jim and Diane in the office we shared. Jim had just been to a briefing, given by **Steve Finnes** on OptiConnect and was sharing what he'd learned with Diane and me.

"The new RISC based systems have been delayed, could be two years, maybe less. There are several large customers whose AS/400s are busting at the seams. The lab thinks that decoupling the applications from the database is a short-term Band-Aid until the RISC systems are available."

"How are they going to do that?" asked Diane.

"They plan to connect small AS/400s to a large AS/400 using high speed fiber optic cable. The small AS/400s will run the interactive application layer, display screens, HLL application code, etc. The database operations will be done against remote files connected via OptiConnect to the AS/400 database server. Batch work will continue to run on the database AS/400, using local database IO operations."

"Do the customers have to move all the interactive work to the client AS/400?"

"No, Dan, they only need to move enough work to allow the database server to function below one-hundred-percent capacity. That's where we come in."

"How so?"

"Diane and I have come up with a Best/1 model to identify the workloads, or applications, that are the most ideal for offloading to a client AS/400."

"I assume you did that via performance data."

"Yes, we isolated work using workstations or user profiles. We then modeled these workloads to determine the size of the client system. Diane and I then went to one of the largest customers to do a proof of concept."

"How did that go?"

"Good news and bad news, which one do you want first?"

"Let's go with the bad news."

"We added an OptiConnect overhead factor, based on the number of sync IO operations which, as you know, would require an IO operation across Opticonnect. In addition, this adds CPU overhead to the client system. The bad news is that it will take at least three AS/400s to accommodate the applications that need to be offloaded from the current AS/400. This is way beyond the customer's budget."

"What's the good news?" I asked.

"Dan, you're going to Disneyland."

The Gold Coasts

Although Disney was one of our customers, the customer in this case was Countrywide, located in Simi Valley, CA, not that far from Disneyland. I already had a reputation for squeezing blood from a turnip; in essence, reducing CPU and IO consumption, allowing customers to continue to run their business applications until the time, and budget, allowed for an upgrade.

Over a two-year stretch I would travel to several customers on both coasts of the U.S.; sometimes with Jim, other times, shortly after Jim and Diane had visited with the customer. Regardless, Steve would lead the charge, running to the sound of large AS/400 customers needing relief while the RISC systems were delayed.

In between these customer visits, Jim and I would fill in our free time visiting customers with just normal performance issues. Some of these customers were outside the U.S.

Auckland, New Zealand May 1995

I was convalescing. I had just returned from Honduras. I had a bad case of the shits; so much so, I decided to see a doctor.

"Mr. Cruikshank, I believe you have a parasite. Were you out of the country recently?"

"I just got back from Honduras."

"Well, that could explain it. You will need to take some antibiotics. Should clear up in a few days."

A few days later I was on a plane, destination New Zealand—a country that was located on a continent I hadn't been to yet.

Help Me

Jim had called me with a request for help. He was on-site with a telecommunications customer in New Zealand. After reviewing performance data, Jim concluded that the current issue was mainly due to the high volume of file open and close operations—my forte.

"Dan, can you come on-site and help me here in New Zealand?"

"My calendar is open."

"Great! If you haven't traveled to New Zealand, Australia, or Asia before then prepare yourself for a long flight, three meals, and four movies."

"Wow, in that case, I'd best get some Depends to bring on the plane with me."

Jim was aware of my latest travel souvenir.

"Ha, ha, I'll see you when you get here."

I booked the next available flight leaving Minneapolis: layover in Los Angeles, and arriving at Auckland, New Zealand, the next day. I arrived early in the morning. Jim had arranged with the hotel for me to use his room in the likely event I wouldn't be able to check-in. Jim was right. What he didn't foresee was my luggage not arriving.

This wasn't the first time my luggage didn't come in on the same plane I did. It was the first time on an overseas trip. It would not be the last.

I was expected to be at the customer's location by noon. I had my sport-coat, as I usually wore that rather than pack it. Other than that, I wasn't dressed for consulting purposes. I asked the hotel concierge where the closest men's store was. He said the hotel had an excellent gift shop, which also sold men's clothing.

"In case of emergencies like this one," he added.

Several hundred dollars later I had a new white shirt, a new tie, a pair of fancy blue jeans ("That's a good look for you," the attractive, female salesperson told me), and a new pair of Italian leather slip-ons—the shoes alone were $300.

It was the best pair of shoes I had ever worn. They were on my feet at many consulting gigs for years to come. Qantas reimbursed me the total amount. My luggage came in on the next flight, later that evening.

Oh, by the way, the performance issue was application related. The usual suspects were involved, lack of blocking, non-re-entrant RPG programs, etc.

The PGJ

Mexico, Central America Fall 1995

Jim and I were standing in the departures screening line at the Benito Juarez International Airport in Mexico City. We were nervous. We had been in Mexico City working for a police organization we thought was comparable to the FBI. On our last night in town, we had found out that the police organization was more like the KGB.

As part of our assignment, we were required to do a POT before leaving the country. We prepared some test data. In the spirit of jocularity, we created fictional profiles of ourselves. Jim was Los Tigre, a wanted bank robber, considered extremely dangerous. I was El Cicatrix Cara Sicario, the scar-faced hitman, a fierce killer, wanted dead or alive.

The line was moving slowly. Each person had to place their bags and other possessions on a conveyor belt. As the bags went through an x-ray machine, one of two lightbulbs would turn on. Green, which meant go ahead, have a nice day; or red, for stop and be searched. We were told the lights were random. In some very rare situations, perhaps some mysterious item in the passenger's possessions might trigger a red light.

We finally reached the belt. Jim went first; he placed his clothes and computer cases on the belt. They went through the machine. The light turned green, and Jim passed through the metal detector. It was now my turn.

I placed my clothes and computer cases on the belt. The computer went through okay—green light. My suitcase went next, not so lucky this time—red light. *Oh, shit.*

Two Weeks Before

Jim and I were in Mexico City to help a police organization improve their case reporting and team assignments. There were five districts overseen by this organization. The problem was that a crime reported in District-1 took forever, if at all, to be reported to the other districts. This resulted in an inefficient use of resources. The appropriate teams were not being assigned in the most effective manner.

We were there to implement a new IBM product named DataPropagator. This was unusual because it wasn't a performance gig; however, it wouldn't be a bad idea to have some performance experts on-site—just in case.

Jim and I would get picked up by our IBM counterpart and taken to police headquarters, where two AS/400s were located. We loaded the product on the main or central AS/400 and set it up to receive and then distribute the data to the appropriate AS/400.

We then loaded the product on the *district* AS/400 and set it up to send and receive data from and to the *central* AS/400. We created test data in the form of crimes committed by various criminals—namely Jim and me.

At the end of the day, we would return to our hotel in the Zona Rosa, strictly prohibited on the IBM list of approved districts. We would change and then go out for dinner. We had found a Spanish restaurant. We couldn't read a word, nor could the server speak English, so we simply pointed at any item that seemed interesting and hoped for the best.

We were never disappointed. As we ate, we talked.

"Have you ever thought about writing, Dan?"

"In a way, I have written a few things—a play and a poem in elementary school, standards and procedures documents, technical stuff mostly. Why do you ask?"

"I have some contacts in the computer magazine industry, and they have hinted to me about writing some AS/400 articles. I was thinking, because of what we've been doing, it might be fun to write some articles together."

"I would like that very much."

The last night Jim and I were in Mexico, we went to the restaurant for a final meal. We noticed the owner of the restaurant, whom we had met, sitting with a man; they were going over a menu. The owner looked up and saw us, waved, and then said something to the man she was with. Later he came over, introduced himself, and asked to sit with us.

He was a U.S. citizen like us, and he was there to help the owner translate the menu into an English version.

"That's an excellent idea," Jim said. "The food is delicious. We've been here almost every night and have never been disappointed."

"Yes, the owner mentioned that to me. So, what do you guys do?"

"We're consultants from IBM. We're here working with an IBM customer, helping the local IBM team with a proof of technology."

"Sounds interesting. Who's your customer?"

"The PGJ," I said.

It was like someone had flipped a switch and instantly all sound died. No conversations between the other diners were happening, nor were the servers serving. Everyone was staring at us.

Our new friend leaned into the table and, in a soft voice, asked, "Do you know who the Procuraduria General de Justicia or PGJ are?"

"We thought they were like the FBI," Jim answered.

"More like the KGB," the guy responded. "These are the guys that take suspects up into the hills and the suspect is never seen again."

Back to Departures

A security guy came over, lifted my bag off the belt, and carried it to a table. He opened it and began rummaging through it. Apparently, the guard was satisfied and motioned to me, then the bag, and pointed at the exit where Jim was waiting.

"Adios, amigo," he said.

I re-packed the bag and got the hell out of there.

Daniel Cruikshank, Inc.
Independent Contractor

Tempe, AZ April 1998

I was working with a software development company. They were in the process of rewriting their application developed for DEC systems to run on the AS/400. They were nearly complete when they ran into a wall—specifically poor performance.

For some reason, rather than going with the flow and choosing RPG—the AS/400 development language of choice, favored by AS/400 code-slingers everywhere—they opted to re-write their application in C.

I made travel arrangements to fly to Phoenix. Prior to leaving I acquired a book—*C for RPG Programmers.* I read it on the flight. I learned enough to be dangerous.

Upon arrival, I met with the president of the company who gave me the history of the project. I summarized what he told me.

"Let me get this straight. You have an application developed for a PDP-1160, written in DIBOL, a COBOL look-a-like, which you decided to rewrite in C. You developed a tool that can convert about eighty percent of the code, the other twenty percent you have written by hand. Correct?"

"That's it, Dan," the president replied. "In addition, none of us know a thing about the AS/400. It's black magic to us. Somehow the C code compiles and runs; however, the performance sucks."

"When you say performance, exactly what do you mean?"

"Specifically, the response time is horrible. It takes at least twenty-seconds for a screen to appear after pressing the Enter key. So, we would like you to review the programs and identify areas for improvement."

"I can do that," I lied, "but first I would like to collect some PEX data. That will give me a good starting point. Sometimes the programs you think are the problem turn out to be okay. I'm sure you don't want to spend a lot of money for me to tell you that."

"Makes sense, Dan, but what is PEX?"

"PEX is an acronym for the Performance Explorer."

"Do I need to buy this from IBM, or did you bring it with you and need to install it?"

"No and no; PEX comes with the OS. It's built in. I just need to load a tool called PDQ, which I wrote to help me analyze the data. PEX can generate millions of bytes of data, depending on what I need to collect."

"Great! In that case, I will introduce you to my top guys and you can do your thing."

The Next Day

I was standing at the front of a conference room. The president of the company was sitting in the front row with several of his top staff. Behind them, occupying the next three rows was the development team. In the back row sat some trainees and some members from the operations side of the house.

The night before I had told the president that I believed I knew what the problem was, but I needed to get some more detailed information from some of the developers—thus the full house.

"Good morning, my name is Dan Cruikshank. I am from IBM Rochester, Minnesota, and I specialize in solving application performance-related issues. Yesterday, I used a tool named PEX to capture the signatures of several of your programs. By this, I mean the way the programs begin, the way they read and write data, the programs that they call—both yours and ours—and how the programs end."

"Question," a developer in the third row raised his hand. "When you said, 'yours and ours' what did you mean?"

"Yours are the programs you wrote, ours are the OS modules that are implicitly executed, based on the complexity of the instructions in your program. For example, when your program opens a file, three OS modules may be executed to complete that single operation. These modules are separated by the *machine interface* or MI. Some OS modules execute above the MI, others execute below the MI. Knowing which of these modules are executing, and how often, can tell me what the performance issue may be."

There were a couple more questions, prompted by my response. Then luckily the president stepped in before I spent the whole day talking away.

"This is all very interesting, but I would like to know what you found, Dan."

The customer had provided a projector that I had connected to my laptop before the meeting started. I brought up my one and only chart. It was a list of module names, in descending sequence by CPU time. The list only contained the top twenty modules. Nineteen of the modules accounted for less than ten percent of the total CPU. The first module on the list accounted for nearly ninety percent—ZFORTIFY.

"It jumps right out at you, don't it? IBM OS modules all begin with the letter Q. For example, the first module underneath ZFORTIFY is QDBGETKY. This module was invoked because your program performed a Read-by-key operation."

A hand went up. "Is that module above or below the MI?"

"The modules beginning with Q are OS modules, thus they are above the MI. Notice the modules that begin with an asterisk [*]. These are the bad boys that exist below the MI. The QDBGETKY module called two additional modules below the MI. Let's see if we can find them. Notice QDBGETKY was invoked or called 3000 times. Aha! The *SETCR and *RETDSEN modules were both called 3000 times. In other words, each IO operation your program performs results in three OS module invocations."

"Is this an issue?"

"It can be, but you don't need to worry about that right now. ZFORTIFY is yours. Who knows what it does?"

The president turned around in his chair.

"Okay, somebody needs to fess up. Who knows what this is?"

All the developers looked around. Finally, a young guy in the back of the room raised his hand. "I know what it is," he said.

"What is it?" I asked.

"It's a module we use for testing. It's called by every program several times during the processing of the program. It stores information in memory, mainly module run times. It should not be in the production version of the programs."

"Thank you," I said, "for standing up. I recommend that, first, you take this module off the production system immediately; second, you delete it forever. Hopefully you have learned that the AS/400 automatically collects the information that your ZFORTIFY program is attempting to do. And it does it in a most efficient manner."

I made several return trips to this customer. They always referred to me as the IBM C programming expert.

Acquired Skills:

Mastered Performance Management and traveled internationally.

PART FOUR

TIME TRAVELERS

The Blue Highway Came Calling

The Pound Puppies

Shortly after Mary Jo and I stopped using alcohol and narcotics our lives changed dramatically. Opportunities seemed to come out of nowhere. Mary Jo was a cost accountant with Schaper Manufacturing, a maker of children's toys, for three years—1976 to 1978. Then in 1979, after completing treatment for drug addiction, she took a big step and accepted the position of production scheduler for the same company. For the next seven years she excelled at her job.

In 1985, Schaper announced that they were leaving Minnesota. Mary Jo parlayed her acquired skills and knowledge into a new job as Production Planner for Tonka Corporation, which would create a new toy—Pound Puppies. Mary Jo played a major role in their success.

The following is from the Tonka Company History web site:

> Tonka introduced Pound Puppies in 1985, a soft dog toy that children "adopted" when they bought it. The adoption ploy was borrowed from Cabbage Patch dolls, which had been all the rage a few years earlier. Pound Puppies sold well, and Tonka's sales and earnings seemed in good shape, more than doubling between 1984 and 1987, to the tune of $293 million. Pound Puppies accounted for more than half of the company's profits in 1986.

It Wasn't All About Me

The Honey Burn

Minneapolis-St. Paul (MSP) International Airport
August 1980

On March 22, 1980, Mary Jo and I were married. We started our new life together long on debt, short on cash, with two heads full of dreams. In addition, we were recovering alcoholics. During the previous two years we had been taught a new way to live our lives, complete with a set of instructions—twelve easy steps to follow.

On Saturday nights, we would go to the airport. Neither one of us was going anywhere—it was a cheap date. We would get a coffee and take it to the observation platform, which was open to the public before 2001. We would watch the planes take off and land.

"Mary Jo, someday we're going to travel, and I don't mean just another road trip in a car. We're gonna travel in style, first class all the way. We're going to exotic places like Hong Kong, Rome, Paris, London, or even China—places we've never been before. We'll see things we've never seen; do things we've never done; meet people we've never met and may never meet again—someday."

"You're a weirdo," Mary Jo would say.

"We're just two weirdos, off to see the world; there's so much to see."

Mary Jo would be the first to get a passport. In 1985, she was responsible for ensuring the production of Tonka Toys' *Pound Puppies*, which were being made in South Korea. Although she never went overseas, she did travel to Spanish speaking "countries" like Mexico and California.

Pound Puppies were a big hit. They accounted for nearly fifty percent of Tonka's net profit in 1986—under the watchful eye of Mary Jo. As a result of her efforts, Mary Jo received Tonka Toys' prestigious President's Award and was named Employee of the Year.

Three years later, I would begin subcontracting for a large organization known worldwide by three characters—IBM.

I was also told to acquire a passport, and within two years I was traveling overseas. Ten years later IBM would hire me. By then I had traveled to four continents and dozens of countries. I would step on the ground of two more continents before I retired.

Ft. Myers Beach, FL March 1980

There were two memorable things that occurred on our honeymoon in Ft. Myers Beach, FL—we both lost our virginity. I'm just kidding. I will say that if we hadn't lost it before then, it would not have happened on our honeymoon trip.

After our wedding reception, held at the Calhoun Beach Hotel on Lake Calhoun in Minneapolis, Mary Jo and I jumped into her white Pontiac Firebird, packed from the night before, and hit the road. We had no intentions to stop, but after driving for sixteen hours, when we reached Locust Grove, GA. we knew we couldn't drive another mile.

We found a hotel with vacancies. We unpacked the essentials, hit the bed, and went right to sleep. In the morning we got back into the car and continued to our honeymoon paradise.

After crossing the GA/FL border we made our first rest stop at a Welcome Center located way down upon the Swanee River—yes, there is a Swanee River. They had some Roman columns along a sidewalk between His and Her restrooms. I remember Mary Jo twirling between the columns like a fairy in a production of A *Midsummer's Night Dream*.

As we passed thru Tampa Bay, St. Petersburg, and Sarasota, Florida, my excitement began to build.

"Mary Jo, you are going to love this."

I had been to Ft. Myers Beach several times as a kid on family vacations, and I was doing my best to keep Mary Jo on pins and needles.

"The road we will drive on from the city of Ft. Myers to Estero Island—aka, Ft. Myers Beach—is lined on each side by royal palm trees planted by Thomas Edison, the famous inventor who had a winter home here. It is now a museum. We need to check it out."

"Sounds interesting, Dan."

"Not only that, in order to access the island, there is a swing bridge."

"What's a swing bridge?"

"It's like a draw bridge, but instead of the bridge being elevated, it swings 90-degrees in either direction."

"Why does it do that?"

"To let the shrimp boats in and out. We are going to gorge ourselves on this trip."

As we approached Ft. Myers Beach, I noticed traffic wasn't slowing down. This was unusual, as the shrimp boats should be coming in with their daily catch.

"Hold on, Mary Jo. Once we go over this bridge up ahead, we will most likely get a view of the island and perhaps a view of the swing bridge in action, especially if we have to stop at the top of the bridge. Funny, I don't recall there being a bridge on this road when I was here as a kid."

"When was the last time you were here?"

"I was fifteen or sixteen, about twelve years ago."

As we got to the top of the bridge, Mary Jo got excited.

"What a view, Dan, it's beautiful!"

"Where's the swing bridge, darn it!"

"I think we just drove over it."

Mary Jo reviewed the TripTik and noticed that the location of our honeymoon motel was almost directly under the bridge. I took the first exit, drove under the bridge, and saw the motel. It wasn't a big chain motel, but the location was great—and it had a pool for swimming and sunbathing. Famous last words.

By the time we finished checking in and unpacking, the day was coming to an end. Mary Jo went to the bathroom. I took that opportunity to rest my eyes; it had been a long day in the car. When I woke up, the sun was shining. I was in bed, under the covers, and still had my shirt and pants on. Someone had taken off my shoes. Mary Jo was lying next to me sound asleep.

Two Beachcombers

"First, let's get some breakfast and then we'll take a walk on the beach. We can go for miles and not see another human being. I had to do that as a kid so I could smoke."

"Sounds like a plan, Dan."

When we finished breakfast, Mary Jo made some plan alterations.

"If we eat out every day, especially breakfast, we'll run out of money by the end of the week and be on credit cards. Let's stop at a grocery store and pick up some fruit, milk, and cereal."

After breakfast we hit the beach. We had dressed in our bathing suits, so we were prepared to get wet in the Gulf of Mexico. We parked close to the pier and used that as a landmark. We began walking. After so many minutes we would stop, take off our sandals, and run into the Gulf of Mexico. We'd goof around and then head back to the beach and keep walking. After the third time I noticed my wedding band was missing. It would have been futile to search for it. Not a good way to start our marriage.

Shortly after we began walking, I noticed there were several others out walking the beach. Every now and then someone would walk our way and ask if we'd heard about *timeshare.*

Today's Special: Lobster

We returned to the motel and changed for dinner. I felt a little uncomfortable, most likely sunburn. We walked under the bridge to the other side where a seafood restaurant was advertising peel-and-eat shrimp. We got a table right away, ordered the shrimp and two iced teas. I was starting to feel lightheaded. I shook it off when the shrimp came. I ate a couple—they were tasty—however, I seemed to be losing my appetite. Worse, I was starting to feel nauseous.

"Mary Jo, I don't think I'm feeling good. Maybe I should go back to the room."

"I'll go with you. We can get a doggy bag for the rest of the shrimp."

We made it back to the motel room and I laid down on the bed. Mary Jo woke me up.

"It's getting dark. Why don't you undress and get under the covers?"

I sat up. I was feeling woozy as I begun undressing. I took my shirt off and heard Mary Jo say, "Oh, my God. You're as red as a lobster."

She helped me get the rest of my clothes off. Except for where my swimsuit covered me, my upper torso and legs were a deep red. And they were starting to hurt. I couldn't lie on my back or stomach. My left side was less painful, so I folded up into the fetal position and prepared to bake to death. Somehow, I fell asleep.

When I awoke in the morning I attempted to get out of bed. My brain was saying get up, you dodo-head, but my body would not respond. I looked at the ceiling.

Oh, HP, what have I done now?

I tried to get up again. This time everything worked. I walked cautiously to the bathroom. Our motel room had a kitchenette with a table for two. I sat in one of the chairs waiting for Mary Jo to wake up. I had no idea what to do. I thought I might need to go to the hospital. Then I heard Mary Jo.

"Dan, I can't get up."

"Just relax. Look at the ceiling for a couple of minutes and then try it again."

A couple of minutes later she sat up and looked at me.

"Oh, my God! What have we done?"

Water Wings

We spent most of the first week of our two-week honeymoon in the hotel room. That was the honeymoon spent in hell. Since Mary Jo had a darker complexion, she was able to leave the hotel room in search of pharmaceuticals. Luckily, they were the kind that could be purchased at a drug store. She was also able to get some good advice from the druggist about sunburn.

"You should take him to the hospital."

"There must be something we can get over the counter that would help?" Mary Jo pleaded. "It's our honeymoon."

The druggist took pity on us and filled a bag with all sorts of ointments and creams. Mary Jo took out her credit card and paid for the potions. She started to walk away when the druggist said, "Just a minute, young lady."

He handed her some sunscreen lotion. "Put this on before you go outdoors again. Repeat it after you go swimming. It's on the house."

By the end of the first week, we felt good enough to go on a tour of the Everglades. We made sure to sit wherever there was shade. After the tour we were heading for the car, when somebody called to us, "Hey, you two, have you heard about timeshare?"

"Yes, not interested," I replied.

"Have you taken a tour?" He kept at it. "It will only take an hour. Indoors, air-conditioned, doesn't cost anything."

I looked at Mary Jo. She shrugged. "Okay," I said.

After the tour, we returned to our motel with our financial honor intact. I saw the sun was low in the west; the swimming pool was shaded.

"Mary Jo, I'm feeling warm. I'm going to jump into the pool. Wanna join me?"

"No, I'm going to wait until we go to Sanibel Island tomorrow."

I dove in and swam underwater until I reached the wall where she was sitting. I popped up, kissed her, and then did a backstroke. Mary Jo started to laugh.

"What's so funny?"

"Haha, the peeling skin, haha, on your arms, haha, has filled with water. It looks like, haha, you're wearing some kiddie water wings."

Back Home April 1980

We were sitting in front of the fireplace in our duplex. We had a fire going. We were wearing our bathrobes and nothing else. We were warming our bare feet by the fire and drinking our cups of strong coffee—hand ground and brewed in our Chemex—we pronounced it She-may—drip system.

When we returned from our "honey-burn," our landlord informed us that he would not be renewing the lease. We had to move out by May 31. Mary Jo was resting her head on my shoulder. She hadn't said anything in a while. I wondered what she was thinking.

Mary Jo

This is incredible. It's like I dreamed it would be, back in treatment.

I went out and bought some incense (I've missed things like that). I was hoping we would get close tonight. I'm kinda scared that I will be awkward, but I want to. I do love to touch him; he has such a sensuous body. I also know he might choose to reject me. But I want to try if I'm ever going to have a real man-woman relationship—and I do know the difference.

Here we are just like I imagined it; scented smell in the air, low lite candles burning, soft fire in the fireplace, and love songs playing on the stereo. I'm lying on the rug in front of the fire, close to my man, firmly—yet softly—caressing his body and kissing him all over.

This is the kind of sexual pleasure I feel I want between two people. And, after our disastrous honeymoon, I know he will be ready.

"Dan, what are you thinking?"

Dan

"I really like that timeshare concept. I wonder if they have that in Minnesota?"

Mary Jo turned her head to look at me.

"That's what you're thinking about? We've been evicted. Where are we going to live?"

I kissed her. "One day at a time, in fact, I think something has just come up."

I nuzzled her neck.

"You're the devil," she whispered as she undid the belt that held my robe together.

Breezy Shores Resort
Detroit Lakes, MN Spring 1982

Mary Jo and I were sitting in the office of the lead timeshare salesman—so he said—for a resort in northern Minnesota, not far from Fargo, North Dakota. I had seen a newspaper ad announcing the grand opening of the resort. Timeshare weeks were on sale. I called the number in the ad and made an appointment. We had dropped Matt off with Joni and Paul and headed northwest on I-94.

"So, Dan and Mary Jo, let me tell you about timeshare."

"Don't need to do that, sir, we know all about timeshare. We're here to buy."

"Well, young fellow, you just made my day. We still have a couple of weeks in prime time, beach access, two bedrooms upstairs, whirlpool in the private bath," he winked at me, "sleep sofa in the main room, kitchen…"

"We don't need to hear all that," I said, "what's the price?"

"These units are going for $4500 a week."

"All the units are the same, right? Two stories, whirlpool, blah, blah, blah, correct?"

"Yes, but not all have beach access. Some are off the parking lot; not much of a view."

"Here's the deal," I looked the salesman in the eyes, "two weeks, back-to-back, prime time in one of the units off the parking lot—$5,000 total for both weeks."

"You can't be serious? Are you?"

"Absolutely; look, those units are not going to sell, and by then you're going to dump them for $500 a week. We don't want to wait. We're willing to buy now. It's a fair offer."

"Why would you want a unit without a view or beach access? Your family and friends won't want to come up here with you. I know I wouldn't."

I looked at Mary Jo. "Who says we're going to come up here?"

We knew all about timeshare, especially the exchange program. We closed the deal.

Calini Beach Club

Sarasota, FL Spring 1983

We were sitting in the two-person Jacuzzi, which was next to the two-person shower stall in the master bedroom suite of the resort that we traded for, using our timeshare weeks in Detroit Lakes, MN. The resort was across from the beach, which practically ran the length of Siesta Key. Matt was asleep after spending the day on the beach helping me build sandcastles or chasing sea gulls.

"Ya did good, Dan," Mary Jo said, just before I nuzzled her neck.

We still own the timeshare after thirty-eight years. In all that time, we have only been to Detroit Lakes twice; however, we have been to some of the most prestigious areas of the U.S.—Hilton Head Island, Sedona, Florida (several times), Las Vegas, Reno, Lake Tahoe, Cape Cod, Virginia Beach, Park City, Palm Springs, San Diego, and the list goes on. That timeshare forced us to take a two-week vacation every year. It was a big hit with our sons, grandchildren, family, and friends.

Two High Achievers

My career seemed to be headed in the right direction. So was Mary Jo's. After I was fired from Schaper, Mary Jo stayed on. She was on maternity leave when I started at Augsburg. When she returned to work, she began hearing rumors that Schaper might be bought by a much larger toy company out east. Those rumors turned out to be true. Schaper was sold and the Minnesota location shut its doors for good. Before Schaper left Minnesota, Mary Jo quickly found work at a much larger toy company—Tonka—where she would become a rock star.

As Mary Jo's career took off, and travel opportunities increased, I became Mr. Mom. I would drop Matt off at daycare, a neighbor who lived a couple of houses up the street from ours. I would still take the bus to work. I would pick Matt up on my way home. I would make dinner for us. Sometimes we would go to Matt's Bar and Grill (the name was coincidental) and order hamburgers and fries.

In 1985 we decided to sell our home on Bloomington Ave. in South Minneapolis. We had discovered a new development in Plymouth, MN. It would be closer to Mary Jo's work. I would have to take a car to work, or to a Park and Ride location.

For Matt's fifth birthday we gave him a puppy. Not a Pound Puppy, but a purebred Cocker Spaniel we named Matthew's Lady Jennifer, or Jenny for short. Mary Jo and I were big fans of the Disney movie *Lady and the Tramp.*

Our home in Minneapolis sold in the spring of 1987. We began construction of our new home in May of that year. At Augsburg, I had created an early version of a blog. I had acquired some software for the 5250-WS. It provided the capability of adding text to the sign-on display. I wanted to encourage work-study students to log into the system first thing, before anything else. I would enter trivia, something about the current date in history. I would also tell jokes and silly stories.

When construction began on our house, I kept up a running dialogue of the process being made: *The ground has been graded, the foundation is in, the framing has started, etc.* I would never finish the blog.

First Class Comes with a Price

COMMON Conference, Texas Fall 1987

"Insert the latch into the buckle and tug on the belt to tighten it around your waist. If you're sitting next to a child, or someone who is acting like one..."

The flight attendant glanced at me as I made a feeble attempt, on purpose, to get my seat belt to latch. Matt, soon to be six years old, laughed before attempting to help me. Matt and I were flying in First Class—on steerage tickets.

Mary Jo's sister, Marci, and Marci's husband, Mike, had just moved to Texas. Although Marci was Mary Jo's sister, Marci graciously filled the role of grandmother for Matt—Mary Jo's parents having died by the time Mary Jo turned twenty.

I had signed up for the COMMON conference before I knew I would be working at SpaceCenter. I thought that going to Texas was a great opportunity for us to spend some time as a family with Mary Jo's sister.

"Mary Jo, Marci, and Mike would like a visit from us, especially Matt. Come with me."

"That sounds like a good idea," Mary Jo replied, not knowing that we would both live to regret it.

When we arrived at the airport, we were placed on standby. There were seats available, but not two together. I stood my ground. At the last minute two seats opened in the first row of first class.

It was common knowledge within Mary Jo's family that she and I were attempting to have another child—without success. Having heard this rumor, Marci did her best to help.

"Mike and I have decided to stay in the guest room, so you two love-birds can have the master suite as you get down to business, if you know what I mean?" Marci said with a wink, wink. "You will probably especially enjoy the Jacuzzi. It is meant for one, but two can use it—if you're creative." Wink, wink.

Later that night, Marci went out of her way to ensure the ambiance in the bathroom was just right for child making.

"The candles are giving off just the right amount of light, don't you think?" Marci said, putting the final touches to our romantic evening in the master bathroom where we would be sharing a one-person Jacuzzi.

When Marci left, I took off the robe she'd provided me, then slipped into the tub. Mary Jo followed suit, dropping the robe, which she had packed, before cautiously getting into the tub. In her best imitation of a sexy voice, she said to me, "Let's get this over with."

We had just gotten comfortable when the bathroom door opened and, using our camera, Marci took a couple of photos.

"You'll thank me later, when you're holding that new little one in your arms," Marci proudly exclaimed as she walked out and shut the door behind her.

That event, plus some major changes that occurred the following year, made sex a very low priority for Mary Jo and me. We did not have any more children.

The price of a first-class ticket does not come cheap on **The Blue Highway.**

A Night at the Opera

Plymouth, MN 1991

Mary Jo

I was hurt and angry about this commuting. I am getting tired of having to take care of everything. Matt is practically growing up without a father. I was so mad at Dan that I rejected his advances, and now I regret it. I can't believe I am doing this, especially after what I wrote in treatment.

I'm too afraid to give my man my idea of sexual pleasure, because it won't be the kind he expects. I'm afraid of being made fun of and being laughed at.

I want to make him happy, but I don't feel I can. I'm feeling alone. Maybe there isn't any man who would want the love I can give.

I am so disappointed because tonight I wanted to give him this pleasure. Now I don't have enough courage to. I'm mad at myself for being so sensitive.

I know that Dan isn't like other men. He is my rock. Why do I hurt him this way?

God grant me Serenity...

Dan

I didn't get it. I knew she was using sex to try and manipulate me. She knew me well enough by then to know that I couldn't be manipulated. The last time she rejected me, I turned away without a goodnight kiss. Rejection is hurtful enough, but it's worse when it's my wife doing the rejecting. I wanted to hurt her in return. It's been three years. I forgot how stubborn we both are.

I felt ashamed of myself. This isn't how a mature adult should act. In fact, sex is becoming the farthest thing from my mind; however, I did miss touching her, the good night kiss and holding each other before we fell asleep. I realized that I was only hurting myself.

I was hoping this opportunity in Wayzata would work out, no more riding **The Blue Highway**. I would be home every day and weekends too. We would be able to rediscover each other again.

God grant me Serenity...

Together

Is he snoring?

"Dan, Dan, wake up, you're snoring! Roll over."

"Huh? What, I don't snore."

I rolled over and fell back to sleep.

Two for the Road

Castel Gandolfo, Italy Spring 1999

I was working with a client on-site at their computer center located in Atlanta, GA. The client was a software development company and I had analyzed their application, making several suggestions that the customer implemented. We ran a basic test using the client's test data; everything worked, and the performance was greatly improved.

The client wanted to scale the application at various workloads. They contacted the Benchmark Center manager in Rochester, MN, to make an appointment. The Benchmark Center was booked out six months. My client did not want to wait that long.

"There is another benchmark facility in Rome, Italy," I suggested.

My client contacted **Charlie Farrell** and they were able to book the center for the next month. They asked if I was available, and it just so happened I was.

"So, here's the deal: the client wants to stay in Castel Gandolfo; it's about twenty miles southeast of Rome, and it's the summer home to the pope. There's a lake, it's very nice."

I was telling Mary Jo about my upcoming travel gig.

"Sounds exciting, Dan."

"Would you like to go with me? The last time I went I had lots of time after work. We could go out to dinner together when I get back to the hotel. You could take the train to Rome during the day. It's a short distance. Come back in time for dinner. I will probably be done early, maybe Thursday, Friday for sure. We can spend the weekend in Rome, fly back Sunday night, or Monday morning. What do you say?"

I touched Mary Jo's hand. "It could be a great opportunity to get away from family and friends and perhaps rediscover each other."

It turned out to be a nightmare—for both of us.

Charlie arranged for a limo to pick us up at the airport. We were driven to the hotel in Castel Gandolfo. We had some time to freshen up before dinner. Mary Jo plugged her 110-W curling iron into a 220-W outlet—it melted. First souvenirs we bought were a power converter and a new curling iron.

The next morning the limo driver picked us up. He dropped Mary Jo off at the train station and took me to the Benchmark Center. I spent the day helping the client attempt to get its software installed. Mary Jo spent the day getting lost.

Mary Jo, On the Go

I got off the train. Dan and I had found the train station—more like a bench—the day before, while we were out shopping for souvenirs.

I wasn't thinking when I plugged the curling iron in. Good thing we were both standing right there. Imagine burning down the hotel on our first overseas trip together.

I had my travel guides and new backpack purse I'd bought in Castel Gandolfo. I studied the map in the guide, recognized a street name—so I thought—and took off.

About two hours in, I realized I was lost. Nothing seemed familiar, nor could I find any of the streets that were on the map. Worse, everywhere I looked there were *Bars*—the word in big, bold letters on the sign above the door to the bar entrance.

Oh, shit, what have I gotten myself into this time? Every direction there's a bar, some streets have more than one, some have three.

Dazed and confused, I sat in an empty chair next to a small table in the street and cried. In between sobs, I used Dan's name and God's in the most unflatteringly way.

"Excuse, Señora. Caffe?"

I looked up, wiped my eyes, and said, "Pardon me?"

"Espresso? Cappuccino?" replied the server who had come out of the bar that owned the table where I was sitting. He then pointed at the sign.

I took a closer look. Underneath the word Bar, in smaller letters, was the word Espresso. It's a coffee bar, I thought.

"Yes, cappuccino," I said, placing my order. "Thank you."

My outlook improved as I drank the coffee. I studied my guidebook. I had a good idea where I was. I finished my cappuccino, paid the bill, and headed in the direction of the train station. But first there were some stops I wanted to make along the way.

Later That Night

We both got back to the hotel later than we thought we would. Mary Jo waited for me in the room. When I finally showed up, we decided to get coffee and dessert. We thought we would have to skip dinner, the time being so late—after 9:00 P.M. Apparently, that's when dinner starts in Italy.

We ordered some pasta and water—no gas. As we ate our food, Mary Jo told me what had happened.

"That seems scary to me. So, you didn't go right back to the train?"

"Nope, I stopped at the Temple of Antoninus and Faustina. It was fantastic. Then I saw several other temples: Saturn, Vesta, Castor, and Pollux. It was wonderful. I saw a couple of Forums, a Basilica, and I finished up with the Spanish steps. I then realized it was later than I thought, so I caught the train and here we are."

"What are you going to do tomorrow?"

"I am going to sleep in, relax in the hotel, maybe do some more exploring of Castel Gandolfo. I am beat."

After dinner we enjoyed a cappuccino and headed for the room and bed.

The next four days, Mary Jo divided her time between the hotel and going into Rome. I spent ten or twelve hours a day helping the customer, or working on other things, while they conferenced with their developers back in the States. At the end of the day, on Friday, the client finally had the software totally installed and ready for testing.

I spent Saturday morning analyzing performance data from the test runs. Mary Jo slept in. Unfortunately, due to the updating, the data had to be fully reinstalled between tests. The client and I decided that we would need a few additional days to complete all the tests. I suggested that we take the rest of Saturday and all-day Sunday off.

That afternoon Mary Jo and I explored Castel Gandolfo and had an early dinner.

"Mary Jo, I'm staying two or three extra days. Are you okay flying home by yourself?"

"It doesn't matter whether I'm okay or not, Dan. I must be at work. I have a job, too."

"I know. This trip wasn't quite what I expected."

"It's okay. This is a beautiful place and I'm glad we came. Let's go to bed early."

"Yes, Mary Jo, when in Rome do as the Romans do."

"You're the devil."

We went to bed.

On Sunday, Mary Jo and I took the train to Rome. Our first stop was the Coliseum where we met the client's team. Mary Jo had already seen it. She and I agreed to meet at another location, and I stayed with the client.

After meeting Mary Jo, she took me on a recap tour of the places she'd been, and we finished up at the Vatican. We took the train back to Castel Gandolfo and had dinner, followed by a cappuccino.

The next morning the limo driver took me to the Benchmark Center and Mary Jo to the airport where she returned home without me. This would become our norm when we traveled, both internationally and domestically.

Sometimes we would fly separately, both to and from the city where I would be working. Mary Jo would go on exploring without me. When Mary Jo returned to our hotel, she would wait for me so we could have dinner together. She would share her adventures and store-bought treasures with me. I would usually have one, maybe two days, at the end of the workweek when we could explore together.

We seemed to be finding a lot more to discover, instead of each other.

A Modern Family

Sedona, Arizona February 2000

Ron, Mary Jo's brother, and Joe (Ron's partner), Mary Jo and I were sitting at a small table in a realty office in Sedona. Earlier that day, the realtor had made several appointments at houses listed for sale. The four of us were on vacation in Sedona. It was Ron and Joe's first trip there. They fell in love with it. We thought it would be interesting to find out what we could get, based on what we thought we could afford.

We had found ten homes in a brochure we picked up while walking through uptown Sedona. After seeing the last house on the list, we concluded that none of the houses came close to what we currently owned in Minnesota. We thanked the realtor and were about to go our own ways, when she told us to wait a minute.

"Folks, that's your list; let me show you, my list."

We looked at each other, shrugged, and nodded our heads. The first home she took us to turned out to be the last home she took us to. The house was in an older neighborhood of Sedona known as The Chapel Area, named after a famous landmark—The Chapel of the Holy Cross, built in the early 1950s. The location was spectacular in terms of views—the number one requirement for Mary Jo and me. Our current home was in a newer neighborhood of Plymouth, MN, but the views were of a cul-de-sac in the front and the neighbor's garage in the back.

Other than the views, the exterior of the house wasn't much. Stucco, brick facade, square windows, tiled roof, surrounded by a wall that needed some work, and so on. In addition, the previous owner had begun renovations on the semi-circular driveway using brick pavers, but never finished. At first, we were not going to get out of the car. Before we could say, "Let's go see house number two," the realtor suggested we go inside.

As we approached the door, we noticed that it was copper plated with a design. We entered the house, and within five minutes decided we should buy it.

From the front door, we could look past the great room at a seventy-foot veranda running along the back of the house, and beyond that was a view of Cathedral Rock, the most photographed monumental rock in the world.

To our right was the front room/dining room combination. To our left was a hallway that led to the master suite. A smaller bedroom was across from the master suite and was adjacent to a second, full-size bathroom. As we entered the great room, we caught our breaths in unison as we looked at the floor-to-ceiling flagstone fireplace, which occupied the entire north wall.

The kitchen, on the other side of the fireplace, had an eating area and island. The countertops were all granite. Meanwhile, the realtor was reciting the specs from the realty listing.

"Three thousand square feet, master suite with bath and jacuzzi, guest suite with kitchenette and bathroom, two-car garage, lower-level storage room, etc. The house is currently in foreclosure; it has been on the market for two years; current asking price is…»

"That's less than what we paid for both our houses," I whispered to Mary Jo, referring to the total value of Ron and Joe's home, and ours—combined.

"I want this house," Mary Jo replied.

"What do you guys think?" I asked Ron and Joe.

"We want this house," they replied in unison.

We made an offer for less than the bank was asking. It was accepted. We were able to qualify for a loan for a second home. Now we only had to do two things: 1-sell our houses, and 2-tell Matt that we're moving to Arizona. Matt was still a senior in high school.

It was only February, plenty of time to get our house ready for sale. Famous last words. When we returned from vacation, Mary Jo was informed that her employer was closing the Minnesota division. If she wanted to keep her position, she would have to relocate to Wisconsin. That wasn't going to happen.

Then we got the news from Ron and Joe. When they returned from Sedona, they met with a realtor friend of theirs who offered to help them sell their house. It sold the first weekend it was listed. They would be out by the end of April.

Mary Jo looked at me and said, "If I'm going to be unemployed, it will be with Ron and Joe in Sedona. You'd best check with your boss to see if IBM Rochester will let you telecommute."

When I returned to IBM Rochester, I met with my manager, **Dan Heithoff.**

"Dan, I'm moving to Arizona. Does it matter if I work remotely 100 miles away or 1000 miles away?"

"No, I don't think so. But first you're going to China."

Freedom

The Flower Child
Mary Jo
Sedona, AZ Summer 2000

I was driving a van up a canyon road. I could see straight out from the driver's window, but I could barely see the ground below the window without sticking my head out. I wasn't going to do that. I knew there was a steep drop-off. I was afraid to take my eyes off the road in front of me, not exactly my ideal job. Hard for me to believe it was number four on my work fantasy list I put together for treatment back in 1979.

Fantasy Job Number 4: Working in a plant and florist shop, almost like an apprentice and working my way up. Sometimes I lack the confidence in myself to be a shrewd enough businessperson. Also, this is a lack of faith in the small—or large for that matter—business society of today.

I can't believe this. Here I am in Sedona, Arizona, and I am an apprentice in a florist shop. The owner of the shop also owns Chic Salon, where Ron works. They needed someone and Ron asked me. I said, "Why not?"

When we first moved out here, I decided not to work. It would be the first time since 1976 that I did not have a job—the year I met Dan—twenty-four years and no longer counting. I'm in for the long haul. So much has happened in our lives since then.

The decision for me now is do I keep working. We have been very successful; I certainly don't need to. Driving a van and delivering flowers is just an attempt to fill a void. I am finding that working in the yard at the new house is starting to interfere with this fun job.

I could offer to do Dan's laundry, underwear, casual clothes and stuff. He did his own while we both worked and raised Matt. He does have his dress clothes sent to the dry cleaners, which is okay with me. He gets reimbursed for laundry expenses. I will talk to him about it when he calls tonight.

I'm starting to enjoy this rediscovery plan of Dan's.

Two Cowboys
Ron and Joe

Mary Jo and I lived with Ron and Joe for six years, until they decided to build a new home about twenty miles away, in Cornville, AZ. Joe died from diabetes a month before they were scheduled to move. I was in Boston training a software engineer to be a database engineer when Mary Jo told me the news.

"Should I come home now?" I asked.

"Ron is okay. The service will be this Saturday, no need to rush."

I left on Friday and caught the flight to Phoenix. During the flight I jotted down a few notes. At the service Ron gave an excellent eulogy. There were tears, some sobs, and maybe a smile or two.

After Ron finished, a couple of other people spoke. The facilitator asked if there was anyone who cared to share his or her thoughts. I looked around and no one was getting up, so I did.

Ron and Joe had made several friends in the community. They attended many events, some of which Mary Jo and I attended, many I did not, mainly due to my frequent traveling. Mary Jo was a regular at the hair salon where Ron worked.

Ron was a very popular guy. Sometimes he introduced me to some of his colleagues, or perhaps to a client, but to many of Ron and Joe's friends I was a stranger. I took this into account as I began my eulogy.

"Hello, my name is Dan. Many of you might have heard Joe describe me as Mary Jo's other asshole."

Ron almost fell out of his chair. I kept going.

"Mary Jo and I are probably the straightest, most conservative couple in the world. Living with the most liberal gay couple in Sedona, and that is saying a lot, wasn't easy. We learned that there were many topics of conversation that should be forbidden at the dinner table—politics, current events, religion, work, just about everything that regular people might talk about. In fact, eventually there were only two topics that would not invoke rage, threats of violence, or physical dismemberment—the weather and poop. When we weren't talking about thunder and lightning, we were discussing the weather."

Mary Jo fell off her chair.

I said a few more things that kept the laughter going. When I finished, Ron gave me a hug. I had to repeat the performance in Minnesota, for family members.

I remember Ron carrying an urn containing Joe's ashes onto the plane. As Ron was taking his seat in the front row, he turned to me and said, "Don't let anyone tell you that Joe and I never traveled in first class."

We told Ron that he could stay with us; but, because the memories of the four of us living together depressed him so much, he moved out anyway. He lived alone for another six years before he passed away in 2012. I also eulogized Ron and, again, I had to repeat that performance in Minnesota. Ron didn't fly first class that time.

If Mary Jo and I had any regrets, it would've been that we never had the chance to watch *Modern Family* with Ron and Joe.

The Art of Bartering

Mary Jo
Shanghai and Nanjing, China
May 24 to June 2, 2002

This is probably the scariest thing I have ever done in my life—going to China.

We spent the weekend in Shanghai after flying for, what seemed to be, forever. We started from Phoenix and made stops in San Francisco and Tokyo before arriving. We stayed at the Okura Garden Hotel in Shanghai, our base for visiting museums and The Bund—the historical financial district in central Shanghai. We carried cards from the hotel that had the hotel's name and address printed in Chinese.

Dan and I met our IBM China host, Joy-E, at a teahouse in Shanghai. He ordered each of us a cup of flowering jasmine tea. When the tea came, he placed a jasmine bulb in each of the cups and then added the hot water. The jasmine flower popped out of the bulb and slowly grew until flowers were floating at the top of the cup.

I must buy some of this before we return home.

Later that day, Joy-E took us to a very popular fast-food place where they specialized in *dumplings*. People were lined up around the block. The dumplings were served in double-stacked baskets with covers to keep the dumplings hot. There were at least twelve dumplings in each basket. They were delicious.

The next day we had to leave for Nanjing on the train without Dan's luggage. When we arrived in Nanjing, we checked into to the Jinling Hotel and I unpacked.

The first thing Joy-E, Dan, and I did was go to a department store. There had to be at least a dozen clerks running around looking for clothes that would fit Dan. I was amazed at how small the people were. I am only five-foot-one, yet I felt like a giant.

Dan acquired two shirts, one pair of pants, and had to get by with the shoes he wore on the flight. He still has one of the shirts, which he now wears on special occasions, like Chinese New Year. Joy-E joined us for dinner.

"Dan and Mary Jo, I've heard from your colleague Steve. He has arrived but is too tired to join us. I thought after dinner we could go bowling, if you wish."

Bowling? There's no way. I once joined a bowling team and they asked me to quit. I wouldn't mind going to bed early.

"That sounds like fun, Joy-E. What do you think, Mary Jo?"

"Sure, Dan, sounds like great fun."

It was hilarious. Joy-E took us to a bowling alley. Some of his colleagues from IBM-China were there. Nobody was really very good, except for Dan—at least he was better than the Chinese guys. At one point, Joy-E was bowling with the ball in one hand, his phone in another, and a cigarette in his mouth. It was a very fun evening.

The next morning Steve, Dan, and I met Joy-E in the hotel lobby. He was with another Chinese gentleman.

"I am so sorry; I cannot take you around the city today as I suggested. Something important has come up for me at the office. I have taken the liberty of engaging the services of a guide to take you to some interesting places today. He speaks good English and will be both guide and interpreter. Mary Jo, Dan and Steve will be very busy the next few days. I have engaged the guide to be with you while we are with our customer. Will that be satisfactory with you?"

"Yes, I appreciate that Joy-E. Thank you very much."

Our guide took us to several interesting places, starting with the mausoleum for Dr. Sun Yat-sen, the first president of the Republic of China. To reach the mausoleum we had to climb 392 steps—it was 94 degrees and humid. We visited the Ming tomb of the first Ming emperor. We saw the Purple Gold Mountain and walked along the Sacred Way. We saw the Zhonghua Gate, aka the Gate of China, and the longest city wall in the world.

On Thursday Dan and Steve went to work. My guide took me to many more interesting sites. My guide was kind enough to take my picture with my camera. On Friday I was on my own. My guide wrote the names of two places—the Confucius Temple and the silk emporium—in both English and Chinese. I would be able to hand these to a taxi driver so they would know where to take me. My guide added the name of the hotel so I could find my way back.

As I was window-shopping at the emporium, my eye caught this cute little jacket. I walked over to the stall. The woman behind a table saw me examine the jacket and she said something in Chinese.

I said, "English?"

She shook her head. She then pantomimed putting the jacket on. I tried it on. The jacket was a perfect fit. I had to have it. I pantomimed how much is the jacket.

Yesterday, before my guide left, he told me that if I buy anything at the emporium, I should not pay the first price offered. I watched as the woman behind the table took out a calculator and entered a number. She then handed the calculator to me. I looked at the number and had no clue if it was good or bad. I divided the number by two, entered the new number, and handed her the calculator.

The woman suddenly held her arms up and wailed as if I had offered her a few pennies. She made such a commotion that women in the other stalls were starting to look at us. She quickly entered another number and handed the calculator back to me. I changed the number and, once again, handed her the calculator.

It got even worse. Not only did she make an even louder racket, but the other women also came over, looked at her calculator, and started making the same amount of noise. The woman punched in another number and handed the calculator back. I was catching on.

I looked at the number and then cried out, "Are you kidding me! My husband will divorce me if I spend this much money. No way can I pay this much!"

I punched another number into the calculator and handed it back. Once again there was much wailing and, I assumed, cursing. Another number was entered, and the calculator changed hands. I thought it was time to end this. I nodded my head, handed the calculator back, and counted out the money from my purse. The woman behind the stall was suddenly all smiles, nods, and bows as she wrapped the jacket and took my money.

I took my treasure and found my way back to the entrance where the taxis were lined up. The first taxi pulled up. I showed the driver the paper with the hotel name. He nodded and opened the rear passenger door for me. I got in and he drove me to the hotel.

That night the guys were supposed to go to an executive dinner. I would be by myself. When Dan returned to the hotel from work, he said I was invited to the dinner.

"Mary Jo, Joy-E says this is a huge honor. You will be the only woman there."

I decided to wear the jacket I'd bought at the emporium.

The restaurant was at least ten stories high; each floor had several rooms, each one occupied with diners. At dinner, we sat at a big, round table. The top of the table turned, allowing us to try different Chinese dishes. I wasn't very good with chopsticks. Dan would somehow pick up the food and place it on my plate.

"Joy-E, why is that older gentleman staring at me?"

Joy-E said something to the older gentleman who said something back to Joy-E.

"Mary Jo, he is the IT CIO for ABC. He says you have honored this dinner by wearing such an elegant jacket."

"Oh, please tell him 'thank you.'"

It was a wonderful trip, beyond my wildest dreams. Once again, I saw many things I've never seen; I went to places I've never been, did things I hadn't done, and met people I've never met—before meeting Dan. I think I'll keep him.

PART FIVE
THE IBMER

Sr. Consultant

Existing Skill Set:

He has an outgoing personality, is a self-starter, has project management skills and writing skills; plus, he knows PL/1, PL/MP, X.25, PL/MI, RPG/400, UIM/Help, APIs, SAM (Spies), TPST (Tips), Office/400, BGU, SQL, PDM, ADM, OCL, CL, DDS, SQL, APIs, X.25, and PC/Support. He has a strong understanding of RDBMS design and implementation.

He is articulate, presents and markets himself well. Most importantly he has shown an ability to work under pressure, to meet deadlines and tight schedules. He has application development capabilities and is familiar with several third-party software applications, including word processing (Word) and presentation software (MS Power Point).

He taught a Computer Aided Software Engineering (CASE) workshop. Is familiar with journal management, replication, and tuning. Has knowledge of customer service best practices. Has performed consulting at customer locations out of state.

Mastered performance management. He has in-depth knowledge of the AS/400 internals, specifically database, journaling, and communications. Has traveled internationally. Assisted several large customers installing Opticonnect.

SQL and Query Optimization

Welcome to IBM

Rochester, MN May 1998

I was sitting in the lobby at the entrance of the IBM facility in Rochester, MN. I was there to fill out an application for employment and then give a blood sample for the drug test. I had handed in my application to the receptionist.

After about fifteen minutes, my name was called. A woman in a nurse uniform was holding the glass door open. This door separated the lobby from a second lobby, which contained small conference rooms used for meetings, interviews, and such.

We walked past the second lobby and came to a wall where several plaques were hanging—awards, patents, etc. We took many twists and turns before reaching our destination—Nursing.

"Okay, Mr. Cruikshank, or should I call you Dan?"

"Dan's fine unless I faint, then you can call me crybaby."

"Ha, ha, this will only take a sec." She said as she stuck my arm and took some blood.

"I guess I picked the wrong day to start drinking again."

"Ha, ha, you're a riot. You're free to go."

I left Nursing, took a left to get to the hallway that connected Blue Building 003 to Blue Building 005, where I took a right and took the stairs to level three. It was only the second floor, but the basement level started at one. I took a left, then a right, and found my way to my new boss's office. The door was open, so I walked in.

"How did it go?" Dan H. asked.

"Fine, I guess."

Dan H. held out his hand. "Welcome to IBM, rookie."

I smiled. That summer I would turn forty-seven.

London, UK October 1998

A software development company, aka the customer, was having trouble with their overnight batch process. The application was in use by several companies in the financial industry. It wasn't a performance issue.

The application was written in RPG. Some of the customer's clients had experienced outages that resulted in a loss of data during the batch process that ran overnight. The customer was looking for a way to restart the application at the point where the interruption in processing occurred. The solution involved an old friend, two actually—journaling and **Charlie Farrell.**

I had spent a week in the UK helping the customer come up with a method for procedural restart. We took advantage of a journal function known as *commitment control* and a complementary bookmarking construct known as a *notify-object*—it isn't an actual object—it could be a file, data area, etc. Commitment control is a feature of journaling, aka transaction logging, that ensures the integrity of the data in the database, should the transaction not complete. The notify-object is used to store the last commit ID of a successfully committed transaction. When used together, they can provide a powerful method for restarting broken batch jobs at the point of failure.

In essence, as a batch job was running and updating data, journal entries containing before and after images of the row being changed were recorded in the journal object, which was normal. In the event of a job failure, any uncommitted database changes were undone, and the last successful commit ID of the transaction was bookmarked in the notify-object. Using the bookmark, with some minor program changes, allowed the customer's application to be resumed at the point of the last successful transaction update.

The change to the application was tested and worked to the client's satisfaction. The client now wanted to test the application in a simulated customer environment. In other words, run the application with a workload that their largest customer would provide. This would be done at the AS/400 Benchmark Center.

IBM Rochester had two facilities where customers could benchmark, or test, applications for issues such as optimal scalability, stress testing, etc. One was in Rochester, MN, U.S.A. The other was located just outside of Rome, Italy. Charlie managed the Italy Benchmark Center.

Rome, Italy October 1998

IBM offered their employees opportunities to take on long-term overseas assignments. The opening for a Benchmark Center manager in Italy was offered and Charlie took it. He now lived in Italy with his family. His kids attended an English language school in Rome. My client had signed up for the benchmark test in Italy and requested that I be there.

The test went great. The application was able to handle the customer's workload. We did various things to disrupt the application: unplugged cables to disk drives, turned the power on and off, etc. After each interruption the data was recovered and the application was restarted from the last successful bookmark.

Before returning home, the client, the IBM team, and I spent a day touring Rome.

The Optimizer Workshop

Rochester, MN Fall 1999

The workshop was highly technical. Jim and I provided instruction on the use of advanced tools for analyzing and optimizing SQL performance. The workshop was intended for system administrators and/or computer programmers, who were responsible for the design, implementation, tuning and maintenance of the integrated RDBMS of IBM's showcase computer system, introduced as the AS/400. Beginning in 2000, the AS/400 would go through several name changes: iSeries, IBM System I, and IBM i.

Since its announcement as the AS/400 in June of 1988, IBM marketing had made a near fatal mistake. They advertised the AS/400 as having a fully functional, self-administrating RDBMS. No DBA required—wrong. Well, to be honest, the AS/400 did not require a DBA if the customer did not use SQL, which was also available for the AS/400—at a fee—another mistake.

Most of IBM's customer base that would eventually move to the AS/400, already had several years of investment in applications developed in RPG/II and RPG/III—the most dominant—or COBOL, which was scarce. These customers had no desire, or need, to replace these applications with SQL procedures, or embed SQL within HLL programs. These applications worked just fine. IBM had provided a special environment where these applications would run without change.

Furthermore, if a customer wanted to take advantage of the new OS/400 operating system, they could migrate from the S/3x environments using the IBM suggested and well-documented approach. This opened a huge market for third-party companies to provide complementary offerings in either migration consultation and/or migration assistance.

In addition, the migration did not require the need to change the existing application's database file structures or access methods. In other words, they were free to continue to use antiquated database design (literally none for most customers) and data access methods—*record level access* (record-at-a-time) versus *set based access* (automatic blocking).

Those customers who understood IBM's vision of the future and were the first to venture into the world of SQL on the AS/400, like those brave, stoic pioneers who attempted to settle and tame America's west, perished like an open bottle of milk in a lukewarm refrigerator.

This could very well mean the end of SQL/400 on the AS/400, and, eventually, perhaps, lead to the end of the AS/400 itself. To avoid this disastrous event, IBM gave the integrated RDBMS, provided free of charge with the AS/400 (like its father the S/38), a new name—*DB2/400*. Changing the name coincided with IBM's plan to eventually provide a single, universal RDBMS that offered consistency across all IBM platforms—regardless of how many more name changes may occur.

Fortunately, a team of IBM DB2 and AS/400 experts, **Michael (Mike) Cain** and **Kent Milligan**, went to extraordinary lengths to address the situation. They developed the AS/400 SQL and Query Performance Tuning and Monitoring Workshop or, known by its acronym—SQLQRYPRFMONW (pronounced Sequel Query Performance Monitor What).

This was the workshop Jim, and I would initially be teaching in Rochester and then eventually all over the world.

The Mission

Jim and I were sitting in the office of Dan H. We were being briefed on our next assignment.

"So, let's make sure we have this straight," Jim was taking the lead. "You want us to impersonate teachers and provide training in relational database performance tuning, in hopes of luring the mythical, computer criminal genius known as The Database Engineer, to a workshop here in Rochester, MN. Once we feel confident that the DBE, as we have dubbed him/her, is an attendee, we will alert authorities that will then take him/her into custody, where he/she, will eventually spend the remainder of their existence in a prison for the criminally insane, or at a very large AS/400 customer location. Is that correct?"

"That's about it; you two are already considered the leading experts in AS/400 system and application performance tuning. Adding DB2/400 to your credentials isn't too much of a stretch."

"I don't know," Jim turned to look at me. "What do you think, pardner?"

"Will it be dangerous?" I was being facetious.

"No, the workshops will be held here in the white buildings, where the classrooms are. You will not be in any danger. We have even provided a new code, Double-Zero, should you need to call for help, without alarming the DBE or other attendees, in the classroom."

IBM used two-digit codes to announce critical events like blizzards, tornadoes or doughnuts (Code-41). The codes were only known by those who needed to know, which was every IBM employee working at IBM in Rochester, MN. Code-41 usually emptied every office.

"Will we need to create the workshop?"

"Negatory; Cain and Milligan, the DB2 guys, have put together the workshop and have done some pilot classes for a few select customers. Everything is ready to go. They just need a couple of presenters with performance skills to teach the workshop."

"How often will the class be offered in Rochester?" Jim asked.

"We're thinking four times a year."

"Will I be compensated for travel expenses?" I asked. "As you know I work from home in Plymouth, MN, a hundred miles away. I really don't want to drive back and forth every day."

"It depends. I will work with IBM Education, who will be adding the class to the current IBM educational offerings and setting the price. So, what do you guys think?"

Jim looked at me. I nodded.

"Sure, Boss, sounds like a great opportunity. What's next?"

"There's one more thing. Your number one objective is to identify the DBE. A secondary objective is to come up with a new acronym for the class."

"What's wrong with SQLQRYPRFMONW?"

Jim and I attended the workshop, along with several other prospects: IBMers and customers handpicked by Mike and Kent as potential instructors to take over the class. The class was divided into two parts: The *Art*, which was presented by Mike, and the *Science*, which was presented by Kent. I found the workshop to be extremely interesting, although quite lengthy. *This workshop will be very hard for one person to deliver, I thought.*

Jim and I were chosen to deliver the workshop. Jim would take over Mike's role and I would be Kent, as the science portion contained more performance details. We would call ourselves Mr. High and Mr. Low. We found out that we would not be the only instructors. Mike and Kent would continue to conduct the workshop—overseas.

Jim and I would be doing the Rochester, MN, version. We performed our first workshop in January 1999 at IBM Rochester. By spring, we would be taking the show on the road. In December 1999, I would be making my first solo appearance—at CFC in Simi Valley, California.

When we performed in Rochester, I would be reimbursed for my expenses traveling from Plymouth, MN, to IBM. I could expense meals, up to the allowed daily maximum for Rochester, hotel, and mileage. I would travel to Rochester Sunday night, stay at an IBM-approved hotel, and return home Friday afternoon. We usually finished the workshop by noon Friday, to accommodate customers with Friday afternoon flights.

One perk we offered for those who came to Rochester was a plant tour. This was usually done on Thursday afternoons, which meant that Jim and I could take the afternoon off since we didn't need to go. Unfortunately, it wasn't enough to get customers to come, especially those who wanted to train multiple employees. It would've been too costly to send three or more. Jim and I would discuss this at lunch.

"Jim, why would they need to train every software developer?"

"Theoretically, they don't. For most customers they would only need to send one. That said, big IBM would not want us to describe this workshop as DBA training, which it is."

"Ahhh, the marketing dilemma bites us in the ass. What if, when a customer asks if they can send more than one, we persuade them to have us come on-site?"

"That might work, except for labs. They would have to log in remotely."

"Maybe we could take a small AS/400 with us."

Our first travel workshop was in Ft. Worth, Texas. We loaded the labs onto a small AS/400 and had it shipped to the IBM office in Dallas, TX. We traveled on Sunday morning before the first day of class. That afternoon we met with an IBM counterpart who helped us set up the AS/400. The class went well, but we both agreed that shipping an AS/400 was a lot of extra work.

Our next travel gig was in Montreal, Canada; international, but not overseas. We treated this one like a performance gig. We did not ship an AS/400—we eliminated the labs. The first day we did questions and answers and used the information we gathered to customize the workshop. We strictly focused on the *Art*, and I did an overview of the Database Monitor. We were done in three days.

My excitement at accomplishing a successful workshop in a non-classroom setting was exhilarating. It was short-lived. Mary Jo called me the night before we were planning to return home and informed me, they'd decided to put Jenny, our Cocker Spaniel, down. She was no longer able to control her bowel movements. It was time; she was twelve years old and had lived a pretty good life.

Dad died a couple of days after Thanksgiving that same year. He was seventy-four. The following year, 2000, Mary Jo and I would move to Arizona. Matt was eighteen and opted to stay behind.

Hieroglyphics

Get Your Kicks with CICS (Pronounced Kix)
Spring 2000 to Spring 2002

The Agricultural Bank of China (ABC) was running a LOB application on a pair of AS/400s, the largest models available. ABC had migrated from big iron to the AS/400s. To handle the large workload, ABC separated the database from the application and moved it to another AS/400. They reconnected the application to the database using a product that was well known to the application developers—Customer Information Control System (CICS) or, in this case, CICS/400.

Steve Dahlby was the owner of the CICS/400 product. He had received a call for help from ABC. They were having performance issues with Steve's product. The current CICS development team was in Mexico. Steve called Dan H. for help.

"Dan, I need someone to go with me to China to help solve a performance issue. We must leave ASAP. Do you have someone available?"

"We just hired Dan Cruikshank; he also has a passport. Why don't you call him yourself and work out the details?"

"Dan Cruikshank, I thought he worked for IBM?"

"That's what everybody thought. It's a good thing we hired him."

Steve called me and we met for coffee in the cafeteria. After explaining the situation to me, Steve asked if I was familiar with CICS/400.

"I thought that was a big iron product. We can actually run that on the AS/400?"

"Yes, Dan, we have for some time. Not too many customers bought it."

"That's understandable; DSPF interaction is handled by the AS/400 OS. So, are they using OptiConnect as the bridge between the two systems?"

"Nope, CICS/400 doesn't use native IO."

"What does it use?" I asked Steve.

"SQL and DRDA."

"Holy shit!"

Distributed Remote Database Architecture, or DRDA, is an open group standard (originally designed by IBM) for allowing databases to talk to one another (reads, writes, etc). DB2 Multisystem was an optional part of OS/400 that allowed a single database to be distributed across systems—up to 32.

I wasn't aware of any customer that was distributing their DB2 database—until I engaged with ABC.

Beijing, China Spring 2000

It had been four years since the RISC systems were made available to customers. Many of the customers that used OptiConnect to buy time until the RISC systems were available continued to use it. For some, due to business growth, it was still a necessity; for others, they now had the capacity to merge the systems back together. They chose not to.

Besides using CICS/400, ABC was also one of the few AS/400 shops that used SQL as the vehicle for reading, writing, and manipulating data. Most of the customers who attended the DB2 optimization workshop were either using SQL from non-AS/400 clients—mainly Java, a platform independent programming language—or they had come from other systems that used SQL as the primary or only method for accessing data. The programmers at ABC were not the traditional AS/400 developers.

Those customers who grew up on the S/3x line of IBM computers were totally clueless when it came to SQL, let alone database optimization. These customers struggled in the workshop. Jim and I would spend most of our time helping them write the SQL needed to complete the labs. We eventually gave the attendees the lab scripts.

In addition, the workshop used a Java based application, Run SQL Scripts, which was part of iSeries Navigator (iNav—the AS/400 was now being called iSeries), to execute the SQL and display the result set.

Many of the AS/400 attendees would use the native "green screen" interface. Unfortunately, not a lot of IBM development dollars were being spent on ancient technology; so, by using non-graphical interfaces, these customers struggled to complete the labs. In this regard, ABC was far beyond the typical AS/400 customer when it came to SQL—they were just lacking database optimization skills.

I told you all of this to set the scene for what happened next.

Upon arrival at ABC headquarters in Beijing, Steve and I met with the customer and discussed our plans for attacking the problem. Steve, with the aid of the CICS/400 developers in Mexico, would review application performance data to identify where the bottlenecks were.

I would review the SQL and Query Database Monitor (DBMon) activity to identify the longest running SQL statements and what, if any, advisories might be available. DBMon captured query optimization information from any query, including OS/400 native queries and SQL, regardless of where the SQL statement originated.

Steve and I came to the same conclusion as to who the main culprit was—SQL—specifically: a lack of indexing.

I was standing in the front of a classroom staring at a couple dozen developers—most couldn't or wouldn't speak English. My IBM counterpart was with me to act as my interpreter, but he wasn't technical. Earlier that day, Steve and I found out that the customer wanted us to fly to Nanjing the next week. It was Friday. I had two hours to deliver a five-day workshop on database optimization.

I had a skill—or a gift—whatever you want to call it. When I read technical manuals, or sat in a technical lecture, my mind would translate what I was reading, or hearing, into pictures—circles and squares. I have been doing this since I can remember.

In addition, I had a speech impediment. I spent one day a week during first and second grade, attending speech class to overcome a lisp. As a kid, I was humiliated by it and barely spoke a word. As an adult, I spoke softly but carried a big stick—a magic marker. I proceeded to draw some diagrams on the white board that was in the classroom (you can find an example of the chart in the appendix).

As I drew, I spoke to the Chinese IBMer/interpreter, slowly and softly. The IBMer translated my words, quickly and easily.

"You have many large tables. They contain many rows of data. Let's call one of these tables—T1"

I drew the table and added some data into the columns.

"You write a query requesting a single row."

I wrote the SQL statement in the upper left corner of the white board.

"You know that the values of ID are unique. DB2 doesn't know what you know."

There was a question. My counterpart spoke to me.

"Dan, does DB2 on the AS/400 not have database statistics?"

"Yes, it does, but unlike other database products, the AS/400 version of DB2 cleverly obtains the statistics from indexes or constraints. Unfortunately, if there isn't an index or constraint over the column in the WHERE clause, then DB2 must guess at how many rows will be returned by the query."

I caught a nod or two.

"In addition, because there isn't an index, DB2 only has one method to read the data and produce the result set—SCAN."

I wrote SCAN above the table and added an arrow showing the table scan.

"The row with the ID value equal to 370 is the very last row in the table. DB2 must SCAN the entire table, gazillions of rows, to find that one row."

Another question was asked.

"Dan, the developers say that during testing the runtime were very fast, even with large amounts of data. How do you explain this?"

"The AS/400 processors are very fast, and you have a large amount of memory. When you test a single query, DB2 can use all available memory and multiple processors. Unfortunately, in production there is more than one query being run at the same time. They all must share the same space. It is going to take longer."

"What must we do to fix this?"

"The solution is easy. Create indexes or constraints that match the WHERE clause selection columns. The first thing that the DB2 Optimizer will do is check to see if any indexes or constraints exist over those columns. DB2 can now make an *informed* decision on what is the best way to process the query—SCAN or PROBE."

As I talked, I wrote PROBE across from the row containing the value 370 in the ID column, along with an arrow pointing to a single row.

"The value 370 is in the last row of the table. The optimizer could not find any additional occurrences, so it chose to retrieve the *relative row number* (RRN) from the index and use that to PROBE the table. Now it will be very fast. A constraint is much better."

"Why should we use a constraint?"

"You must tell DB2 what you know. Just because there is only one value does not guarantee to DB2 that this will always be the case, unless there is a constraint, such as a primary key, that guarantees uniqueness."

Normally, during an SQL optimization workshop the difference between SCAN and PROBE was covered on Day-1, typically involving three or four labs and most of the day.

We were out of time. I was sure I would be back, and I was right. Steve and I returned a couple of times a year over the next two years. After reviewing the database monitor data during the next trip in 2001, I noted that there wasn't a single DB2 performance issue. All the current issues had to be resolved by Steve and his team.

Saturday of the first trip, Steve and I visited the Forbidden City. We made plans to tour the Great Wall on our return to Beijing. On Sunday, we flew from Beijing to Nanjing. From there we drove to a small city of five million or so. We attended a meeting there and then returned to Nanjing for another meeting.

Our IBM counterpart informed us that ABC was satisfied with the recommendations we had made and did not see a need for any more meetings. From Nanjing we drove to Shanghai, where we booked flights back to the U.S. I never saw the Great Wall, nor would I see it in any of the dozen or so return trips I would make to China.

I returned to ABC in 2001 and 2002. Mary Jo came with me on that last trip.

Going Solo

Fall 2002

Jim took the latest early retirement plan being offered from IBM around 2002. IBM offered a great package and Jim couldn't resist. The package included free training in a new career. Jim chose a course on how to charter sailing cruises.

I was on my own. Not that I hadn't traveled on my own, but it was nice to have someone to spend dinner with. Jim also made sure that we did not put in overtime, something I was notorious at.

Moscow, and How

Red Square Moscow, Russia October 2006

I was sitting at a small table in the lobby of the Metropole Hotel. I had just completed my first day of the SQL optimization workshop. The lobby was the only place in the hotel where WiFi was available. It was a Monday night, disco night in Russia. I knew this because several women in little, black dresses kept walking by. I heard someone talking to me. I turned to see a woman wearing an extremely short dress standing next to me.

"You want woman?" she asked.

"I'm sorry. I don't dance."

"Ha, ha, ha, you are very funny American; you get special rate, half price, da? I show you dance."

She thrust her hips at me—a universal gesture I've seen in several countries by women of the evening who did not speak English. I guess she doesn't have to draw me a picture.

"I'm sure you're an excellent teacher, but I must refuse. I have much work to do."

She made another universal gesture with her middle finger and walked away. I closed my laptop and headed upstairs to my room. So much for email, it can wait until morning.

The Prior Friday

I didn't think I was going to make it to Russia. A request for an on-site optimization workshop had come to my manager (I no longer reported to Dan H.) from a Russian IBMer, located at the IBM facility in Moscow.

"We need this workshop immediately. Many of our most important AS/400 customers are asking for this information. We have no one here to do it. You must help us."

My manager checked to see if I was online. She sent me a text urging me to call her about my availability. When I confirmed I was available she told me to begin making travel arrangements. Most importantly, I needed a visa in order to enter Russia.

I checked my passport and noticed there were several blank pages in the back. I went online to the visa web site, filled in the blanks with my travel information and printed out the mailing labels for the shipping company. I went with the 72-hour turn around offered by the San Francisco visa fulfillment location, as that was closer to my home in Arizona.

I made airline reservations. I would fly out of Phoenix on Saturday, October 14, arriving in Moscow on Sunday, October 15. The workshop was scheduled for Monday thru end of day on Friday, October 20. My return flight would be on Saturday, October 21.

Kent had been to Moscow and suggested I stay at the Metropole on Red Square. I normally would've stayed closer to the IBM location; however, how often do I get to go to Moscow? I booked the Metropole.

On Monday, October 9, I received a call from the visa provider.

"Mr. Daniel Cruikshank, I am sorry to inform you that you do not have any valid visa pages in your passport. We will need to add additional pages. This will delay our promised delivery date."

"I don't understand. I checked my passport, and I was sure there were several blank pages available. Is this not the case?"

"There are blank pages, but these are not valid for Visas. They are for additional information, if needed."

"I was hoping to have my passport back by tomorrow. How soon can you get the passport to me?"

"We cannot guarantee the exact date, but we need three days to add the extra visa pages and then complete the visa process. We can ship it overnight on Friday, October 13, to arrive first thing Saturday morning. That is the best we can do."

The next two days I was a nervous wreck. Even if the passport arrived at my house Saturday morning, I still had to get to Phoenix to catch my flight. It was approximately a two-hour drive from my home in northern Arizona to the airport. I made an executive decision.

I booked a Friday morning flight from Phoenix to San Francisco. I arrived just before noon. I took the train from the airport to downtown San Francisco. I found the visa location and waited there for my passport. I then took the train back to the airport and returned to Phoenix. I stayed overnight at the Hilton Airport and caught my flight on Saturday. I even had time to have dinner at the San Francisco airport before flying back to Phoenix.

Moscow, What Now?

I arrived in Moscow some time on Sunday, October 15. I took a bus from the airport to the Metropole. Kent had also suggested I book a car at the hotel, rather than driving a rental. I was able to make those arrangements at the hotel front desk when I checked in.

The next morning, I was in the lobby at the scheduled time. A man dressed in a black suit came through the hotel doors and approached me. I think I was the only person in the lobby. He introduced himself and asked if I was Mr. Cruikshank. I said yes and he turned around and gestured with his hand that I was to follow him.

We got into a black sedan and he drove me to the IBM location. It took about an hour. When we arrived, I asked if he would be here at 5:30 P.M. to pick me up. The workshop was scheduled from 9:00 A.M. to 5:00 P.M., Monday thru Friday. He confirmed it.

After the workshop, I packed up my laptop and headed for the pickup location. I arrived there about 5:15 P.M. It was cold out. I realized that I wasn't dressed properly for Moscow in October. I was wearing my business suit.

I checked my watch—5:45 P.M. I noticed a couple of dark sedans parked further away. They were both running. I walked in that direction. As I got closer, a door opened and a person I did not recognize got out of the car. He approached me.

"Mr. Cruikshank?" he asked.

"Yes, that is me."

He introduced himself as the brother of the other driver, who could not get here to pick me up. "Some other activity; I will be your new driver."

I got into the sedan and we drove away. I thought I would never see my home again.

My new driver brought me to the hotel without incident. I thanked him and wondered who was picking me up tomorrow.

Code Hard: With A Vengeance

Center City, California, U.S.A.

I was sitting with several men in a conference room, located within the 20th Century Studios building. One of the guys was telling me about the building's history.

"So, the towers are about three-quarters complete, and one of the executives decides to use it in a movie."

"Do you mean Die Hard, with Bruce Willis?" I asked.

"You got it. This room was under construction at the time. Bruce probably ran through here barefoot, cutting his feet on broken glass."

"I guess he finally left his footprints on Hollywood Boulevard," I quipped.

The guy laughed. The other guys smiled at us, probably not getting the joke or, more likely, they didn't care for the movie. They were Russians, and they were responsible for the application I had reviewed. I was set to deliver my findings.

"So, you will tell us what is wrong with our code, da?"

"Yes, but theoretically there is nothing wrong with your code, per se. It is the way you are using OPNQRYF."

"The IBM command for queries?"

"Yes."

"I knew it!" The guy slapped hands with his cronies. "So, you will fix this piece of shit, smart guy from IBM."

"I can tell you how to fix the problem, but OPNQRYF is working as intended."

"That isn't possible. You have just told us that it is the command, and the command is IBM's, not ours. You must fix it."

Was that the sound of a safety being released?

"Let's review the issue. You complained the batch job, running overnight, is taking too long. It doesn't complete in time, so the morning crew is waiting for it to finish before they begin their work. Is that right?"

"Yes, but you said it is an IBM command issue, not our program's issue. Fix it now."

"Yes, I did. I captured performance data from last night's run and discovered that every time this OPNQRYF command runs, it builds a temporary index, which takes twenty minutes. After ten minutes, the same OPNQRYF command is run again, and it creates the temporary index again. This repeats several times during the entire run."

"OPNQRYF isn't our command, it is yours, Mr. IBM Guy, and you will fix it. You will not leave until this is done and the batch run is improved, understand?"

"Okay, I can fix it, but I must have access to the production machine so I can create an index which I believe will solve your problem."

"You want to access our production system? Such a thing is not possible during the day. Can this not wait until the weekend?"

"Do you want to wait another three days and pay me to sit around, drinking coffee, talking about Bruce Willis movies, at $10,000 per week?"

"We cannot allow you to do this on our production machine. Creating indexes is very time-consuming and cause problems for everyone. We have no idea how long it will take to create this index."

"It will take twenty minutes," I said.

It took about half an hour, due to the other activity running on the system. That night the batch job completed in two hours, about six hours before the morning shift would begin work. I left without getting Bruce Willis's autograph.

The Small World

Brazil, SA July 2003

I arrived in Sao Paulo at the International Airport. From there I took a one-hour bus ride to a domestic airport where I met my IBM counterpart. She had made my travel arrangements. From the domestic airport we flew to a smaller city in central Brazil.

The customer was experiencing performance issues when attempting to utilize embedded SQL in their applications. Embedding SQL is a term used to describe the process of executing SQL statements from within a compiled program object. During the compilation process, the SQL statements are converted to internal API calls. These calls are made directly to the SQL optimization engine. In other words, they are optimized the same way as an SQL statement executed dynamically.

At the end of the week, my colleague and I caught a domestic flight back to Sao Paulo. By the time we collected our luggage, my colleague said, "Hurry, Dan, we have less than an hour to make your flight at the international airport."

She flagged a taxi and explained the situation. We left the domestic airport. I remember my colleague encouraging the driver to hurry up in Portuguese. She obviously made her point. The driver literally drove on sidewalks as he weaved in and out of the traffic and pedestrians.

I made my flight with minutes to spare. My first-class seat was still available.

The New Mr. Low

Argentina SA

When I agreed to become an instructor for the database optimization workshop, I believed I would be doing it for a couple of years. That was not to be. I would continue to teach the course until I retired, either solely or sometimes with another performance expert.

Mike and Kent were not as active in the workshop, as they had become involved in strategic planning. I enlisted a member of my team, **David Lewis**, to become Mr. Low during standard optimization workshops—the section that covered detailed performance topics, typically the last half of the workshop. Dave and I would do our last workshop together in Argentina.

I made a total of three trips to Argentina, all to Buenos Aires. It was during one of those trips that Dave accompanied me. We had a day to kill before returning home. We spent most of the day walking, terminating at a sidewalk restaurant across from a famous cemetery—lots of tombs and crypts to check out.

Shortly after we sat down at a table our server arrived. She was very attractive, like many of the women I met in Buenos Aires.

When the waitress approached the table, I said, "Buenos tardes, señorita."

The waitress sized us up as North Americans, and responded, "Good evening, sirs, can I take your orders?"

Her English is impeccable, so much for my Spanish.

"Yes, I will have a hamburger and a Coke, please."

"I will have the same," Dave responded.

I was impressed with her English. The waitress left and we talked and studied the graveyard until she returned with our orders.

"Thank you." The waitress turned to walk away. "Oh, miss, excuse me, but I have a question. If you don't mind?"

I spoke slowly and enunciated each word.

"Yes, what is your question, sir?"

"You speak very good English. Did you learn it here in school?"

"No, I'm from America, originally."

"Oh, that it explains it, I guess. What part of America?"

"I grew up in Golden Valley, Minnesota."

"No way! I grew up in St. Louis Park, Minnesota. We were neighbors."

"I'm from southern Minnesota," Dave chimed in.

It's such a small world.

The Case for the Missing DBE

The Check Engine Light

Seoul, South Korea Winter 2004

I was working from home when a call came in from **Anil Madan**, who was currently on-site at Hyundai of South Korea. The AS/400 check engine light had come on and he wasn't quite sure what to do.

"I best come on-site," was usually my first response. It was Friday. I booked a flight to Seoul and was outbound on Saturday. I barely had time to kiss Mary Jo goodbye.

The Hyundai software developers were utilizing APPC and embedded SQL within a COBOL program running on an AS/400 to retrieve data from an IBM big iron system. The SQL result set was stored in a host array, a working storage area defined within the COBOL program.

The problem that caused the check engine light to come on was the expected results obtained by the SQL query were not correct—so they assumed. The Hyundai software developers wanted to know why.

First, there was no check engine light that came with the AS/400. That was just me taking liberties because the customer was a car manufacturer, and I would come to own a Hyundai Genesis. Second, back when I was teaching myself SQL, I wrote an APPC program to test the efficiency of returning result sets from one computer to another. Although I used RPG as my programming language of choice, the process was the same.

After a few tests, I was able to isolate the problem—the AS/400 tire pressures were low. Not really, although the analogy of the check engine light is appropriate. When an SQL error occurs, an error code is sent to the calling program, in other words, the internal check engine light or SQL Error Code, comes on. It is the programmer's responsibility to check the error code value after retrieving the result set to determine the next steps. An empty result set isn't an error.

Information about the check engine light is returned in a separate structure referred to as the SQL Communications Area (SQLCA). The programmer needs to validate the return code. A positive return code (e.g., 0, 100, etc.) indicates a successful execution of the SQL statement.

Any data returned replaces any data that is currently stored in the host array. The positive code of 100 indicates the SQL statement executed successfully, but no data was returned as a result of executing the query. In this case, the host array remains as is.

The programmers were not checking for code 100. They assumed that the host array would be cleared. Wrong. The previous results still existed, giving the appearance that wrong data was being returned. The solution was to check for SQL code 100 within the program code and clear the host array using the proper COBOL instructions, if this condition was true.

The New Model

I was at Hyundai in South Korea. They had requested that I come back for two weeks to review their SQL statements, due to a new problem. In this case, there was no check engine light. This involved a change to the engine itself—the AS/400 Query Engine.

In the beginning, when IBM created the AS/400, the engine used to optimize a query (SQL, OPNQRYF, AS/400 Query, etc.) was referred to as the *Optimizer*. Around the turn of the century IBM introduced a new query engine that did not replace the old engine—there were now two optimizers. To distinguish between the two, the old optimizer was referred to as the Classic Query Engine (CQE). The new optimizer was named the SQL Query Engine (SQE). There were two major differences.

The first difference, as the name implies, was that SQE optimized SQL statements only. This would change in the early teens of the twenty-first century. The second, more significant difference was that SQE was developed below the MI—at the hardware layer. CQE was developed above the MI—it remained part of the OS.

Those who followed the AS/400 knew that anything developed below the MI as System Licensed Internal Code (SLIC) was very slick indeed. By that, I mean not only fast, but it added a bushel-load of new bells and whistles. SQE came with database self-tuning features—say goodbye to Dan.

Not so fast, I'm not dead yet.

The problem Hyundai was experiencing occurred after an upgrade to the latest OS on their production system. Suddenly, business reports containing summary lists were no longer appearing in the correct order.

The following is an example of a summary SQL statement:

SELECT CountryID, SUM(Qty) AS Total_Qty, SUM(Sales) AS Total_Sales, COUNT AS Total_Items

FROM Table1

GROUP BY CountryID

Before the upgrade the result set contained one summary entry for each distinct value in the CountryID column and the CountryIDs were in ascending order.

"Dan, can you explain to us what happened?" asked the attractive Korean IBM customer service representative, who spoke English better than I could.

"In the U.S. we call this a 'happy accident.' To explain this, I must describe the optimization sequence of events. The Optimizer has but one goal—minimize the cost of the query. It does this by eliminating IO. It considers many factors including the speed of the disk drives, the amount of memory, the speed of the CPUs, the day of the week, ..."

"No, it doesn't, Dan," interjected the IBM customer representative.

"You're right, I am exaggerating to make a point. The CQE optimizer wasn't as smart as SQE. As it optimized the query, it considered the environmental attribute of the query, which happened to be *ALLIO. In other words, the optimizer was free to choose all methods. It determined that the use of an index, keyed on CountryID, Qty and Sales, was the most efficient way to return the entire result set. All the data it needed could be found in the index—no need to access the underlying table."

"Why did this change?"

"The new optimizer, SQE, has improved statistical measurements and methods in which to gather the information it needs to make a better implementation method decision. It chose to use parallel techniques to read the data from the tables and then merge the threads into the result set. The SQE optimizer had no reason to return the results in any sort of order."

"But the results should have been in CountryID order, the way they were before the upgrade."

"Neither Optimizer knew that. There was no information in the SQL statement that specified a particular order. GROUP BY does not define the order of the result set. The data was in order by CountryID because the CQE optimizer chose to use an index to complete the query. The index happened to be in the order desired. It was just a happy accident."

"I don't understand."

"The SQL Architecture states that there is no guaranteed order of the result set without specifically defining the sort order by use of an ORDER BY clause. If the SQL statement had this clause, then SQE would have created a plan that ensured the result was in order based on that clause. To ensure order, you must add the ORDER BY clause like this."

I wrote the correct statement on a white board that was in the conference room.

```
SELECT CountryID, SUM(Qty) AS Total_Qty,
SUM(Sales) AS Total_Sales, COUNT AS Total_Items

FROM Table1

GROUP BY CountryID

ORDER BY CountryID
```

The query was run, and the result set contained one summary entry for each distinct value in the CountryID column and the CountryIDs were in ascending order.

The Code Slingers

Boston, MA Fall 2005

I was sitting at a workstation in the Computer Center of a large retailer of office supplies aka The Customer, located in the Boston area. The Customer was having some system performance issues. They were a large IBM user, having several AS/400s along with a few IBM big iron systems and several PCs. The combined processing power of the five or six, maybe seven, AS/400s they owned, equaled, or exceeded, the total processing power of all the other systems.

Converting the AS/400 to RISC and utilizing PowerPC 64-bit processors made the AS/400s capable of executing billions of instructions per second (IPS). For example, the performance analysis reports all had to be changed to report in nanoseconds (one-billionth of a second) instead of microseconds (one-millionth of a second) otherwise the reported values were zero. The new AS/400s rocked.

Unfortunately for The Customer they weren't rocking, and they strongly made their disappointment known to IBM upper management. Like they say, shit rolls downhill, so there I was.

The initial problem was hardware related. IBM Rochester had identified the problem, provided a solution, and things were back to normal. To appease The Customer, IBM offered to send a performance expert on-site free of charge to review the current systems under the service offering known as a System Health Check. I was available.

So, here I was, minding my own business, completing my summary report, when my body suddenly stiffens. I turned around in my chair. There were three guys standing in the doorway. They had a look I remember from my childhood days. Tough guys. Only these guys were worse. They were computer programmers, RPG/400 code-slingers, based on the way they stood—loose, ready for action.

"You the performance guy from IBM?"

"Yes, can I help you?"

"You that Cruikshank guy, wrote all those BS stories like SQL being better than RPG?"

"Yes, I have written several articles about SQL and RPG performance. Most of my articles are about the differences in data access methods—set at a time, used by SQL, versus record at a time, used by high level languages such as RPG."

"Whatever; still bullshit. SQL is shit."

"What makes you say that?"

"Here's the deal: we have an application, batch job, runs overnight, taking too long. End users are getting upset. I read one of your articles. In it you talked about blocking, how SQL takes advantage of these new instructions, and shit like that. I thought I'd give it a try. Wrote an SQL INSERT statement. We had to manually kill it after two days."

"A simple INSERT statement shouldn't take that long. There must be more to it than that. Was this an INSERT with a sub-select?"

"See, that's the problem with you PhD rocket scientists and all your bullshit talk. We're just RPG programmers. We don't know a sub-select from a fucking submarine."

"Listen. I don't have fancy college credentials. I was an RPG programmer like you guys. I was lucky to get a job with IBM where I was taught how to measure AS/400 performance, specifically the performance characteristics of different HLL programming products. It sounds to me like your INSERT statement has a complex SELECT, defining the data set to be inserted. Is that the case?"

"Yeah, I didn't know that's what it was called. To be honest, I did some more research, read another of your bullshit articles. It talked about using an index to improve the performance of an SQL statement. Are you shitting me? A fucking index?"

"Did you try creating an index based on the columns, I'm sorry, fields defined in the WHERE clause of the sub-select?"

"Okay, let's get right down to the issue. Yes, I created a logical file with key fields matching the fields in the WHERE clause. It made a fucking difference, but it still took three times as long as the RPG program being used. I did some more reading, tweaked the LF, and even added another. Got it down to six hours. That is still way too fucking long. When I heard you were here, on-site, I couldn't pass up the opportunity to tell you to your fucking face what I think of SQL and your bullshit."

"Hey, I appreciate you coming to tell me face to face. I respect you for that, more than you know. Just one more question. Did you use Visual Explain (VE) to visibly show how the SQL statement will be implemented?"

"Say what? Visual Explain? What the fuck is Visual Explain?"

"It's a tool used by database engineers to understand an SQL's access plan. Do you have the SQL statement? I have the VE tool. I can explain it to you."

He looked at the other members of his gang, who shrugged.

"Sure, here you go."

He handed me a sheet of paper that had the SQL INSERT statement written on it. I brought up the Run SQL Script tool. I typed the SQL statement into the tool, checking my typing several times to make sure I got it right. My laptop was connected to one of the customer's AS/400 test systems. This system was used for Quality Assurance (QA) and had a complete set of production data.

I checked the tool settings and ensured I was in explain-only mode. This setting allowed me to start the SQL Query; however, the SQL Optimizer will stop once optimization is complete, kill the query process, and display the SQL Access Plan in a VE diagram, basically circles and squares, a language I fully comprehended. When the VE diagram completed, I wasn't too shocked.

Just what I suspected; the query plan is being generated by the CQE optimizer.

The VE diagram clearly showed the steps the SQL engine will take to implement the SQL INSERT statement. Since the insertion of data into a database is done by a single instruction, the VE diagram only showed the plan for the sub-select. It was a four-table join using indexes to retrieve that data. The plan included the creation of a temporary index, the first clue that this might be CQE. The icing on the cake was the subtle differences in the diagram shapes used for CQE versus SQE. The implementation was terrible. I explained the Explain to the complaining code-slinger.

"So, because it is using CQE, and because there is a JOIN involved, and because the optimizer has decided that an index join would be the fastest way to complete the query, the optimizer has decided that it must create a temporary index to satisfy the join-by-index requirement. As you can see, the estimate to run the query is very time consuming, most likely due to the creation of the temporary index."

"Cut the crap, CQE, SQE, FQE, who gives a shit? Are you saying that I need to create another LF?"

“It depends. I think we should first determine why the CQE optimizer is being used. CQE was introduced on the S/38 in 1987. It’s ancient. Is it possible that one of the files on the FROM clause is an LF?”

“Yes, they all are.”

“Okay, let’s change the FROM clause to use the underlying base table names. Do you know the names of these tables?”

“What’s a base table?”

“My bad; in AS/400 speak, they are physical file objects or PFs.”

“Oh, okay, here you go. I thought we needed to use the LFs because they contain the sort keys and such.”

“My colleague, Mike, always says, ‘Don’t tell DB2 what to do, tell it what you want.’ For example, if you want the query result set to be in a certain order then just code the sort order in the ORDER BY clause and let DB2 figure out how to order it.”

I replaced the LF names with the base table they referenced. An LF on the FROM clause of an SQL SELECT statement forced a CQE implementation. I had hoped to get a much better implementation plan by allowing DB2 to use the new SQL Query Engine (SQE). (Shortly before I retired, SQE was enhanced to optimize SQL statements, which referenced LFs.)

“Okay, that should do it. You guys ready?”

The code-slingers nodded in unison. I checked the settings, double-checking for Explain Only—I didn’t want the query to run. I pushed the button. The plan appeared very quickly. I noticed two things right away: the plan had changed, and the symbols were SQE types.

“It’s different. Let’s check the estimated run time. It appears to be, ummm, 27 seconds. Well, we got the optimizer to use SQE, which is good. Let’s see if there are any advisories; perhaps we can make it better.”

I was yammering to hide my shock. This couldn’t be right. Was it 27 minutes? That would still be impressive.

I looked again. I was about to bring up the index advisory display, when the lead code-slinger stopped me.

“Run it.”

“Okay, but let’s just check the index advisory first. The estimate doesn’t account for system usage…”

“Run it.”

“Let’s keep in mind that it is only an estimate. It’s possible that there is a huge discrepancy in the amount of the data on this machine, versus the production machine."

"RUN IT."

"Sure."

I pushed the Run button. The hourglass symbol appeared. My brain was working overtime.

What do I do if this takes forever? Get up fast, push the chair behind you. That should hamper the middle guy. Spin right, take out the guy on your left, then an elbow to...

The hourglass symbol went away. A message appeared at the bottom of the display: SQL Query completed successfully. I displayed the Joblog. There was a message stating that many rows were inserted into... Another message read: Actual run time 57 seconds.

I turned around and faced the code-slingers. They were staring at the display. They had the same looks they'd had when they first came in. The middle code-slinger turned around and walked out of the room, followed by the other two.

There were two members from operations in the room who had been quietly watching the entire event.

"That was incredible," one of them said.

"I thought I was done with my report summary," I said. "I guess not."

I went to the bottom of the Executive Summary paragraph of the report I was working on prior to the visit by the code-slingers and added the following:

Recommendations

> It is strongly recommended that the position of Database Engineer (DBE) be created and filled when feasibly possible. This should be considered as one of the highest priority action items. As this is an emerging role for the administration of the AS/400 RDBMS, known as DB2, it is highly possible that a person with the requisite experience, as described in the Addendum, may not exist. IBM can assist in the training of the best possible candidate and provide interim support as needed.

Sedona, AZ January 2006

I got a call from the chief database architect (CDBA) for The Customer.

"This is Dan," I spoke into my phone.

"Hello, Dan. I'm the CDBA for DB2 here at the supply company. We met last November in Boston. You had recommended that we hire a database engineer. Is that right?"

"Yes, it is. I remember you. So, have you begun looking for a candidate?"

"We have and we've made an offer. The candidate has accepted. They can start in two weeks. I was calling you to take you up on your offer of training. We had to settle on an individual that is already an employee, has good communication skills, knows the business and the AS/400, but isn't strong in SQL or DB2. We're hoping your training program can bring him up to speed."

"I'm sure it can."

"How long does it take?"

"You should budget for full-time, on-site training for at least two months, then every other week for three months. That would include my billing rate, travel, and living expenses."

I gave him my current billing rate.

"I think this is reasonable. We currently have IBMers on several projects. Just so you know, you are a bargain compared to their rates. Can you start in two weeks?"

"Yes, I can."

Boston, MA
January 2006 thru May 2006

I was sitting in the lobby of The Customer where I met the CDBA. He brought me up to the database team area. There appeared to be over a hundred people sitting at workstations, inside of cubicles.

"Are all these people on the database team?"

"Yes, mostly for Sequel Server, almost one per server; then there are several for the IBM big iron DB2."

"Interesting, all of these DBAs for of all those computer systems, and you don't have a single one for the six or seven AS/400s that pretty much run your business—hmmmm."

We approached two cubicles, one empty, the other occupied.

"Dan C., I would like to introduce you to Dan Kowal, our newly hired DBE."

Dan K. stood up, turned around, and held out his hand. It was the middle code-slinger of the three that confronted me last November.

"Hi," he said. "What you did was the most impressive thing I've ever seen. I want you to teach me how you did that."

"I will be glad to," I said to Dan.

I commuted from Arizona to Boston for the next five months. I hadn't finished the training when my assignment was interrupted due to the death of Joe. Dan K. and I kept in touch over the years. He was one of the few people whom I considered to be DBE worthy.

Modernization

A Cold Case

Rochester, MN, U.S.A.

Jim and I never came across the elusive, computer criminal genius, aka the DBE. I had given this some thought. I put myself in the DBE's place. Why wasn't the DBE showing up at this workshop? What's missing?

And then it hit me. The workshop isn't attractive to someone who probably has credentials like mine—programming, specifically RPG, and a bit of an authority issue. Someone who likes working alone, who doesn't want to be an administrator but wants to be a developer, creating solutions that solve problems using database constructs—indexes, embedded SQL in RPG, SQL procedures, in other words—an engineer.

During the first two years I was teaching with Jim, I had free time to experiment with some of the performance benefits that SQL provides, versus traditional HLL IO operations. I developed some additional labs that utilized these new capabilities. When I started teaching the workshop on my own, I added these as topics and used my prototypes as labs. I called it: *Database Modernization*

The Dan Plan

I had developed a methodology for replacing existing database physical file objects—created using the native CRTPF command—with a physical file created using the SQL CREATE TABLE statement, without having an impact on existing applications. In other words, programs referencing the new objects did not need to be re-created. They simply continued to work as if nothing had changed.

An analogy would be the process of replacing the basement of an existing home with a new, more solid foundation, which also contained modern plumbing and wiring. When the old home is placed on the new foundation and reconnected to the electricity, water and gas supplies—the faucets run, the toilet flushes, and not vice versa.

The process employed the following methods for re-engineering an existing database:

Reverse Engineering (RE)

Generating an SQL data definition language (DDL) CREATE TABLE statement from an *existing* database object, regardless of how the object was created.

Database Refactoring

The process of replacing a database object with a new object created from a more robust version of source code; without changing the attributes that are currently visible to the applications

Validation

Validation is achieved by comparing the record format ID (RFID) of the before-and-after database objects. It is further proven by testing existing applications to ensure they continue to execute as intended without the need to recreate the other objects that make up the application.

Objective

The intent is twofold:

a) To take advantage of new database function that provides additional levels of security

b) To ease the implementation of future, modern applications

The *key* to making this work was an internal Primary-Key (PK) constraint, for lack of a better term, known as the *record format ID* (RFID). The RFID established relationships between files and programs. If the RFID remained intact when modifying a file's record format, then the relationship between the program and file remained sound.

When a program opened a file, a check was performed between the RFID PK of the file and the RFID FK of the program. If they didn't match, then a format level-check error occurred. This was meant as a failsafe, should the programmers not do their due diligence when making changes to files. Without this check, changing the attributes of columns might result in erroneous results.

The RFID was based on an algorithm that considered the number of columns in the record format, the attributes of the columns, and the format name. At the time, SQL defined files did not provide a means to name the record format, as this wasn't a part of the SQL standard. The default for SQL files was to name the record format the same as the file object name. This automatically resulted in a new RFID, even if the SQL file name matched the name of the physical file it was replacing.

As shown in the "Dan Plan" diagram, I circumvented this SQL shortcoming by inserting a logical file with the same name as the physical file being reverse engineered between the program and the new SQL defined physical file. The file type wasn't a part of the RFID value, thus the programs continued to run as if nothing changed. Some people referred to this as a "hack." I called it modernization.

One of the huge benefits of this technique, which I didn't appreciate at the time, was that by replacing physical files with logical files I was inadvertently creating a database abstraction layer. Theoretically the new SQL table could exist anywhere within the same computer, or on a different computer altogether—anywhere within the world.

Still trying to get your head around this. There is another technology that, coincidentally, uses that same acronym, but in a different context—*radio frequency ID* (RFID). This technology is commonly used in hotel keys. The RFID FK on the card key must match the RFID PK of the door lock for the door to open. This creates an open data path for your feet, allowing you to enter the room. The guest can change but the key RFID remains the same.

Although I called the inability to rename a format a shortcoming of SQL, it really wasn't. SQL used other means to ensure the integrity of the data. For example, when writing an SQL SELECT statement, best practice is to only specify columns required for the result set. If the underlying base table is changed, by adding new columns, SQL statements not referencing those columns continue to run as if nothing happened. Specifying ALL columns on a SQL SELECT statement wasn't a problem, as all columns, including new columns, would be returned. Well, if you were using embedded SQL with a host-array, then you had to ensure that the host-array included all columns in the result set. Best practice: only list the columns you need.

Rochester, MN

Winter—It Was Cold

The “Dan Plan” was coined by **Nicole Merritt**, an IBM marketing representative, who was attending the Large User Group (LUG) conference held at the IBM Rochester facility three times a year in Rochester, MN. Nicole was there with her customer—an employee of Bank of America (BOA).

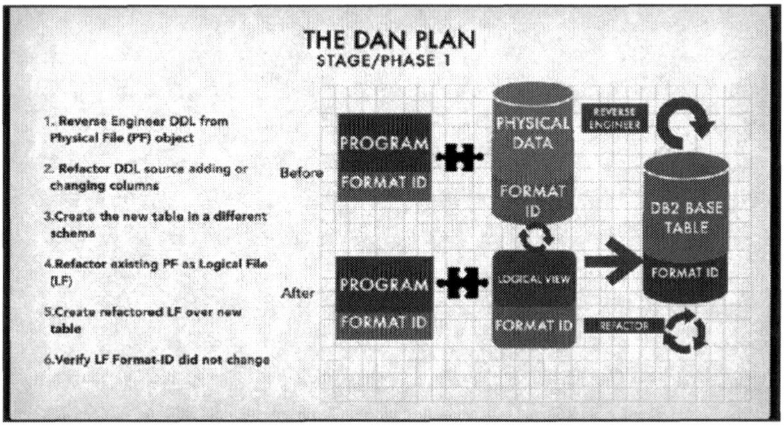

Database Modernization

This was the annual meeting that focused on Operations and where IBM highlighted new features and functions made available in the prior release. In addition, attending customers were given updates on undisclosed, upcoming hardware and OS enhancements. All customers attending had nondisclosure agreements with IBM.

Nicole had approached me during a customer briefing between BOA and the IBM Database Architecture team. **Mark Anderson**, chief architect for DB2 on IBM i, and **Robert (Rob) Bestgen**, chief architect for the SQL Query Engine (SQE), provided BOA with a deep dive into the latest DB2 and SQL features. I was sitting in the back of the conference room.

“Hi, I’m Nicole, the new IBM client representative for BOA. You’re Dan Cruikshank, right? I’ve heard quite a lot of good things about you from the client. I wanted to introduce myself. BOA has been implementing several new software changes, mostly Web stuff, since Bob M. left.”

"Hi, Nicole, nice to meet you. That Web stuff is probably the reason Bob left. I only hope this new bunch is listening to what Mark and Rob are saying."

"I'm just a client representative; I don't understand any of it."

"My previous employer used an analogy that I really liked. It involved a pyramid, the strongest structure known to humankind. If the base, or foundation, did not remain intact, i.e., the base of the pyramid did not grow horizontally, as the pyramid grew vertically, then it was inevitable that the pyramid would collapse. This is what happens when Web or Client-Server type applications take precedence over the database, DB2 in this case," I explained to Nicole.

"The application programmers create functions that could be performed by the database. We call that *application centric* programming, versus *data centric* programming. Eventually, the applications become top heavy—the database can no longer handle the load. Visually it would look like an upside-down pyramid and, like that pyramid, the applications will eventually collapse. It normally happens at the worst possible moment, and then the customer is on the phone with IBM. When I present this topic to user groups and clients, I usually say, 'That's when IBM calls me in.' I then tell my audience that I am the last person you want to see come through your door. I take names and I kick ass."

"How do you address this issue?" Nicole asked.

"I usually recommend that the customer create the position of database engineer, or DBE, and promote one or more individuals from the application development team to become a DBE or DBEs, as the case may be."

"How do they become DBEs?"

"I come on-site, and I train them, especially if they're located in California," I grinned. "That is my plan."

Nicole laughed. "The 'Dan Plan.' I'm having dinner with the client. I thought maybe you could explain the 'Dan Plan' to them."

"My pleasure; what time do I need to show up?"

The Table Turns

Denver, CO Fall 2000

I was presenting the Dan Plan to a group of developers. At that time, it did not have a name. I simply called it "modernization." The developers had an application written in COBOL, originally for their Wang computer. They had migrated the application to an AS/400, with minor changes to the application code. Things were going fine until their client base began asking for analytics. In other words, their clients wanted to begin mining their data for trends and other bits of gold they could use to expand their business. The LOB for this customer was stock trading.

The big issue wasn't performance. When the COBOL application was migrated to the AS/400, the developers simplified the task by *not* taking advantage of *external file definitions*. In other words, the file definitions were stored within the COBOL program, which wasn't accessible to the stock trader's clients.

According to the five stages of database modernization—starting with Stage One as defined in the Dan Plan—the application was at Stage Zero.

"I didn't know you had a Phase Zero." **Lou A.** was Italian, from Australia. Apparently, *phase* is Italian-Australian-English for *stage*. Lou A. and I were discussing the approach to modernizing the customer's database.

"Not in the Dan Plan, Lou," I replied. "Most of our customers who migrated from IBM S/3x platforms converted to externally described files as part of that process. Stage One requires the files to be externally defined."

"What do we need to do?"

"We start with Stage Zero. Or in other words—from scratch," I smiled.

One of the most important parts of the Dan Plan was to acquire a proper set of data modeling tools. There were some tools provided by IBM to ease the transformation from program described files to externally described files; however, these were mostly for use with RPG coded programs, and the tools had been deprecated.

I had used data modeling tools on OS/2 and Windows platforms for their graphical interfaces and SQL generation capabilities; however, they lacked the ability to import AS/400 DDS, nor could they generate it.

In the case of this customer, that didn't matter. The DDS files they created simply contained two defined fields: one which defined the key for the data in the file, followed by a *great big field* (GBF). The key fields and the GBFs mapped to the COBOL File Descriptors (FDs). It would have been worthless to reverse engineer the existing DDS to SQL DDL, the first step in Stage One, because someone would still have to hand code the individual fields—which defeats the entire purpose of using a data modeling tool.

I searched for a new data modeling tool that generated both AS/400 DDS and SQL DDL. I found one—Visible Analyst for Windows. I acquired permission from my IBM manager to purchase it. While I became familiar with the functions that came with the tool, I reviewed some other products the company offered. One of those was an MS-DOS based product that would read COBOL FDs and translate them to SQL DDL.

The COBOL developers had used a common practice of coding the FDs in copybooks. During the compilation of the COBOL source the FD would be copied into the source code. This allowed modifications to be made to the COBOL FD in one place.

I ordered the COBOL FD conversion tool from Visible Analyst—it was free. I had the customer send the COBOL FDs as text files to me via email. After I received the email, I downloaded the text files. There was one text file per COBOL FD.

Following the instructions for the conversion tool, I entered the name and location of a text file, the name and location of the converted DDL text, and a file extension. I ran the tool and reviewed the generated SQL DDL—the syntax was standard SQL. I uploaded the generated sql file into the IBM i Navigator Run SQL Scripts tool. There were no syntax errors. I pushed the Run button—the table was created successfully.

I wrote a white paper, *Migrating from DDS Created Physical Files to SQL Tables*, which explained the process I used to transform the archaic DDS language to the industry standard and strategic SQL DDL.

Approximately five years later, the white paper would be used as the basis for the Redbook *Modernizing IBM eServer iSeries Application Data Access - A Roadmap Cornerstone.* My name would appear on the cover, which other than the white paper was my only contribution to the Redbook. However, the original white paper used as the basis for the Redbook, was woefully out of date—five years is a lifetime in computer years.

I published a series of articles on database modernization—as of 2005:

Modernizing Database Access: The Madness Behind the Methods, April 2005

Performance Comparison of DDS-Defined Files and SQL-Defined Files, May 2005

Replacing a DDS Physical File with an SQL Table, May 2005

Analyzing Data Access Methods, August 2006

My thinking was to introduce those developers who were contemplating a database conversion project, based on the Redbook techniques, to the current state-of-the-art best practices for database re-engineering.

The new techniques included the notion of a DBE, which I would later introduce in an IBM white paper:

The Emerging Role of the Database Engineer on IBM AS/400 Systems, June 2006.

The Big Bank of Hong Kong (BBHK)
Hong Kong, China Fall 2012

Jim Denton, aka JimDT—Jim's BBHK name so as not to be confused with Jim Diephuis, aka JimDP, BBHK's name for him—and I were sitting next to each other at a conference table in the middle of the application development area. It was after 6:00 P.M., getting close to our normal quitting time. We had already put in a full day.

We kept an eye out for Lou A., who had been in a status meeting forever with the BBHK management team discussing our fate.

Will we be returning home tomorrow, or will we be making travel changes?

Finally, I saw Lou A. approaching. His face was expressionless.

"Dan, what do you think?" asked JimDT.

"He's not carrying a pizza," I replied with a grin.

JimDT laughed because I had told him about my troubles with management during the OA project.

"Guys," Lou A. said as he pulled up a chair, "here's the deal. I have agreed with BBHK that we won't leave Hong Kong until we have our report complete. We will continue to work here for another hour, then leave and catch the train to the airport hotel. There we will grab a quick sandwich, change clothes, pack our stuff, meet in the lobby, and finish up the report."

"Will we then just head to the airport and catch our flights?"

"If the report is finished."

Lou A. must've caught me rolling my eyes.

"Guys, I am serious. We will complete that report, however long it takes. I'll tie you up in your chairs if I have to."

Lou A. got up and headed back to where he came from.

JimDT looked at me and said, "I am so glad I packed my handcuffs."

We both laughed, more like giggled. We were very tired and hungry.

"He should've brought pizzas," I said. We both laughed again.

Denial of Service

Hong Kong, China April 2004

The upper echelon of BBHK wasn't happy with IBM. The Hang Seng stock exchange did not open on time. This was due to a hardware failure that prevented the BBHK's very large AS/400 from being available; service had been denied to the stock exchange.

IBM Hong Kong customer engineers had identified the problem and fixed it; however, BBHK was down, castors up, for about 24 hours. The hardware failure wouldn't have been as costly if HHBK had been utilizing High Availability (HA)—a product offering available to AS/400 customers that utilized high speed connections to replicate images of the primary system database changes onto a replica, or mirrored, database created on another AS/400. If the target database was within the same location, but on a different AS/400, then it was referred to as local or Metro. If the target AS/400 was located a long distance away, then the database was referred to as remote or Global.

Metro Mirror was best suited for local outages, such as a hardware failure like the one that was incurred at HHBK. Global mirror was intended for disaster recovery, such as a tsunami, which could destroy all of Hong Kong. The global mirrored system could be located thousands of miles away.

After several discussions between IBM and HHBK, it was decided that IBM would put together a team of the best and brightest AS/400 SMEs in their respective fields. Not only did this include hardware specialists, but also experts in the area of communications, security, IBM Websphere, IBM MQ, HA, system performance and, most importantly, in my humble opinion, database and application performance.

Chuck King, who was currently based in Hong Kong, would be the on-site IBM project manager. Chuck chose one of the leading experts in HA—to lead this team, remotely from Rochester, MN. I was chosen as the application performance specialist. **Bobby Daniels**, based out of Atlanta, was my counterpart, doing the system or hardware performance analysis. Lou A. couldn't join us due to other commitments. We made travel arrangements, which included the necessary visas and letters of invitation.

Our mission was to identify potential single points of failure, hardware and/or software, and make recommendations, short-term and long-term. We spent eleven days in Hong Kong. I gathered large quantities of PEX data, my tool of choice for identifying software inefficiencies in the customer's applications—all developed in-house at BBHK using RPG.

We returned to our home bases. For me that was Rochester, MN, even though I lived in Arizona. I was fortunate, as this allowed me to work alongside several members of the team who were based in Rochester and lived there. It also gave Mary Jo an opportunity to travel with me and visit with family and friends in the Cities. If it was a short trip, then I would stay in the Cities with her; otherwise, I would stay in Rochester.

Once we had all turned in our specific reports with findings and recommendations, Lou A. would compile these into a single report with an executive overview section. We also needed to prepare a presentation for our scheduled return trip in July. I was explaining this to Mary Jo.

"Want to go to Hong Kong with me July the fourth? I will have three days of work then we can spend several days exploring Hong Kong, Kowloon, and maybe each other together. What do you say?"

"Is it much like Nanjing and Shanghai?" Mary Jo asked.

"Better. Everyone speaks English, and Bobby is bringing his wife. That means you will have a companion while I'm working."

It was our best trip together. Hong Kong is one of the most beautiful cities on earth, in my opinion. There is a diverse population, meaning there are several restaurants from a variety of cultures to choose from. The only downside was wearing a black suit in temperatures of 100 degrees Fahrenheit and basting in 100-percent humidity.

We stayed at the Mandarin Hotel for both business and pleasure.

When the work was done, the rest of the team returned to their respective home bases while Mary Jo and I stayed at the hotel—on our dime—for several more days. We explored Kowloon; Mary Jo had been there with Mrs. Daniels and was able to show me around. We took a day trip to Macau, a gambling haven off the coast of China.

Before we left, Chuck talked to me about the possibility of my taking a six-month assignment in Hong Kong.

"Mary Jo, this couldn't have happened at a better time. Ron and Joe can stay at the house in Sedona. We pay our share of the bills like we normally do."

"Dan, I'm happy in Sedona. Count me out."

I turned down the offer. I wasn't going to do it alone. I would return to Hong Kong several more times before I retired in 2016.

Days of Wine and Espresso

Milan, Italy December 2009

I was back in Milan. I was teaching a workshop on database modernization to the programmers who worked for a small software development company. This was my first workshop with a set of labs that were not based on the optimization workshop. These labs included proof of concept exercises that proved the main premise of Stage/Phase One of the Dan Plan—database objects could be changed without impacting the application layer.

I spread the workshop out over four days. I didn't have that much lecture material; the workshop was mostly labs and I wanted to provide enough time to complete them. In addition, I expected there might be a lot of handholding, which would eat up the clock. I was wrong. The programming team was sharp. They completed the labs successfully, working together. I was impressed.

Massimo Marasco, my IBM colleague would meet me at the subway station where the IBM bus would load IBMers to take them to the Milan IBM site. Since I was going to the customer site, my colleague would drive me to the customer location. On the last day of the class, **Simona Pacchiarini**, who worked for IBM Italy, based in Milan, invited me and my colleague to have dinner with her and her husband, Renato, at their home.

On the way there, I asked my IBM colleague if he could help me pick out a wine to bring to dinner, as I did not drink, but thought I should bring something with me. Dinner was excellent. My colleague drove me back to my hotel. On the way there we were involved in an accident. Neither driver stopped to exchange insurance information.

The Boondoggle

Orlando, FL

I was attending an IBM Technical Conference. It was an award for being recognized by my peers as having strong, technical skills. I was at breakfast. Like always, I was one of the first conference attendees there. It was Friday morning, the last day. I would travel back home that afternoon. I always started the day with a good breakfast, especially if it was free.

The trip was better than I expected. There were two sessions that I attended and thoroughly enjoyed. One was about being a lone practitioner—someone who can work alone without supervision—which fit me perfectly. The other was presented by a young, black woman who talked about her experiences coming to work for IBM as a professional hire—like me. She used humor and some of her stories were hilarious.

I was thinking about all of this as I wolfed down my breakfast. The chair next to me was pulled out and a man asked if I would mind if he joined me.

"Be my guest," I said, as I motioned for him to sit down. I noticed that we were the only ones at breakfast.

Breaking the ice, he asked, "What do you think of the conference?"

"To be honest, I thought this was just going to be some boondoggle, but in retrospect, I think I really enjoyed it."

"That's good, because I don't speak at just any boondoggle."

It was then I recognized him as the keynote speaker and an IBM Fellow, the highest level of recognition an IBM scientist, engineer, or programmer can achieve.

Springboks, Tex-Mex, and Coffee

The Dan Plan would eventually become a service offering that JimDT and I would teach around the world, as a team or individually. JimDT had been teaching the optimization workshop in Europe. IBM decided to move the Benchmark Center from Rome to Montpellier, France. Charlie decided to return to the U.S. He was followed by Dan F., JimDT, and Neil W.

In 2010, I traveled to countries located in four continents: Africa, Asia, Europe, and Mexico (North America). The extraordinary thing about this was that the trips spanned a period of three months, beginning in late August and ending in late October.

The Last Record

Cape Town, South Africa August 2010

This trip, like many others, happened as a result of an HA study for a client located just north of Cape Town. The client was in the medical industry and had several small AS/400s running homegrown software, written in RPG/II on a System 36. The applications still ran in S36e mode. The HA expert was quick to recognize a Dan Plan opportunity in the making.

As it turned out, it was much more. The fact that the applications were running in the S36e space was the first clue that this was another Stage/Phase Zero implementation. There would be several steps required before this client would be granted access to **The Blue Highway**—the road to modernization.

Education, and a lot of it, would be the first speed bump to overcome. This was apparent as I talked to the customer about reusable ODPs.

"To make the ODPs reusable, you must first make the program reentrant, that is, remain active. To do this, you must replace the Last Record (LR) indicator with the Return (RT) operation or indicator."

"Excuse me, Dan. I assume you do not know much about RPG."

"Why do you say that?" I asked, incredulously.

"Everyone knows that you need to set on the LR indicator in order to end the RPG program." The questioner of my RPG manhood looked around the room, getting nods of approval from his fellow programmers.

"That was true in the seventies when you were running on your S/36 and reading card decks, but that isn't true today."

The LR indicator in RPG got its name because it was associated with the last card, or record, in a deck of cards that was being read by the MFCU card reader. The last card had a /* in the first two positions. The purpose of this card was to signal to the RPG program that the last card, or record, had been processed and it was now safe to end the program.

A contentious discussion, or debate, ensued, culminating with my challenge that they create a POT program, containing a single file and a single instruction, Return, coded within the RPG calculation specifications.

I also suggested they create a similar program, except this program would have a single file (not the same as the other program) and two instructions: SETON(LR) followed by Return.

The programmer created the programs, compiled them, and used the CALL command to execute each program. They both ran successfully, i.e., no errors.

"Okay, you were right, we don't need to use LR," the programmer conceded, "but, what was the point?"

"Do this. Enter the DSPJOB command then select Open Files from the menu."

The display showed that the file from the program using Return was still open. The file from the second program did not display.

"Because the file is still open, it can now be reused, eliminating the overhead of the file open process. By removing LR you have made your program *re-entrant*. When the program is called again, the program activation process does not occur. Less work, better performance."

I recommended that they contact the IBM Rochester CTC to engage with them to help with the programming effort to eliminate LR, amongst other things.

"In order to modernize, according to the Dan Plan, you must be at Stage/Phase One. You're not even close. I can come back once you're ready for Stage/Phase One. Then we'll have even more fun."

I couldn't wait. The DBA for Microsoft (MS) SQL Server, an alternative to IBM's DB2, who originally wanted the client to move off the AS/400 to a more "modern" computer, was now excited to be a part of the Dan Plan. He took me out to dinner the night before I was to return home and introduced me to Springbok, aka Gazelle. It was delicious.

Database Engineering

A DBE Suspect

Dallas, Texas September 2010

It was my second trip to BOA's Dallas location. I had been there once before to conduct a non-lab version of the optimization workshop. The attendees were the big iron DB2 team. They had acquired the responsibility for the administration and maintenance of CFC's DB2 for i database. They were confused. I believe I gave them enough to get their feet wet. They were impressed with DB2 for i's Visual Explain (VE) tool, the graphical version of the EXPLAIN tool **Ed Simon** and I used at the Indianapolis customer location sometime back in the last century.

"It's much better than the mainframe DB2 VE," one of the attendees shared with me.

Now I was back to present database modernization. There were a few of the same DB2 for i optimization workshop attendees, including the manager. Also in attendance were the AS/400 system administration manager, a couple of AS/400 RPG programmers, and Thudyen Phan.

I had met Thudyen during a performance review of CFC's overnight batch process. Thudyen worked on a CFC team that was made up of mostly RPG programmers who did non-application development—they were more like systems programmers typically found in big iron shops. Their role was to enhance AS/400 system functions by providing more user-friendly capabilities. Thudyen was the exception.

I believed Thudyen was assigned to me as an understudy to learn everything I did so the CFC team could become less dependent on IBM Rochester for performance analysis. Thudyen and I became good friends.

This engagement involved analyzing the overnight batch processes. I had jumped through hoops to get permission to use the PEX tools—CFC had a PEX related system crash in the not-too-distant past. I assured CFC that the bug that caused the crash was fixed. They agreed to allow me to collect PEX data only if I did it on-site during the overnight batch run. I agreed.

Thudyen was a short, Vietnamese woman with looks and mannerisms like Mary Jo's. She was always prepared. When she learned that she would be shadowing me during the overnight process, she packed a care package consisting of fruits and nuts. She would slice the kiwi fruit into equal shares and place them on napkins she had also provided, along with the appropriate utensils—that was so Mary Jo.

I taught her how to use the PEX tools to capture program signatures and how to create summary charts using Query Management Facility (QMF) for Windows. I now used this tool instead of my PDQ tool. QMF was shipped on the AS/400 as QM/400. Like anything else involving SQL on the AS/400, it was rarely used, if ever—except by me. QMF for Windows, the latest version of QMF, provided the ability to execute the SQL from a PC and produce various charts and graphs using the SQL result set.

When BOA acquired CFC, Thudyen remained with the CFC team. She became my protege. I taught her how to use my RPG tools that called the SQL APIs to monitor and collect SQL performance data. The SQL detailed monitor came with OS/400—Dan's tools did not.

When the SQL Query Engine (SQE) became available, around the turn of the century, the SQL Summary Monitor APIs were deprecated. By default, the CQE optimizer collected detailed statistics about the query plan—the steps taken to implement and run a query (SQL, OPNQRYF or Query/400). The APIs were available under the controlled openness initiative for customers or software vendors to provide summation of the detailed query plan data.

Being the crackerjack programmer that I was, I wrote a set of RPG programs to start and end the summary monitor collection. I gave these programs to potential DBEs and trained them on how to use them. One day, a bug in one of the summary monitor APIs resulted in my customer's AS/400 becoming non-responsive

The problem was solved, and I was politely asked by Rob (the SQE architect) to inform my customers to stop using the APIs. Rob explained to me that SQE collected the same data as my tools, only in real-time. This was referred to as the SQE Plan Cache (SQEPC). It was a huge enhancement.

I passed the information on to those customers who were still using my APIs, including BOA. Thudyen requested additional training in the use of the SQEPC. Specifically, how the SQEPC can be used to produce the same reports the QMF tool provided. I returned to BOA's Mortgage Division to train Thudyen in the use of SQE and how to dump the plan cache.

The most important takeaway from the modernization workshop was the importance of the role of the DBE on the AS/400. It was nowhere near the role of a DBA on big iron DB2. This person had to know programming, application performance tuning, SQL, database optimization, and AS/400 HLL program products like RPG and COBOL.

The second most important takeaway from the workshop was for me to identify a candidate from the group of attendees who had some of the skills necessary to become BOA's initial DBE. I knew enough about BOA's mortgage application, formerly CFC's, to know they would need more than one.

I knew the first one I would nominate was attending the workshop—Thudyen Phan.

The Database Modernization Workshop

Mexico City, Central America September 2010

As the need for database optimization and modernization grew, so did the Rochester team. At first, these workshops were filler; they soon became full-time jobs. Our team was a motley crew of several IBMers, who were becoming household names when customers talked about AS/400 database.

Besides me, the team consisted of Mike, Kent, JimDT, Rob Bestgen, **Tom McKinley** (DB2 development team), **Doug Mack**, and **Hernando Bedoya**. JimDT had ended his Montpellier assignment and maintained residences in Rochester, MN, and Minneapolis, MN. JimDT, Tom, and Rob all came from the Rochester lab as former developers of OS components.

Doug and I were the only members who did not live in Minnesota. I had lived there for fifty years, but not in Rochester. Hernando was originally from Columbia. He had moved to Rochester to manage IBM Redbooks pertaining to IBM i (AS/400). He was now our Spanish language presenter of the optimization workshop. For modernization presentations in Spanish speaking countries, he would bring someone else in while he came up to speed.

This was why I was in Mexico City presenting the modernization workshop to a group of programmers working for Banco Azteca. Hernando had sold the workshop to the client and made all the travel arrangements.

When we arrived at Banco Azteca, we had to go through security. Hernando went through the metal detector and waited while the security guard examined his papers. He motioned Hernando to go on and then motioned for me to come through the detector. I made it through without setting it off and handed my passport and IBM badge to the guard. He seemed to be taking longer to review mine. Thoughts of PGJ came to me.

The guard looked up from my passport and said, "Arizona? You do not like us."

"It wasn't me," I said. "It was some other guys. I just moved there from Minnesota a few years ago. We love everybody."

The guard smiled and let me through.

The workshop went well. A couple of nights before the end of the workshop, I received a call from an IBM client representative, asking if I had a few minutes to talk about his customer. I said sure.

"My customer is rolling out a new application worldwide to over ten thousand stores, and they have run into a brick wall. I called the PR-JOFC, and they gave me your number. Can you help them?"

"I don't know, I need more info. What kind of application? Web, or green screen?"

"Let me put you on speaker. I'm with the customer now."

I waited a couple of seconds for the caller to figure out the speaker button.

"Hello, Dan. I am going to let the customer tell you about the application."

The customer came on.

"Hi Dan, we are rolling out a new web-based application written in Java. We were hoping to have all ten thousand of our stores enabled by next week. Apparently, we have maxed out the AS/400 after rolling out less than a few hundred stores. Can you come on-site and help us?"

"Unfortunately, I am in Mexico until the end of the week. Then I will be going to Europe for three weeks. When you say Java, are you using SQL for data access?"

"Yes."

"Okay. Here is what I want you to do. Is someone from operations on the call?"

"Yes. Here he is." The op guy came on the phone.

"I am going to send you instructions for saving the SQL Index Advisory table. I then want you to compress it into a zip file and email it to me. I will then reinstall it on my AS/400 in Rochester. I will remotely review it and see if there are some low hanging fruits in the form of index advisories. If so, then I will send those to you with instructions for installing them. Okay?"

An index advisory occurs when the optimization engine cannot find an index or constraint that matches the columns coded in the WHERE clause of an SQL statement.

"Okay. How soon can you get back to us?"

"I will get back to you tonight. I think I am an hour ahead of you. By the way, what customer is this?"

"We work for Starbucks."

"I love Starbucks. I was just thinking that I can now say, 'IBM proudly serves Starbucks.'"

"Yeah, that is funny, as long as you can fix our problem."

After restoring the saved data, I discovered that there were many index advisories. I made some notes about whether Starbucks had a DBE on staff. If not, then on-site training was on the table, along with a free cup of coffee.

I sent a follow-up email with about twenty indexes to create, based on the index advisory. I looked at the time.

I better get some sleep; I still have a full day of class tomorrow—more like later today.

I didn't hear back from Starbucks while I was in Mexico.

Combining Business with Pleasure

Optimization, Relaxation, Modernization

Europe

It was our thirtieth wedding anniversary—March 22, 2010, to be precise. I was booked to present the database optimization workshop for one week in London—in October the same year. This would be followed by a trip to Milan, Italy, two weeks later. I took advantage of the opportunity to fill the open week with a great anniversary gift that matched our gift-giving style. We no longer gave store-bought gifts to each other on our anniversary, birthdays, or holidays.

I talked Mary Jo into coming with me and spending the intervening week together in Paris. I had been to London and Milan several times. I had been to Lille, France, but had only traveled thru Paris. This would be Mary Jo's first trip to London, Paris, and Milan, not her first trip to Italy. That one turned into a disaster. I was hoping for some rediscovery time—three weeks' worth to be exact.

The SQL Workshop

London, UK Late September 2010

Originally, the London workshop was scheduled to be held in London. The customer decided to move it to a smaller town, east of London—Tonbridge. I had booked a room for us at a Hilton in Dartford. We could've stayed in London, and I would've taken the train to Tonbridge; but Mary Jo was okay with taking the train to London. She had her guidebooks.

The new class location was accessible by train, but I would need to leave Dartford quite early to take a train to London and then catch a train to Tonbridge. I would not be able to arrive at the location with enough time for setup before class began. We made the move to Tonbridge. It had a train station next to our hotel. It was older but had more character—and characters.

Mary Jo had a wonderful time exploring London. The class went extremely well. The hotel where we stayed served breakfast and dinner.

On Friday afternoon, Mary Jo and I went to London together, hit some places she hadn't made it to, finished with a great dinner, and returned to the hotel.

The following morning, I got up early and went downstairs for coffee. There was an older gentleman wearing a hat, standing at the hotel reservation desk. This wouldn't have been remarkable if it wasn't for the fact that the hat was all he was wearing. Apparently, there was a problem with his luggage. I think he was trying to make a point.

30th Wedding Anniversary
Paris, France October 2010

We caught the train to London and transferred to the train to Paris. We stayed in Paris for a week. We had a hotel room near the Arc de Triomphe just a block off the Champs-Élysées. I was amazed at how many Starbucks there were in the neighborhood.

We were able to tour Notre Dame, the Palace of Versailles, and the Louvre. The museum contained many old and new works of art, and much to our pleasure—a Starbucks.

We visited the cemetery where Jim Morrison, lead singer for the Doors, was buried. The cemetery reminded me of the St. Louis cemetery in New Orleans. The ornateness of the style and size of the cemetery monuments were now making sense—most likely the French influence.

DB2 Modernization Workshop
Milan, Italy October 2010

From Paris we took the train to Milan, Italy. That night we had dinner with my friend and colleague, Simona, and her husband, Renato.

I had first met Simona while doing performance work for a large bank in Milan. I arrived on a Sunday morning and spent the day exploring. That night, Simona and I met for pizza and she gave me directions to the bank. There were two incidents I remember clearly which spoke volumes about Simona's character and why I liked her.

The first involved the restrooms at the bank. They were marked separately, 'Men' and 'Women.' During our lunch break Simona suggested we stop and use the bank restrooms before we went to the restaurant. I went to the men's room and Simona went to hers. The men's room had individual stalls and one urinal. The urinal was occupied so I grabbed a stall, shut the door, and did my thing. When I finished, I opened the door and was slightly shocked to see Simona standing there.

"The women's bathroom is out of order. I must use yours. I will meet you outside," she said, as she pushed me out of the way.

I was reminded of Mary Jo telling me that she would sometimes brazenly go to the men's room at this or that event and use it because the line at the women's would be too long for her to wait. She was way ahead of her time.

The other incident occurred while we were meeting with the programming team. I was discussing techniques to improve performance of several programs written in the RPG/IV programming language. The programmers insisted that I review the programming code in the program compile listings. I was having trouble explaining that's not how it's done.

I was getting frustrated. "I need to capture a performance signature of the program, then I can make informed recommendations."

Simona was killing time flipping pages in a program compile listing. I knew, based on the amount of paper used by that one program, that attempting to find a performance issue without the aid of a tool was foolhardy. Suddenly Simona spoke out with some excitement in her voice.

"Dario!" she said, addressing the programmer, and handing him the compiler listing. "Here, tell Dan, [it sounded like Don] what this word is."

Simona was pointing at a grouping of code on the compiler listing. I could tell that the line of code was a comment. As I followed her finger, I could see the word she was pointing to. Dario's red face confirmed my suspicion. I know the word *fuck* when I see it—in any language.

Back to the Present

At dinner, Simona was talking about her new home, how she was spending time in the garden doing this and that. At one point she stood up to show how she moved a plant from here to there. I looked at Mary Jo. She was captivated. Gardening was her passion.

Simona gave me directions for getting to the IBM facility where the workshop was being held. The first day was spent finding the restrooms, reviewing the technical set up, and making sure my remote presentation clicker worked. Everything went smoothly.

Mary Jo's day was just as good. She had no trouble using the subway system. She spent most of the day near the Duomo, a famous cathedral in Milan built over the ruins of some ancient Roman structure.

The next day was the first day of the workshop. I met Simona at IBM. The first thing was to have our morning espresso from the vending machine. The attendees gradually showed up and we settled around the espresso machine. Simona then herded everyone into the classroom where we did formal introductions, going around the room. It was then time for break and more espresso.

We returned and I began the presentations. I would get through two or three charts and then a man in the front row would turn around and start yakking with the folks behind him. I would patiently wait until he finished and then proceed. Two or three charts in, he would repeat the same behavior. Something had to be done.

We broke for lunch—espresso and a sandwich. I asked Simona if I could speak with her in private. We stepped away from the group.

"Simona, you have to talk to that guy in the front row. He's becoming a distraction."

"Oh, no, Don, he is telling the other attendees that he has read your Redbook and database modernization articles and everything you are saying is really true and works. This is very important to our customers. They can be very skeptical."

When class resumed, I made sure that I paused after making an important point so the guy in the front row could add his two cents worth. The workshop ended on Thursday. It was a great success. Everything went smoothly.

Mary Jo and I spent all day Friday touring Milan. Unfortunately, we were unable to get into Santa Maria delle Grazie to view *The Last Supper* painting by Leonardo Da Vinci. We toured the Duomo and climbed the stairs that took us to some outdoor walkways at the top of the cathedral. The views were incredible.

The Database Engineer (DBE)

IBM Proudly Serves Starbucks

Seattle, WA Late October 2010

Upon returning from overseas, I decided to give Starbucks a call for an update. I asked my customer contact how things were going.

"We have made significant headway, but we're starting to run into some roadblocks."

"So, my index recommendations helped?"

"Oh, yeah, they sure did."

The initial improvements made by creating the twenty indexes allowed the application to be installed in nearly fifty percent of the Starbucks stores. I was given a contract to come on-site and work with the operations staff to find more improvements.

Once I arrived, I was escorted to the operations center where I would work with operations staff to find more indexing, or other opportunities that did not require application changes. The probability was high that some applications would require changes.

Around mid-morning I asked one of the system administrators, "Say, what's a guy have to do to get a cup of coffee around here?"

The system administrator jumped up and said, "I thought you'd never ask. Follow me."

We went to the break room for our floor. This was no ordinary break room. It resembled the inside of a typical Starbucks store.

"What's your poison?" asked the system administrator.

"I'll take a tall, dark roast, thank you."

"That's it? Each employee is a trained barista. You don't want something fancier?"

"Plain, strong coffee will do for now. I may have an espresso this afternoon."

Before I left, I *strongly* recommended that Starbucks create the position of database engineer. The next time I returned, I met the new DBE.

The CASE for Xcase

BBHK, Hong Kong
2010 thru 2014

Between 2010 and 2104 Lou A., Mike, JimDT, JimDP, and I would make several trips to BBHK. The majority of those involved some form of database modernization and/or re-engineering project. The projects were driven by many factors, with HA being primary, and modernization secondary; however, modernization would become our longest engagement. If we weren't on-site then we were engaged off-site, usually in Rochester, MN. Sometimes I would be on vacation, working on or finishing a report. Or I might be creating a proof of technology and/or concept using my templates.

One of our biggest accomplishments, although we were not there to see it thru to fruition, was the database engineering endeavor that involved the Dan Plan and thirty-seven different databases. Each database represented a different country. Each country had made custom changes to the original database format. This appeared to be impossible to accomplish. Xcase to the rescue!

Rochester, MN

While in Rochester I was approached by one of my colleagues who mentioned a presentation being done by this guy from Israel. He was pushing a new application modernization tool his company developed. I found the room and joined the presentation in progress.

The company name was Resolution Inc. The representative's name was **Eli Muyal**. The product Eli (pronounced Elly) was presenting was called Xcase. It was a Graphical User Interface (GUI) tool, which automated the Dan Plan, based on the Redbook version published in 2005. I introduced myself to Eli and commented on how well he followed the Staged/Phased approach. I asked him for his business card and said I would keep in touch.

I had condensed the original five stages of the Dan Plan to three phases: Phase One now combined Stages One and Two; Phase Two was now Stages Three and Four combined; Phase Three was simply about moving forward. The most important feature of Phase One was re-factoring.

Thru various POCs, I had learned that I could do more than just convert the original DDS PF to an LF and build it over an SQL table without changing the RFID; I could also add new columns, change the attributes of existing columns, and even drop unused columns—without a single existing application being aware that I had done this.

In addition, several changes were made to SQL CREATE TABLE, CREATE VIEW, and CREATE INDEX statements; the most important was being able to specify a record format name—the key ingredient in Phase One of the Dan Plan. This allowed the SQL INDEX record format to be shared by LFs referenced in HLL programs as a *surrogate file*. The surrogate file was the name coined by **Paul Conte**—an industry expert in relational database design—for the LF used instead of the original PF. The question was: can Xcase do this as part of its initial conversion phase without causing existing programs to break?

I kept in touch with Eli. I sent him scenarios that I wanted him to tryout on the Xcase tool. He would run the test and report back that the tool was able to do what I suggested.

"It worked beautifully!" he would reply.

It's Greek to Me

Athens, Greece Summer 2013

I was at the IBM Technical Conference standing in front of several IT professionals, few who spoke English, some who understood it if I spoke slowly. The rest were there because of the topic—Database Re-Engineering.

How do I dumb this down? It's not that the audience is stupid, it's the material. This is brand new stuff; there isn't an existing IBM Redbook on this—yet. Sure, I wrote a white paper on the topic, and I've published several articles. The original 2005 Redbook version of reverse engineering DDS physical files to SQL tables was in the process of being re-written slated for 2014. Have all these people read some or all of these articles?

I was suddenly stricken with stage fright.

Would the audience get the message? I don't speak the language; it's Greek to me. Will they understand my colorful Scottish/Scandinavian/Minnesotan English accent?

Using the seat-of-my-pants method I came up with a solution. I abandoned my carefully prepared presentation—complete with stick figures, circles, and squares—and proceeded to tell the story of the Three Little Pigs and the Big Bad Wolf.

"Once upon a time, there were three little pigs who needed to protect their data." I slowly spoke to the audience, "The pigs tried to build a database using straw. That was easily breached by the big bad wolf. The pigs opted for sticks—not good. Once again the database was breached by the wolf."

"Enough of this nonsense," the boss pig yelled. "We must bite the bullet and bring in an engineer to help us."

"Their cry for help was heard by IBM who provided a DBE who showed them how to take their sticks and straws, mix them with some mud, and bake them into bricks. They then built a state-of-the-art brick shit-house database. They were never breached again."

Simona attended the session. Later she said to me, "Don, I loved the little pigs story."

Later that night, Simona and I got on a bus that took us to a very popular—and probably expensive—restaurant, provided to conference attendees and IBMers. After dinner, a group of musicians provided entertainment, mostly Greek music using stringed and percussion instruments; however, the last number was an instrumental version of Led Zeppelin's song "Kashmir." It was fantastic.

The next day, after making my final presentation, I went to relax in the hotel's executive lounge with other IBM speakers. I joined *Steve Finnes* and we compared notes. We left together, and on the way out I stopped for a bottle of water. Being the goody two shoes that I am, I asked the lounge attendant if it was okay for me to take the bottle with me. She said no, so I put the bottle back.

As we were walking away, Steve said to me, "Do you know what your mistake was?"

"Asking for permission?"

"Right. Make them run after you and then ask for forgiveness."

"Lesson learned."

Crash and Burn

Simi Valley, California Fall 2014

I was at BOA's Mortgage Division, which occupied the same building that once was home to CFC. I was sitting in a conference room with a representative of BOA and my friend Matt, the customer client representative. We were waiting for the director of software development to join us. I would be giving my pitch on data centric versus application centric software development.

The director arrived and we introduced ourselves. The new director quickly informed us that he had very little time, so no charts or graphs, just QA.

"Dan, in as few words as possible, tell me why Data Centric."

"DB2 for i."

"Do you mean DB2/400?"

No matter how hard IBM tried to change the perspective of the AS/400 thru name changes, it just couldn't get past the image of green screens and dumb terminals.

"No, sir, DB2 for i; an integrated RDBMS, delivered for free with the IBM i OS, implemented at the SLIC or hardware layer. Many of the enhanced features of DB2 for i are only available by using SQL, DDL, or DML. These data centric techniques are best limited to database engineers. This team of individuals should be the only IT personnel allowed to create database objects, manipulate database structures, and tune the database. This allows application software developers time to focus on creating the required business applications. Any questions?"

"Okay, I get that, but I intend to build a data abstract layer that would exist on another platform. All application access would be through this layer. Who would be responsible for… why are you smiling?"

"Sir, IBM i comes with a built-in virtual layer known as Single Level Store or SLS. There is no need to create a data abstract layer. DB2 for i takes advantage of SLS, as does every object that exists on IBM i. All objects must be in virtual storage before they can be accessed. That has been part of the architecture since this platform was called a S/38."

"This is very interesting, Dan; however, I am running late for my next appointment. When can we meet again?"

I was about to answer when Matt kicked me under the table.

"If you're available this evening, IBM would love to take you out to dinner so you and Dan can continue this discussion."

"I believe that would work. I will invite a couple of other members of my staff so they can hear this."

"Excellent," said Matt. "I will email you with the restaurant name and location."

Dinner was attended by Matt, myself, the director, and two of his immediate subordinates, along with a woman I had met at the BOA location in Dallas a few years before. She was knowledgeable in AS/400 administration and I believe was there for translation purposes. I repeated to the other members of his team what I had told the director earlier.

Without much discussion the director stated he would stick to an application centric approach. He thanked Matt for the free dinner.

The Data Cruise

Ocean Vessels

Miami, FL Summer 2013

I was sitting in a conference room located in the headquarters of a major ocean-going cruise line. I was working on a report where I was recommending that the cruise line create the position of database engineer. The cruise line already had a database architect and several database analysts.

Like most of my engagements, it started with a phone call and then a request for me to be on-site. I would check my calendar and then suggest some dates when I could be there. Sometimes it would be the next day, other times it could be a week or two. This one was different. I could work remotely.

The Problem

The client was implementing a new application to handle several sophisticated promotional offerings, e.g., the first several customers to book a cruise would get discounts. The database architect had created and implemented a well-designed relational database; except for the key-data used to establish relationships there was little, or no, data redundancy—this wasn't the problem.

The problem was the choice of data access method. The client had chosen a tool that was highly regarded in the industry as the best of breed for accessing data from a relational database. The tool provided a data abstraction layer, in essence, separating the application processes from needing to understand the complexity of the database design. Not a bad idea, except the IBM i had already done this and had been doing it since 1978—as the S/38, AS/400 and eventually the IBM i.

The tool provided this type of support for those computer systems that did not come with an integrated RDBMS—IBM i did. Thus, the tool would be perfect for any other computer system where the RDBMS was an add-on product.

Mistake number one.

In addition, the person, or persons, who coded the data access methods, chose a technique that retrieved rows from DB2 for i—one row at a time.

Big mistake number two.

They then built a virtual layer, aka data abstraction, which provided the data to the application programs as a single view. Again, the IBM i already had this capability. It was called an SQL VIEW. An external application, using SQL, would simply perform the data access operations against the view, not the physical data. Okay, but as I said earlier, the database was well designed, which meant it was normalized to at least Third Normal Form (3NF. The database consisted of twenty-seven base tables, and some applications needed a piece of data from each table. This was the problem.

The process of accessing the data from twenty-seven tables one row at a time, then rebuilding the database image on the system that contained the applications (written in Java), and subsequently displaying the result on the UI device, was taking several minutes, if it finished at all.

Resolution

The solution was simple. I recommended the use of an SQL JOIN to return a single result set to the Java application. There would be no need for the additional overhead created by a tool that mimicked the built-in capabilities of IBM i and DB2 for i.

My first step was to gather database access data during the execution of the customer's transaction process. I was given a sign on to the customer's test system. I started the Database Monitor (DBMON) tool over the job that was serving the customer's transactions. I then had the customer execute the transaction. It took several minutes to capture and download the collected data remotely to my IBM laptop.

From the captured SQL SELECT statements, I identified the tables being accessed and the primary key fields. Using IBM Data Studio—my tool of choice for designing and creating the circles and squares that represented a relational database—I reverse-engineered the customer's database into SQL DDL statements. In addition to the SQL SELECT statements, DBMON captured the SQL WHERE clause values. These were the values used to define row filters, e.g., promotion codes, dates, etc. I used that information to populate my replica database with test data.

There were a total of twenty-seven distinct SQL statements, one for each table being accessed. I used these statements to create a single, SQL JOIN statement. I ran the SQL statement against my replica database. The result set appeared in less than a second. Of course, my database only contained the rows that were in the result set. The real test of response time would be made against the customer's data—millions, if not billions, of rows.

I received credentials to log in to a test system that contained a copy of the production system data. I connected and ran the statement against the test system. The answer appeared in my Java based SQL scripting tool in less than twenty-seconds—without tuning.

Aftermath

I wrote two reports for the customer. One was an Executive Summary explaining what I'd done, how I'd achieved my results, and why they did not need a third-party data access tool, plus a recommendation to create the position of DBE.

The second report was for the existing database architect and contained the detailed process to "modernize," by adopting SQL as both the data definition and data access language, replacing the antiquated DDS and RPG methods used in several other legacy applications that I had a chance to review.

As a result, I was engaged by the client as a consultant to help them achieve these goals. It never happened. I was stuck in a conference room and given the keys to the kingdom. I became a surrogate DBE—not what I had in mind. I passed that work on to someone else as soon as I could.

River Boats

Boston, MA Spring 2014

The following year, after the ocean vessel gig, I found myself speaking to a user group in Boston. I had two sessions and was free to leave the following day after the second one. I had extended my trip by one day to meet with the CIO of a small riverboat cruise company. This meeting was arranged by the company's IBM customer rep on behalf of the CIO.

The CIO was new to the AS/400. He came from a MS Sequel Server environment. He was totally confused by the terminology being used by the programming staff—RPG, DDS, physical, and logical files, WTF? He needed to talk with someone who spoke SQL. The IBM marketing representative searched the IBM consultant database and found me.

"DB2 for i is one-hundred percent SQL ANSI Standard compliant," I explained to the CIO. We were sitting in his office after I was shown around the department.

"If that's true, then tell me, Dan, what is a physical file?"

"First, you must understand that the IBM i architecture is object oriented and thirty-six years old—about my age."

The CIO laughed. I kept my hair short, but it still didn't hide the amount of silver threads that covered my head. My hair had gone through several changes: pure white, brown, now gray—like the AS/400; S/38, iSeries, now IBM i.

"To answer your question, a physical file or PF is an object, like a base table in SQL parlance. It is where the physical data is stored."

"So, do these PFs need to be converted to tables so they can be accessed by SQL?"

"No; however, I strongly recommend that PFs representing core business objects—customers, boats, passengers, crew, etc., be converted to base tables. This is normally carried out by the DBE using graphical tools, e.g., IBM's Data Studio (IDS) or Infosphere Data Architect (IDA). I also recommend that the new base table be isolated in a library separated from the application libraries."

"What are libraries?"

"Schemas."

At that moment, the CIO quickly got out of his chair and promptly displayed his middle finger at someone standing outside the window of his office. That someone returned the gesture using both of his hands. This caused the CIO to counter by smacking his upper arm, producing a raised fist, which he shook, keeping his middle finger raised for emphasis.

"Where I come from, we just say, 'Hello, how ya doing?'" I said to the CIO. "We don't display a lot of emotion like they do out here in the East."

"He's a Yankee fan," the CIO replied. "We do this every spring at the beginning of the baseball season. So, where were we?"

Vertigo, Don't Ya Know

Sedona, AZ October 2015

I was strapped to a gurney and being rolled out to an ambulance parked in the driveway in front of my house. I had been given something to stop the nausea and dry heaves, but it did not seem to be working, as they wouldn't stop. Each dry heave made my stomach clench.

I had woken up suddenly about 4:00 A.M. with a strong urge to vomit. I got out of bed and was heading to the bathroom when I stopped. The house appeared to be spinning. I was home alone. Mary Jo was spending the weekend at her sister's in Colorado. She was due home that day.

I always thought if I ever took a drink again and survived, I would wake up, half-naked, in some alley in Tijuana. Well, the half-naked part was right. And no, I hadn't been drinking. Later I would be told that I had an episode of vertigo.

I got down on the floor and crawled to the bathroom. I spent the next forty-five minutes dry heaving into the toilet. I was lying on my back when I decided I should try to get back into bed, near a phone. I reached the bed. I pulled myself up, turned to the right, and laid myself down. I wasn't near the bed.

I fell and hit my head on the corner of the nightstand. I wasn't sure if I was knocked unconscious. At some point, I rolled over on the floor and decided I needed to get to the phone and call for help. The 911 operator assured me that help was on the way.

The pants and shirt I'd worn the day before were still on the chair where I'd left them. I made it to the chair, put them on, then sat there and waited. I realized the front door was locked. I crawled to the front of the house and made my way to the front door. I reached the door handle. Just as I opened the door the first responders were coming thru the screened security door.

"Come on in, I've just started coffee."

I still had my sense of humor. As I rode in the ambulance, dry heaving, I thought about some of my recent work events, now in the past; I was sure they would be my last thoughts.

Homeward Bound

December 2012

I made my last Christmas trip to Asia in 2012. That one was extra special. I had a case of food poisoning in China, and one of my worst cases of gout ever in Malaysia. To top it off, after arriving at LAX International Airport from a long trip overseas, I was greeted by the news of another Elementary School shooting—Sandy Hook.

June 2015

I made my final visit to an institute of higher learning—Ritsumeikan University in Kyoto, Japan. Not only had I worked at a college, but I had also been engaged with many community colleges, vocational/technical schools and universities who owned AS/400s—for educational and administrative purposes.

The first day there I was sitting in the lobby of the Holiday Inn waiting to meet the customer representative. I noticed a Japanese woman approaching me. With each step she would bow her head. When she was within speaking distance, keeping her head down, and not looking directly at me, she spoke, "Daniel-san?"

"Hello," I responded. "I am Dan Cruikshank, with IBM."

It was then that she looked at me.

"I am honored to meet you, Daniel-san. I have researched you on the internet. You were the director of the administrative computer center for Augsburg College in Minneapolis. I attended St. Thomas College in St. Paul, Minnesota. My colleagues and I are very excited for you to be here."

"Thank you, shall we get started?"

My last night there, **Jin-Ming**—a colleague from IBM Rochester who could help with translation if need be—and I were taken to dinner by the customer representative and her team. After dinner, they presented us with red colored ties that had the university name on the front. Tomorrow we would be meeting with the president of the university.

"Please, Daniel-san, wear this tie tomorrow," the customer representative said to me.

Jin-Ming and I had worn suits the whole week we were there—sans ties. I had packed ties, but opted not to wear one, assuming Jin-Ming, who had been to the university before, knew the proper dress code. I decided to return in November but, due to a side effect of the vertigo episode, I was forced to cancel the trip—I had lost my ability to walk.

The Last Redbook

October 2015 thru January 2016

I was diagnosed with ataxia, the loss of motor skills, as a result of hitting my head when I fell. I was told with the help of physical therapy, I would fully recover. It would probably take a year, perhaps eighteen months. My brain was still fully functioning.

I had to cancel a return trip to Kyoto, Japan—Mike filled in for me—and a speaking engagement at the IBM Technical Conference in Nice, France. Simona covered that one.

I had been working with JimDT, Simona, and the DB2 team on a rewrite of the SQL Procedures Redbook. It was near completion. I volunteered to continue working on the Redbook from home, as I was unable to travel.

During my recovery, Mary Jo walked with me every day, holding me upright as I gradually became able to walk by myself—with the aid of a cane.

"Not the kind of rediscovery I had in mind, Mary Jo," I told her as we walked around the neighborhood.

I thought that my traveling days were over. I told my manager, **Laura McGuire**, that I planned to retire at the end of the year, unless I was able to take advantage of an earlier retirement option. I told her I could still think and was able to work on the Redbook.

I completed the Redbook by the end of January 2016, just in time to take a trip to Iowa.

The Final Four

The Last Trip to Italy Spring 2016

I was sitting in the passenger seat of Simona's red Alfa Romeo Giulietta. We were driving from Milan to a city in Umbria, where I would be conducting my final performance of the SQL Optimization and Tuning Workshop. We never came up with a new acronym, nor did we ever find the elusive DBE.

It was still winter-like in northern Italy. The skies were growing overcast with dark, threatening clouds. It wasn't long before some snowflakes started falling from the sky. Simona was traveling at a decent rate of speed. I had noticed the red color of brake lights in the highway up ahead. Simona wasn't paying attention.

"Look, Don! Prada!" she was pointing at the Prada building on the left side of the highway. I was watching the brake lights of the cars in front of us coming up close, faster than I was comfortable with.

"That's great, Simona, but I think the cars are stopping up ahead."

"No problem, Don, I will mind the road; you must look at Prada."

Shangri-La—The Last Boondoggle
Manila, Philippines July 2016

As usual, the engagement began with the customer needing specialized consulting. The customer insisted that only the best and brightest from IBM be sent. They were busy; but JimDP and I could be there immediately.

We coordinated our travel schedules and met at the international airport in Manila. We had booked the IBM-approved Shangri-La hotel. The next day we met our IBM counterpart and walked to the customer location. We were given a small meeting room. We unpacked our laptops and waited for the customer. And waited. And waited.

We finally left. After returning to the hotel, we went sightseeing, and then to dinner. The next day we returned to the customer location, unpacked our laptops, and waited. At noon, a customer representative came to our conference room.

"I am sorry, but the customer is very busy. Please go to lunch and then maybe they can meet this afternoon."

We left for lunch. When we returned, we were told the customer was busy, but should have time for us tomorrow. We went back to the hotel. We spent the rest of the day sightseeing and then went out to dinner.

The next day was a productive full day. The day after that wasn't. By noon we decided that we were wasting our time. We told the customer we were leaving and that they should contact IBM when they had more time for us.

We changed our flight schedules and returned to the U.S. I would never return. JimDT did go to the customer later that year and conducted the training exercises that JimDP and I recommended.

Ghana, with the Wind
Africa August 2016

My last international trip was to the country of Ghana on the West coast of Africa. Due to our highly successful trip to Manila, JimDP and I teamed up again. Before we left, I mentioned to JimDP that I would be wearing a suit. JimDP packed appropriately.

The first day of our trip, JimDP and I needed to convert our money. We decided to get picked up at our Holiday Inn. As we were being driven to the customer location, we asked the driver if we could stop at a currency exchange. A few minutes later, the driver pulled the car over, got out, and spoke with a group of men on the side of the road. The driver came back to the car, told us he had negotiated a good exchange rate, and then asked for our U.S. cash. He went back, made the exchange, and came back with our Ghanaian currency. It seemed like a good rate to us.

The wardrobe suggestion was a good call on my part. The customer representative was a VP and we spent most of our time presenting concepts of database optimization and reverse engineering to him and his team. Although JimDP, the customer, and I were all dressed to the nines, it didn't help with selling our typical modernization re-engineering strategy. The customer was using a third-party software product and could not modify the application code.

Other than that, the trip was excellent; however, I did leave a newly acquired iPad in the seat pocket of the airplane during my trip from Phoenix to Minneapolis, where I met up with JimDP. I called Delta Airlines from Amsterdam and provided Lost and Found with the information. When I returned to the States, my iPad had been recovered and was waiting for me when I got home.

Dan, Can You Come Home?

Minneapolis, MN November 2016

I was staying over the weekend in Minneapolis. Mary Jo did not come with me on this trip to Minnesota. She would only return between Memorial Day and Labor Day, less chance of being caught in a blizzard. I was scheduled to speak at a user group in Madison, WI, the following week. I was having dinner with my sons, Dennis and Matt. We were celebrating their birthdays, which were in November.

After dinner, I got a call from Mary Jo. She was having a medical emergency and asked me to come home. I called Laura that evening and explained the situation. I would have to cancel the speaking engagement. I needed to go home. It wasn't the first time Mary Jo had called me to come home, but it was only the second time in nearly thirty years. The first time was when Mary Jo had been diagnosed with breast cancer in January of 2012. I was in Hong Kong. I caught the next flight home.

Laura called Mike, but he wasn't available to fill in for me. She was able to contact JimDT, who said he could take my place. Jim was staying in Minneapolis. I had rebooked my flight to return to Phoenix. It was scheduled to leave for Phoenix mid-afternoon. Jim and I met at the IBM branch office located in downtown Minneapolis, which was walking distance from Jim's condo. We went through the topics that I had planned to present. Jim said it was fine; he would have no problem.

We shook hands and I said goodbye. I would not see Jim, or anyone else at IBM for another two years. As of December 31, 2016, I was no longer the IBM guy who could perform magic with AS/400s—I was just a guy.

Acquired Skills:

Mastered Query Management Facility (QMF); iNavigator (iNav) and Visual Explain (VE). Became familiar with several third-party software applications, including word processing (IBM Lotus Word), presentation (IBM Lotus Freelance), and several industry specific solutions (Visible Analyst).

Mastered IBM database design and development tools, Data Studio, and Infosphere Data Architect (IDA). Also mastered IBM application development and management tools (Rational Suite).

Has publish numerous articles and contributed to several IBM Redbooks.

He is recognized as one of the leading experts in his field—worldwide.

EPILOGUE

"I have but one regret. *I may never see Palmyra."*
~ Dan Cruikshank

BBHK, Hong Kong
Sometime 2012

I was in a meeting with BBHK management. With me were Mike and Lou A. We were making a final presentation on the process we were going to use to re-engineer thirty-seven databases, representing the same number of countries and almost the same number of languages, into thirty-seven SQL defined databases that were identical; including incorporating the core fundamental elements that made a relational database relational—primary keys, foreign keys, and referential integrity. Each database would take advantage of Unicode, an encoding standard for translating text-type data stored in a database and presenting the text back to the end-user—in their language of choice.

JimDT, who wasn't in the meeting, had done some POTs in Rochester, MN, which proved that text type columns could be converted to Unicode and, by using the Dan Plan, not cause the existing applications to break. I had contacted Eli and asked if he could implement this in Xcase. He tested it and responded, "It is working beautifully."

"So, Dan, just so I understand what you are saying. You have a process that will replace each database regardless of the language and mismatched formats. And you believe you can do this in weeks, not months or years. Do I understand you correctly?"

"Yes, that is correct, sir."

"How do you intend to do this?"

"I don't intend to do it. There's this guy who is phenomenal. He has created a tool called Xcase that has fully automated the Phase One process of the IBM database re-engineering methodology. The tool is based on a process that is defined in an IBM Redbook and supported by several articles and customer testimonials."

"And you're comfortable recommending this tool and the guy that created it."

"Absolutely," I replied, winking at Mike. "I invented it."

Sky Harbor International Airport

Phoenix, AZ August 2020

The plane set down on the runway for Phoenix International Airport. It was a short trip. I had an aisle seat back in steerage with Matt. My days of flying Business or First Class for free were long gone. Then again, all the seats on Southwest Airlines are Business Class—mind your own business, that is.

I liked the aisle seat. I could pop right up when the buckle-your-seatbelt light went out with a ding sound. I would always wait. I could tell who the newbies—or the elitists—were. They jumped out of their seats when the plane stopped.

This action was usually followed by the inevitable:

"Please remain in your seats until the plane comes to a complete stop and the captain turns off the buckle-your-seatbelt light. This is your signal that it is safe to move around the cabin."

I would say it along with the attendant, like it was the national anthem. Ha, ha, the rookies, or crookies, would always look around like I used to when I would stand up and read, "I am the first one to reach this spot in the test," before realizing that I was supposed to read everything before doing anything.

Follow the directions, you jerk.

There, there, Dan, Mary Jo would've said if she were with me. You've got all the time in the world now. Remember, you were one of them once.

She's no longer with me. Once again, she's gone ahead without me. She's in a place she's never been before, seeing things she's never seen; doing things she's never done; meeting people she's never met, or some she met and can't forget. She's waiting for me to come home again, after my work here is done.

We were informed that it was safe to move around the cabin, so I got up. I grabbed my computer bag from the overhead; even though I could check two bags for free, I always kept my MacBook with me.

As I got off the plane, I caught Matt's eye and pointed in the direction of the bathrooms. My first stop was the men's room, which would probably have a gender-neutral name in a few years—if not sooner.

I walked to the sink, looked in the mirror, and saw my face.

It was ironic in a way. I had spent the last twenty plus years traveling the world, affecting change, while pursuing a mirage with a name—database engineer. I never found him, or her, although I met several viable candidates. In almost every case, they were pretenders or, at best, dreamers, looking for the elusive pot of gold at the end of the rainbow.

The exceptions were the ones who wanted to be DBEs and would have been perfect; however, they were never able to convince upper management—those fools—that the need was there.

As I stared at my face, I realized that my days of searching for the missing database engineer had finally come to end. I could now put that case to rest, pursue something else, something fun like gambling—or just writing.

I have finally found the database engineer.

The DBE is me.

D.R. Cruikshank

May 2021

AFTERWORD

The Last Road Trip

Dan and Mary Jo

Cottonwood, AZ June 10, 2020

We were sitting in triage at the ER of Verde Valley Medical Center. We had been there for nearly eight hours. Mary Jo was experiencing abdominal pain so severe she would double over when a spasm occurred.

When we first arrived, Mary Jo refused to take narcotics for the pain. After several hours, the attending physician talked her into taking, "The smallest dose of Fentanyl ever prescribed for humans." After taking the drug, Mary Jo asked if she could go to the bathroom. She didn't make it. She soiled herself and apologized profusely for making a mess.

About an hour later the emergency team were debating if she could go home or should be admitted. The latest attending physician was studying the various monitors that provided the vital statistics she needed in order to make an informed decision.

"I just can't let her go home," she said. "We're going to have to admit her."

"Mr. Cruikshank, you will have to leave now. You cannot accompany her to her room. Covid rules you know," the attending nurse told me.

I looked at Mary Jo. She was staring at me with a look I had seen several times before in my life—the thousand-yard stare. I walked over to her and held her hand. I kissed her on the lips one last time. She was non-responsive. I looked into her eyes. The Mary Jo I had known for over forty-three years was no longer there.

I Folded Mary Jo's Underwear

Our final road trip began on the morning of June 10. Mary Jo had slept for twelve hours. I was looking in on her when she awoke with a start, "What time is it?"

"It's past 10:00 A.M. Are you okay?"

"Yes, is it still Hump Day?"

Wednesday, Hump Day, meant Casino Night.

"Yes, it is."

"Great, I have to take a shower," Mary Jo said, as she went into the bathroom.

About an hour later she came into the front room where I was reading.

"Dan, I have some pain in my lower back. It's really bad."

"Should we go to Urgent Care or the Emergency Room in Sedona?" These were both in Sedona, about a fifteen-minute drive—without traffic.

"Let's go to Immediate Care in Camp Verde. We'll be closer to the Casino."

The doctor at Immediate Care did not have the proper facilities to diagnose Mary Jo. We left for the Emergency Room in Cottonwood, another twenty miles away. We had just driven twenty miles to Immediate Care.

The road was a new 4-lane with a 55-mph speed limit. I drove a few miles over the limit—ten or twenty or thirty, who's counting? It was during this drive that Mary Jo made her underwear request between screams of pain.

"Dan." *Scream.*

"Yes, Mary Jo?"

"After I get checked in, you will have to bring me my underwear." *Scream.*

"Okay. I will throw some in your Go-bag."

"They're still in the dryer. You will have to fold them first." *Scream.*

"It's just underwear."

"You [breath] must [breath] FOLD [deep breath] them first." *Scream.*

We arrived at the Emergency Room in Cottonwood, where I could wait with Mary Jo. Mary Jo had just gotten all hooked up when a nurse showed up to take her to Radiology for a cat scan. He unhooked everything. When he brought her back, he partially hooked her up again.

Our nurse, Emily, came in with some liquids, antibiotics, and pain relief medicine. Mary Jo had told her earlier she would not take any narcotics. She is a role model for recovering addicts everywhere. Emily had found some extra strength Tylenol that was used at the zoo for elephants giving birth. It did not stop the pain.

After eight hours of comings and goings, the late shift doctor did not like Mary Jo's numbers and decided she should be admitted. The doctor asked Mary Jo if the pain was under control. Mary Jo said no. Another doctor showed up. He was like an old-time country doctor used to dealing with patients who only came to the hospital if a bone were showing.

"Mary Jo, we cannot manage the pain without the help of narcotics. Most patients are happy to get the morphine drip. Here is what I am going to do. I am going to give you the world's smallest ever dose of fentanyl. Is that okay?"

"Mary Jo, I won't tell anybody," I said. "It's been over eight hours. Take the damn fentanyl."

The next day, Thursday, Mary Jo's care coordinator called me at home. Mary Jo had requested that I bring her iPad, which contained some meditation exercises she was doing as part of her therapy treatment for anxiety disorder. When I got to the hospital, I had to give the iPad to security—no visitors.

As I drove home my cell phone rang. It was from Mary Jo's cell phone. It stopped after three rings. I called her back. There was no answer. I received a text from her phone, "I can't talk now."

I called our care coordinator. She had not been updated. She did some calling and found out that Mary Jo had been moved to the ICU.

A short time later, the doctor called. "Mary Jo is very sick," he said. "Her white blood cell count is very high. Her BP isn't good. We moved her to ICU. She is on a respirator. She has an infection. It isn't Covid, but we have not ruled it out. In other words, we know it's a dog, we just don't know what breed."

Friday morning, I received a call from another doctor. "Mary Jo is critically ill. We are going to try another focused MRI, followed by a short version of a colonoscopy, and if we still don't know what it is, then we will need to do exploratory surgery."

I called our son, Matt, and told him that Mom was very sick and he should fly out here.

Later that day, Mary Jo was in surgery and I was folding her underwear. *It's so tiny.* About 5:00 P.M., I called Mary Jo's attending nurse. Mary Jo was back in ICU, asleep in a medically induced coma. They discovered that her fallopian tubes and ovaries were "dying," so they were subsequently removed. The doctors believed this to be the root cause of the infection and pain. They would bring her back from the coma the following afternoon, Saturday.

I drove to Phoenix on Saturday morning and picked up Matt. We stopped at a Starbucks near the hospital, and I called for an update. Mary Jo had woken up by herself. She had been given a sponge bath. She was able to communicate with the nurse, but she was still intubated and could not communicate with us. Matt and I went home—no visitors.

The news wasn't good. Mary Jo was very, very sick. She had sepsis and had gone into septic shock. She was heavily sedated, and now she was on life support.

The next day, during a Zoom meeting with Palliative Care, the doctors asked if Mary Jo had a living will. "It's only a precaution," the doctor said. "Due to her critical situation, should she suffer heart failure, it would require extraordinary measures to revive her."

A month before, Mary Jo and I had discussed this very thing with our lawyer as we prepared our trust. We had both agreed—No extraordinary measures. The paperwork was completed. Nothing was left but the signing on July 29, more than a month away.

But now Mary Jo was literally on her deathbed. I looked at Matt, and he nodded his head. I gave the health directive, "DNR—Do not resuscitate."

Before I went to bed on Tuesday night, Palliative Care warned me there was little time left. "We will do our best to keep her comfortable," the nurse said. "You must stay close to your phone in case we call. Do you understand what I am saying, Dan?"

At 4:00 A.M., Wednesday, June 24, 2020, I received the dreaded call from ICU.

"Yes," I said. "We'll get there as soon as we can."

I hung up and walked into the kitchen where Matt was working remotely. "It's time."

Matt and I drove twenty-four miles to the Cottonwood Emergency Room and arrived in less than twenty minutes. The security guard, who was waiting for us at the back door, escorted us to ICU. The hospital appeared to be deserted.

We were shown to Mary Jo's room where she was wearing an oxygen mask that was keeping her alive. We spent the next ten to fifteen minutes holding her hands and saying goodbye with our eyes.

At approximately 5:00 am. MST, Mary Jo Cruikshank went castors up, with Matt and me at her side.

Life after Mary Jo

Mary Jo
My Traveling Companion

I have been beating myself up over that missed phone call. I believe it had to do with the decision to intubate her. I'm sure Mary Jo did not want to go through that, and she wanted me to concur with her—I would've concurred.

After talking about it with Matt, we agreed that Mary Jo did not make that call. Someone else was using her phone. We came to that conclusion after learning that Mary Jo's cousin Joni, had also received a call. Someone else using her phone would logically call me first, then Joni, who was probably right after me in her favorites list, or her emergency contacts.

On the other hand, by missing that call, Mary Jo did live for another twelve days. Time to say goodbye to Matt and me one more time. Time to allow family and close friends to Zoom in and see her one last time.

I believe our higher powers intervened in our lives and brought us together. I believe they intervened one last time, preventing me from answering that phone call, and allowing us to say goodbye with dignity and honor.

The disease of alcoholism has no cure. There is only one solution—complete and total abstinence. I believe it was our abstinence from alcohol and drugs that made us very successful in our careers. I also believe that by abstaining from sex, as Mary Jo grew older and lost interest in intercourse, we became best friends forever—with benefits that were far more lasting and memorable than the physical act of sex could ever be.

What Might Have Been

It's easy to look back on my life and wonder what might've been.

What if is a question I often heard during my IT career, as a customer of IBM and eventually as an employee.

What if I'd never taken that first drink, finished high school instead, and gone on to engineering school?

What if I'd gone to work at my grandfather's company?

What if I'd met someone and lived happily ever after?

What if I'd never met Mary Jo?

Bottom line—I would not change a thing. Yes, we made sacrifices. I missed out on a lot of family events. I could've been a better husband and father. The past is the past; I am still moving forward.

I am starting a new career.

I've got more books to write.

Serenity
When the Grieving's Over

Once again, Mary Jo has gone ahead without me.

I find solace in the Serenity Prayer.

God grant me Serenity to accept things I cannot change.

I can't,

hold her hand anymore;

hug her and listen to her talk;

kiss her good night, hello, or goodbye;

or compliment her every day.

Nor can I ever stop loving her.

Courage to change things I can.

I can,

hold my grandkids more often;

listen to others more closely;

find new relationships;

And be there for family and friends.

And Wisdom to know the difference.

I know I can rediscover the type of love Mary Jo gave me; and I now can give—once again.

ADDENDUM

STATE OF MINNESOTA

DEPARTMENT OF EDUCATION

SECONDARY SCHOOL EQUIVALENCY CERTIFICATE

This certifies that Daniel Robert Cruikshank

has, on the basis of the General Educational Development tests (high school level), demonstrated achievement equal to or above the minimum standards prescribed by the State Board of Education, and is hereby awarded this Secondary School Equivalency Certificate.

Dated at St. Paul, Minnesota November 2, 1970

Commissioner of Education

F 41-29 (Rev. 1-70)

Credentials

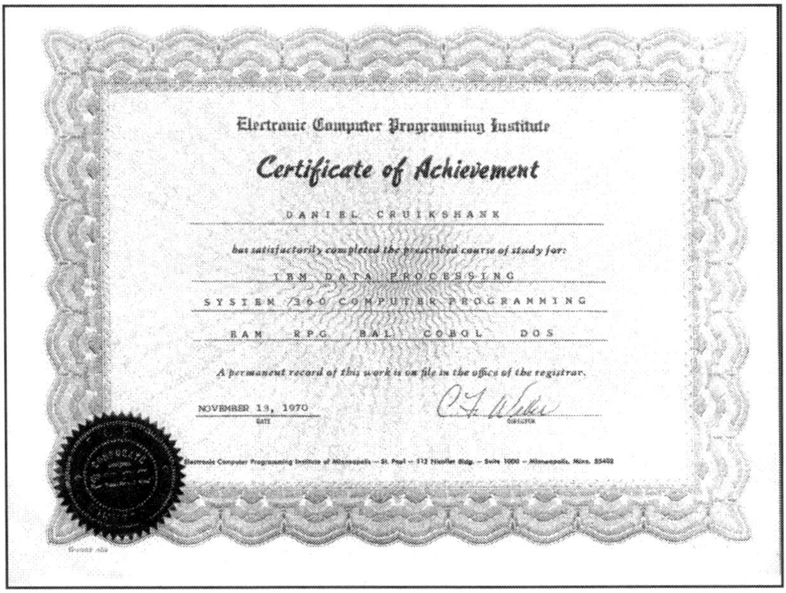

Electronic Computer Programming Institute

Certificate of Achievement

DANIEL CRUIKSHANK

has satisfactorily completed the prescribed course of study for:

IBM DATA PROCESSING

SYSTEM /360 COMPUTER PROGRAMMING

BAM RPG BAL COBOL DOS

A permanent record of this work is on file in the office of the registrar.

NOVEMBER 13, 1970

DATE

DIRECTOR

Electronic Computer Programming Institute of Minneapolis — St. Paul — 512 Nicollet Bldg. — Suite 1000 — Minneapolis, Minn. 55402

12-18-81

TITLE: Administrative Computer Center Manager

REPORTS TO: Vice President of Finance & Management

COORDINATES WITH: All Data Processing User Departments and any agencies affecting the Data Processing operation.

BASIC FUNCTION: Under the general direction and guidance of the Vice President for Finance & Management, plans, organizes and controls the activities of the administrative computer center including systems analysis, design programming and computer operation activities.

RESPONSIBLITIES:

1. Personally oversees major personnel, administrative and data processing problems, controlling all activities under jurisdiction.

2. Confers with and advises coworkers and subordinates on administrative policies and procedures, technical problems, priorities and methods.

3. Provides overall direction to insure that assigned activities are completed in the most competent, effective and efficient manner.

4. Establishes time-line completion dates for both training of personnel and implementation of data processing objectives. Consults, advises, and coordinates between user departments as necessary for proper integration and correlation of work objectives.

5. Analyzes proposed and actual projects in terms of machine capabilities, costs of man and machine hours. Provides overall program organization, improving service where and when possible and redesigning use where and when feasible.

6. Prescribes storage of data documents.

REQUIREMENTS: Degree: BA; RPG II experience of 3-5 years required; systems conversion experience preferred. RPG III experience preferred.

Augsburg College ACCM Job Description

International Business Machines Corporation

Information Systems Group
National Marketing Division

This is to certify that

D. CRUIKSHANK

has successfully completed

S/38 APPLICATION PROGRAMMING FACILITIES

and in recognition thereof is awarded this certificate

FEBRUARY 12, 1982

IBM

J.P. CURIE, DIRECTOR OF EDUCATION
INFORMATION SYSTEMS GROUP
NATIONAL MARKETING DIVISION

International Business Machines Corporation

Information Systems Group
National Marketing Division

This is to certify that

D. CRUIKSHANK

has successfully completed

S/38 RPG III STRUC PGMNG SKILL WKSHOP

and in recognition thereof is awarded this certificate

MARCH 5, 1982

IBM

J.P. CURIE, DIRECTOR OF EDUCATION
INFORMATION SYSTEMS GROUP
NATIONAL MARKETING DIVISION

International Business Machines Corporation

Information Systems Group
National Marketing Division

This is to certify that

D. CRUIKSHANK

has successfully completed

S/38 IMPLEMENTATION I

and in recognition thereof is awarded this certificate

APRIL 2, 1982

IBM

J.P. CURIE, DIRECTOR OF EDUCATION
INFORMATION SYSTEMS GROUP
NATIONAL MARKETING DIVISION

S/38 Training Certificates

MARY JO CRUIKSHANK

4875 Deerwood Lane
Plymouth, MN 55442
(612) 557-0452

OBJECTIVE

A challenging operations/marketing management position that utilizes my extensive experience and demonstrated skills in all aspects of planning.

PROFILE

Experienced in planning, scheduling, inventory and purchasing. Results-oriented with excellent organization and analytical ability. Background includes knowledge of accounting and computer experience. Extensive interaction with overseas suppliers has broadened comprehension of cultural differences in business. Proven ability to meet corporate objectives.

PROFESSIONAL EXPERIENCE

TONKA CORPORATION 1985-1988

Senior Production Planner (1987-1988)
Production Planner (1985-1987)

- Prepared weekly master production schedule from Master Production Plan, maintaining minimum levels of inventory and stable manpower.
- Responsible for material planning and requisitioning. Majority of material imported from offshore vendors; monitored production and shipping performance, providing opportunity for direct and constant communication. Acquired extensive knowledge of business theories, practices and cultural differences.
- Implemented Advanced Manufacturing Accounting Production System (AMAPS) on an IBM mainframe computer.
- Served as member of task force, responsible for setting control files and data elements to determine business operations.
- Updated and converted all B.O.M.'s.
- Recipient of President's Award for Employee of the Year (1985) as a result of exceptional progress in communication and barriers overcome.

SCHAPER MANUFACTURING COMPANY 1976-1985

Production Scheduler (1979-1985)

- Prepared annual master production schedule from current marketing forecasts.
- Participated in implementing MRP System for production department.
- Developed and maintained weekly and daily schedules; prepared manpower requirements and equipment usage.

Mary Jo's Resume 1988

Customer Application		System/38 X.25
Are you awake?	—>	Zzzzzzzz
(waiting)	<—	I am now. What do you want?
I'm horny.	—>	(waiting)
(waiting)	<—	I'm not.
What if I do this?	—>	(waiting)
(waiting)	<—	You're the devil.
Perhaps you would like some of this?	—>	(waiting)
(waiting)	<—	Keep that up and you better be good to go.
Oh baby, I'm ready. What if I try this?	—>	**Protocol Violation**

X.25 Handshake Sequence

```
                 TSA Demo
Select one of the following:
   1.  Work with objects
   2.  Work with programs
   3.  Work with objects and programs xref

Selection or command ===>1
F3=Exit F4=Prompt F12=Cancel
```

```
              Work With Objects
Type options, Press Enter.
  1=Add 2=Change 4=Delete 5=Display
Opt Object Type Description
_
5...PGM1......*PGM Work with objects list

Parameters or command
===>
F3=Exit F4=Prompt F5=Refresh F12=Cancel
```

```
   Display Object Description(DSPOBJD)
Press Enter to continue.

Object . . . . . . : PGM1
Type . . . . . . . : *PGM
Description........: Work with objects list

F12=Cancel
```

TSA Demo Panel Work Flow

International Business Machines Corporation

Highway 52 & Northwest 37th Street
Rochester, Minnesota 55901
507-253-4011

July 14, 1989

Mr Ronald B Silverman
Keane, Inc
102 South Broadway
Suite 205
Rochester, MN 55904

Dear Mr Silverman

On behalf of the Testing Support Application (TSA) team, I would like to acknowledge the contributions of the following people to the project-level external design (IO) of the Performance part of TSA.

Contributor	Contribution
Dan Cruikshank	Development team technical team leader, data base normalization, and technical design considerations
Sue Kennedy	Development team project manager, performance data base design coordinator, IO moderator, panels, panel flow, development perspective, development vendors' representative.

We appreciate your support in this effort as well and look forward continuing to work with you and your team in the further development and implementation of TSA. Thank you!

Sincerely

Steve

Stephen J Cyr

cc	D R Cruikshank	Keane TSA team	
	C L Hartley	45N/006-2	IBM Rochester, MN
	S E Kennedy	Keane TSA team	
	J G Kloc	45N/006-2	IBM Rochester, MN
	B J McLane	274/020-3	IBM Rochester, MN
	J W Newcomer	479/030-3	IBM Rochester, MN
	S J Oenning	51D/006-2	IBM Rochester, MN

Steve Cyr Customer Satisfaction Letter

KEANE

Ray E. Becker
Vice President & General Manager
Information Services Division

January 19, 1990

Mr. Daniel Cruikshank
4875 Deerwood Lane
Plymouth, MN 55442

Dear Dan,

Congratulations...you have earned a **K-preciation** pin for your fine work at IBM.

We have received a copy of a letter to Ron Silverman from Stephen Cyr of IBM. He acknowledged the contributions of you and Sue Kennedy in the external design (IO) of the Performance part of TSA.

He went on to list your contributions to the project, one of which included, Development Team technical leader. In addition, Sue Kennedy supported Mr. Cyr's comments with a very informative letter detailing your contribution. Clearly you've proven that you have what it takes to be a Keane "Essential Professional".

Thank you, and keep up the great work.

Sincerely,

Ray E. Becker

REB/kmu

cc: J. Keane
D. Klatman
T. Rossman
Personnel File

Keane, Inc. • Ten City Square • Charlestown, Massachusetts 02129 • (617) 241-9200

Keane K-pin Award Letter

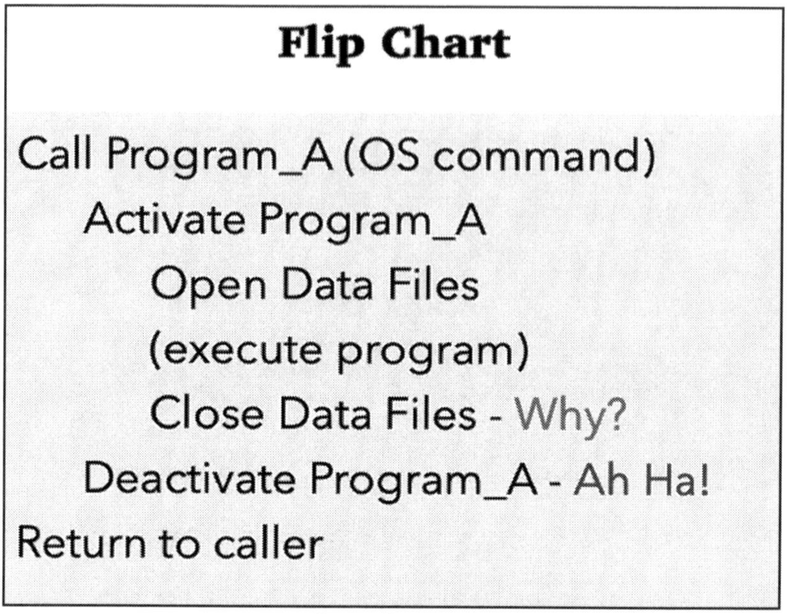

Call-Level Hierarchy

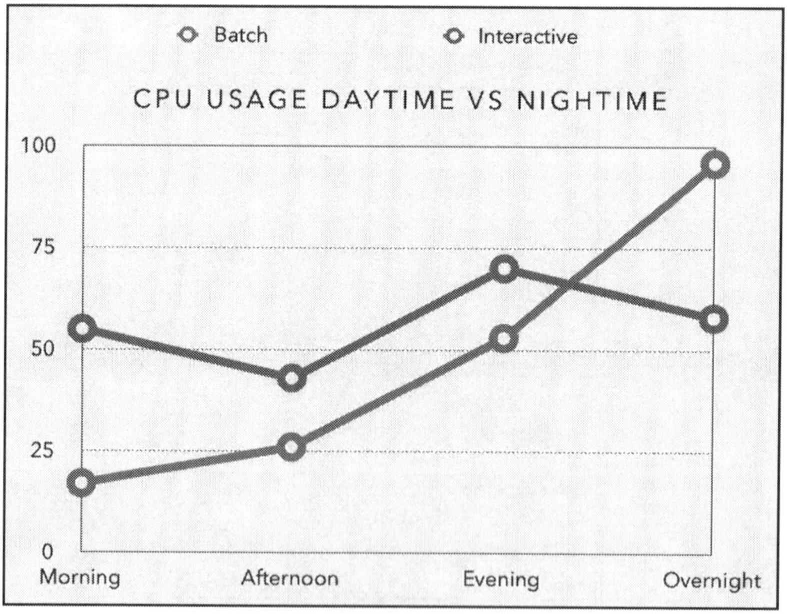

CPU Usage Night vs. Day

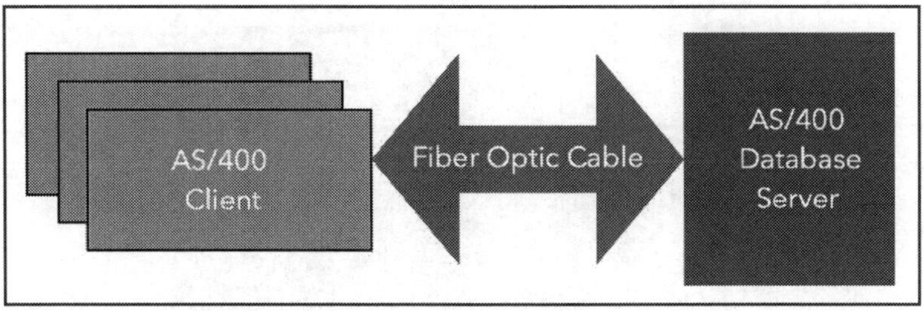

Opticonnect Conceptual Diagram

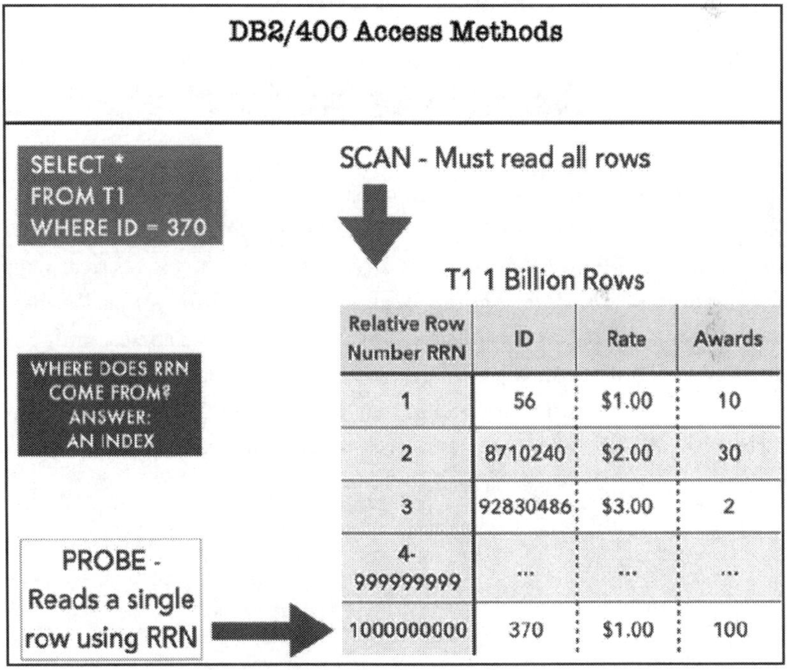

SQL Access Methods

About the Author

D. R. Cruikshank is retired and lives in northern Arizona. This is the author's second memoir. His first book, *The Franklin Trail,* is about the author's childhood, driven by his therapy sessions during his treatment for alcoholism. *The Blue Highway* begins where *The Franklin Trail* ends.

The author has published several technical articles and co-authored several technical manuals on software and database re-engineering. If you are interested in reading any of these publications type "Dan Cruikshank IBM" into your web search tool of choice.

Made in the USA
Coppell, TX
05 November 2026

11302985R00188